FAREWELL LEICESTER SQUARE

FAREWELL LEICESTER SQUARE

Henry Hollis and Dan Wooding

Wm MacLellan (Embryo) Ltd.

Front cover picture courtesy Terry Rand
© 1983 by Henry Hollis
First published in Great Britain by Wm MacLellan (Embryo) Ltd
Printed and bound in Great Britain by
Clark Constable (1982) Ltd, Edinburgh
ISBN 0 85335 258 5

I dedicate this book
to my Dad, Blind Bill.

Foreword

The Road Stars were a part of London's West End life that I had been thrown into in 1952 when I learned that I had, at last, passed an audition and been offered a job at the famous Windmill Theatre.

I often wondered what had made the Road Stars, with all their obvious professionalism and wealth of talent, take to the streets instead of the boards.

I am delighted that the publishers have let Henry Hollis tell the story HIS way, spelling mistakes and all (although I suggest the reader studies the glossary of the various esoteric slang words before reading it). It's a wonderful, unique Cockney medley of laughter and tears.

Bill Maynard

Chapter One
Blood bruvvers

A geezer once said to me, 'Harryboy, why don't ya write ya life story?'

'Leave awf!' I said, 'I can't even write my own bleeding name!'

Well I pissed around wiv the idea for a few days, and I fawt, *That's not a bad idea, that.* So here goes.

My story began in the East End of London. It must have been the Bow Bells that woke me up in my muvver's belly on 12 May 1922. That's right, I am a cockney and proud of it. My poor old Mum must have gawn frew hell to bring me into this world. I can see her now – five foot two inches tall with auburn hair and blue eyes. When God was dishing out angels' wings he must have forgotten hers. She never seemed to stop work and she was as tough as old nails. My old mum worked herself potty to bring up us five saucepan lids.

Yes, there was five of us, three saveloys and two girls. She was up at six every morning, winter and summer, washing the bits and pieces we had to wear, and she was hours on end scrubbing the floorboards to make them white. You see, we had no lino or fancy rugs, just bare boards and a couple of old mats. We couldn't afford lino. Her kids were her life and gawd help anyone who tried to harm them. She was as wise as an old owl and as cunning as an old fox, but we loved her dearly.

The house we lived in was a right old dump. It had free little bedrooms. Mum and Dad had one bedroom, my two sisters had anuvver, and me and my bruvvers Bill and Albert had the uvver bedroom. We had a small kitchen wiv a copper in the corner. This was for boiling dirty washing in, and when the old lady had the fire going in it on wash day the steam from the hot water used to run down the walls and drip awf of the ceiling. Poor old Mum would have sweat running awf of her. I was born in that dump we all called home.

I shall never forget that address as long as I live. It was 68 Broomfield Street, Poplar, London E14. The old girl kept it spotless, but no matter how much she tried we just couldn't get rid of the bugs and it seemed the more she scrubbed the more bugs we got. In them days the walls were plastered wiv lime and horse hair, and the bleeding bugs used to breed in the wall. They just kept on coming so there wasn't much we could do about it.

The times the council fumigated that dump was nobody's business.

'Ya know wot muvver,' I said to the old lady, 'ya don't want to pay any rent this week, and if the landlord wants to know why ya ain't paid ya rent, tell the old barsted you had to buy food for the bleeding bugs.'

But no matter wot the council did, they just kept coming, the barsteds.

Apart from looking after us saucepan-lids (kids) and the house, my poor old Mum would go round Whitechapel scrubbing doorsteps for the front-wheel skids (yids) just to make ends meet. Ya see, my old Dad was blind, and he was a busker. A busker is a man wot goes round the streets playing a musical instrument. Well, my old Dad played the concertina. He was very well known round the East End and everyone called him Blind Bill.

My Dad was five foot six tall wiv silver-grey 'air and a silver-grey moustache. His eyes were once blue until he was blinded in the First World War, and then they went a watery grey. He always carried a white stick and walked upright. Ya could almost see ya face in his boots wot yours truly had to polish for him. He did most of the fings himself, but the old lady always had to cut his food up for him, and if we were lucky enough to have meat, she would cut it up for him, and place the meat at free o'clock on his plate and that way he knew where to find it.

He always wore the old-fashioned collar and fronts. They were stiff wiv starch, so all the old lady had to do was to scrub them on the kitchen table, let them dry, and he always had a clean one to put on. He always wore a white pocket handkerchief in his top pocket even though it was a bit fredbare. He was very clean, my Dad, and a very gentle creature.

I can remember taking home a small sparrow that I found lying in the road injured. I told my Dad about this tiny mite. 'Show me,' he said. Even though he couldn't see, he always said show me. I placed the tiny creature in his cupped hands, and I watched him feel it so gently. That little creature knew he was in safe hands: his tiny little eyes seemed to be looking up at my farver.

'He's a pretty little fing, Dad,' I said, 'Do ya fink we can make him better?'

'If God wants him to survive he will survive,' the old man replied.

Every morning and last fing at night, my Dad would hold that tiny creature in his hands. I tried feeding him wiv milk and bread. Arfter about four weeks, he was ready to leave the security of his rescuers.

One sunny morning, the old man and I took him into the back yard. The old man opened his hands. For a moment that little creature sat in the palm of my Dad's hand chirping. The old man ran his finger over the tiny sparrow's back.

'It's time to go little feller,' he said. The little bird chirped and then took flight.

'He's flying Dad,' I said, excitedly. The old man smiled.

'That is what God wanted son,' he said.

The sparrow landed on the gutter of the roof, rested for a while, gave another chirp and then flew away for ever.

Apart from being a hardworking man he was very talented. He had only to be shown how to play an instrument once, and he would have it mastered in a few hours. But wiv all the instruments he played the concertina was the one he used most.

I fink that when my farver lost his eyesight he was given extra senses. He could play five different instruments, he could tell the time wiv an ordinary watch by feeling the hands and I would sometimes pull his leg about playing wiv marked cards.

Sometimes I would take him to the park if it was a nice day. We would sit on a bench, and I would watch him lift his face towards the sun, and wiv the warmf of the sun on his face he would say, 'It's a lovely day son.'

I can remember him making my youngest sister and me stand by the old kitchen table to see how much we had grown. My youngest sister and I were the only two children that he had never seen when we were born. He would feel the top of our heads and say, 'Ya will be up to the kitchen sink before ya know where ya are.'

He must have had a hard life when he was a boy if old grandfarver Hollis was anyfing to go by. Even when my Dad was a man, I never ever heard him answer his farver back.

'Ya must have respect for ya parents son, as they brought ya into the world,' he once said to me.

He deplored violence and he hated swearing. As us boys got

11

older and if we should happen to swear in the house, he wouldn't remind us of it, he would just give a little cough and we knew he disapproved of our language. And because of that we never swore much in the home.

He could write in Braille as well as longhand. His longhand writing wasn't all that good but you could understand it. I remember he once went away to a blind home for a holiday, and he sent my Mum a letter in longhand. It started alright, but as he got to the middle all the words began to run togevver. We all larfed but we could still read it. That was the only holiday he ever had. They sent him to Hastings and he liked it so much he said he wouldn't mind ending his days there.

He must have suffered a lot of pain when he first lost his eyesight, my muvver told me that he had several operations on them. But it was no use, he finally went totally blind. His children were his life, and he did all he could for us. My muvver took care of him frew all his suffering and he was very grateful to her. They were the best of partners. They had their arguments like every married couple, but their love was a very strong bond. Between them they provided for us kids. They did the best they could, and they did it wiv all the love and care we could wish for.

I never questioned my Dad much about the way he became blind. When I did ask him once he said, 'It is wot God wanted, son.'

I remember my uncle Harry saying once, 'My bruvver Bill 'as got a lot to fank his bleeding country for. They sent him awf to bleeding war and he ended up like that, the poor barsted.' And that is how I know that my old Dad lost his sight in the First World War. He never spoke much about the fings he had done. He was a quiet man. I should really say a gentleman wiv the ways of an angel.

The trouble wiv this world today is that there are so few gentlemen around. I fink people should touch each uvver more, like when you shake hands. It wouldn't hurt to put your hand on a person's shoulder. This would bring people closer togevver and bring more love to the world. As I see it, man's made a right old mess of it.

My old Mum put her 'art and soul into looking arfter us lot. My bruvver Bill was the eldest, then came Albert, then Lily, then yours truly Henry, and Rene was the youngest. Rene never went out busking as she was too young. By the time she was old enough the bloody war had started. Bill took my Dad out busking a long time before I was born and, when he started working in a factory, my bruvver Albert took over the job of taking the old man out. Each day Albert had to leave school early so he could take the old man round to the dog-biscuit factory to catch the workers coming out.

Busking was very hard in those days as there wasn't much money around and ya had to work very hard to make ends meet. Ya see, us being the fird generation of buskers, we had our own language. We learnt this language from our farver and he learnt it from his farver. Even up to this present day my children speak this language. My farver's farver started busking years and years ago. How he started I don't know. Ya see I was only a twinkle in my old man's eye when grandfarver Hollis started busking. My dad started busking wiv his farver, same as I did wiv mine.

Years ago, that's a long time before I was born, some old geezer who was on the throne at that time, granted a charter to a team they called the strolling players. Ya see, busking is like prostitution, it is one of the world's oldest professions. As for the buskers' language, I don't know where that came from. All I know is that the 'ole of the family spoke it including my muvver.

Our family used it as far back as I can remember. It's a mixture of French, Italian, and Romany. The *joegars* of today don't use it as they don't know it. None of my children or bruvver's children have followed in our footsteps so we are the last of the fird generation of buskers. There was none we could hand the language down to.

In busker's language a boy is called an '*ome*' and a girl is called a '*Palone*'. A friend is called '*jaggs*' and good is '*bona*'. Bad is '*bold*' and look is '*varda*'. Coppers are '*scarps*' and dogs are '*buffers*'. Legs are '*scotches*' and tits are '*traysalties*'.

If we saw a good-looking girl coming down the street we would say, '*Varda the bona palone wiv the bona traysalties ya jaggs.*' And that meant, 'Look at that lovely girl wiv the nice breasts.'

Or ya could say if she had a nice pair of legs, '*Varda ve bona palone wiv la bona scotches ya jaggs.*' In uvver words, 'Look at that lovely girl's legs mate.'

To '*bottle*' would mean to collect the money. '*Medzers*' means money. '*Slang*' is picture queue. '*Miltog*' means shirt. '*Batarlies*' are shoes or boots. '*Joegar*' means busker. '*Feelies*' are children. And there are lots more.

13

The money goes like this: a harpenny is a '*medzer*', a penny is a '*saltie*', twopence is a '*dooey saltie*', threepence is a '*tray saltie*', and so on. A pound is a '*font*' and two pounds is a '*dooey font*'. It is just like pennies but you say '*fonts*' instead of '*saltie*'. As for shillings they are called '*beonks*', so one shilling is a '*beonk*' and two shillings is a '*dooey beonk*'. Let's say you wanted to say two pounds ten in buskers' language, it would be a '*dooey font medzer*', meaning two and a harf, harf being a '*medzer*'.

If you were to meet anuvver busker in the street you would say to him, '*Voke the palaree ya jaggs*,' which means, 'Do you speak the language mate?' But there was a limited few that spoke the language. The buskers of today wouldn't understand it at all as they are either students or dropouts. The students go busking if they need a new instrument or if they need help wiv their studies, but the dropouts we have no time for. they do it for '*bevvy*' (beer).

The students we didn't mind as they were doing it for a good cause. But as for those layabouts, we didn't want to know them at any price. If one of them was to come up to us in Leicester Square, Albert would say, '*Johnalderly the bold ome ya jaggs*.' In uvver words, 'Tell that old barsted to piss awf.' Ya may fink to yaself that there was no difference between them and us but believe me there was a great difference. For one fing, we never drank the money away that we earned, that was for our families.

My sister Lily started busking when she was twelve. She was only four foot five with blue eyes and auburn hair.

'Don't forget,' Dad use to say to her, 'if anyone ask ya how old you are tell them you are fourteen or we won't be able to get into the boozers.'

I can see her now, dressed in a long black coat that looked two sizes too big for her and a pair of old 'igh 'eel long-legged boots that my old mum had bought her awf of the secondhand stall in the market. Before Lily took the old man out it was Albert's job. But once Lily was old enough Albert started working on his own. I learnt a lot from Albert and have a lot to fank him for. So ya see the 'ole lot of us was buskers except Rene. So ya can see we all took turns in leading out dad frew his darkness.

He was a good 'un my old dad, and you would never hear a bad word from him. Mind you, if ya ever was to put him out gawd help ya. I remember the old lady upset him one day, and he swung his walking stick round, and yours truly got it right in the kisser. I walked around for about a fortnight wiv two bleeding heads. Yes, he was a good 'un my old dad.

'Dad, there's a bug running up the wall,' I used to say to him.

'Hit him wiv the hammer son so's he don't fill it,' he would say.

Those summer nights in the East End was murder. We couldn't sleep for those bleeding bugs so to amuse ourselves we would sit up 'arf the night on the front doorstep waiting for the rats to come out of the bone-yard opposite. The bone-yard was where they used to pulverise meat bones and turn them into soup. We would frow all sorts at them bleeding rats, and sometimes we would put down a rat cage, and if we copped one of those 'orrible old rodents we would let one of the dogs have it. If there was free or four neighbours about at the time wiv their dogs, we would all line up wiv our dogs at the ready, and someone would let the rat lose. We would slip the old dogs from their leashes and awf they would go after the rat. There wasn't a better dog track in the whole of the East End than ours, and those old rats didn't like it one bit.

We always had a dog as far back as I can remember. It was the old man ya see. He loved animals and he always said that if ya were kind to animals there would always be a place for ya in heaven when ya died. (I bet my old Dad got his place all right.) We used to call our dog Peter. Boy, did he love those old rats, and could he have a fight.

Even right up until the last he had a fight. As I was taking him to the RSPCA shop to have him put down he had to have his last punch up. Ya see, poor old Peter got this bad ear and it made all one side of his face swell up. Well, I told the old man, and arfter he had felt around poor old Peter's ear he said, 'I fink we will have to take 'im to see the RSPCA man down at the shop in Grundy Street and let 'im 'ave a look at it.'

When the geezer at the RSPCA shop saw poor old Peter's ear he said, 'I'll give you some cream to put in it, but if it is no better wivvin a week I am afraid I will have to put the poor old chap to sleep. Ya see, 'e 'as got wot we call a canker, and it can be very bad for him. It could cause fits if we can't clear it up.' I felt the old man's fingers grip my arm and I knew wot he was finking. All the way home the old man didn't have much to say.

'Don't worry Dad,' I said. 'He'll be all right.'

'I hope so son,' said the old man.

All that week I kept putting cream in poor old Peter's ear, but it made no difference and it was as though that poor old dog knew it was his last week wiv the old man. He just hung around him all the time. Now and again I would see the old man put his hand down to feel his ear and he would gently rub him on the head. The day came for us to take that poor old dog back to the RSPCA shop. 'We have got to take old Peter to see the vet today, Dad,' I said to my old Dad.

'Yus, I know, son,' the old man replied. 'We will take him arfter I've had this cup of tea.'

'Well I watched the old man drink his tea and I could see he wasn't hurrying it.

'Do ya fink there is any change in his ear, son?' he said.

'No Dad, I fink it is worse than it was last week,' I said. I watched him drink the last of his tea and I said, 'Shall we go, Dad?'

The old man put his hand down and stroked the old dog's head. He hesitated for a moment and then he said, 'You take him son.' Just then the old dog licked his hand as if to say 'Goodbye pal'.

As I took that old dog up the street he never even looked back. It was as if he knew I was doing it for his own good. As we got to the RSPCA shop some old bird came out wiv her dog on a lead and on seeing Peter, this dog made one dive at him, and before I knew what was 'appening, the old bird let go of his lead. Well, I never saw such a commotion in all my life. Old Peter turned round and got hold of this dog by the scruff of the neck and shook it like a rat.

'Oh me dog! Oh me dog!' was all that the old bird could shout.

'Ya shouldn't have let the bleeding fing awf the lead, missus,' I said. I managed to pull poor old peter awf of this other dog, and I said 'You'd better piss awf wiv him missus, or he will end up being dead.' And that was the last punch up old Peter was to have.

It seemed funny going back without him. When I got indoors, I said to the old man, 'He's gone Dad,' and the old man replied, 'All right son.' The next fing I knew the old man had vanished to the bedroom, and I knew the reason why.

Our poor old dog Peter was only a mongrel, but we gave him all the love and care we would have given a thoroughbred. I can remember going and picking him from the litter. We got him awf of a man who lived a little way down our street. This old geezer used to bite the tails awf of puppies if you wanted one wiv a little tail. It broke my 'art when the RSPCA put poor old Peter to sleep. I don't know how they put him to sleep. I just turned my back on him and walked away crying.

But those days in the East End of London were one round of laughter and tears. I take arfter the old lady for being small. I only go to five foot two, and, as they say, good fings come in little parcels. Besides, there is an advantage in being small: you can duck and dive from old Bill a bit lively. I wish I had a pound for every time I scarpered from the Law when I was busking in the West End of London. I would be a very rich man now. All I had to do was to dive into the crowd and they couldn't see me. Well, who wants to get nicked anyway?

When you are born in the East End as I was, you get a knack for earning a few coppers. I got the knack at about the age of nine. My mate Fred and me used to go round Whitechapel on Saturday mornings lighting the fires for the front-wheel skids. Arfter sundown on Friday night Jews would pack up work until Sunday. It was against their religion to do any work so we would light their fires for them. We would knock on the door and shout, 'Fire Light!' and if ya were lucky enough to get a punter (customer) you would go into the house, rake the old ashes out of the fire grate, re-lay the fire and light it, and for that ya would get a penny. Well, I mean, if ya was lucky enough to get four punters at a penny each it meant you had earned fourpence, and that was a lot of money in them days. Mind you, ya didn't get a penny from all of them, and some of them used to try and get out of paying ya.

I had one old geezer try it out on me one morning. It was freezing cold outside. I had just lit his fire for him and it was burning lovely.

'There ya are guv, ya wouldn't get a better fire in bleeding 'ell,' I said and held out my hand for the money.

'Vot ya want?' he said.

'Me bleeding money,' I replied.

'Piss owf ya. Ya gets no bloody money here,' he said.

'*Ya old barsted*,' I fawt.

'Right,' I said. 'I'll piss awf all right.'

I did not more and pulled out me manhood and pissed all over his bleeding fire. As I was doing so I said, 'No bleeding money,

17

no bleeding fire.' Well there was steam everywhere and the stink, phew. It was enough to make a skunk cry. The old yid was coughing a spitting all over the gaff.

'Michamachina on ya, ya old barsted,' I shouted as I ran frew the door.

Well the old Yid went mad, but he couldn't do nothing for coughing. Ya see, that is the worst thing ya can say to a Jew. It means 'have a fit and die in it ya old barsted.' He went cold that morning without his fire.

My mate Fred Barker was about five foot tall wiv fair hair, blue eyes, and a fresh complexion. His dad worked for the local council driving a water cart, and he used this to wash down the market when it was closed. All the kids would run behind it barefooted.

We never had boots in those days. We couldn't afford them, so we had to make do with plimsoles, out of Woolworth's. They would cost ya a tanner a pair. They were handy, them old plimsoles. Ya could creep about all over the gaff in them and ya could get up to all sorts of capers. At night we would creep round the back of the boneyard and watch the courting couples making love. At a given signal we would all shout, 'Ya dirty old barsteds,' and we would run like the wind. Laugh . . . ya should have seen the birds trying to pull up their strides. If we knew who they were we would shout out, 'We know ya, ya dirty old barsteds.'

I can't remember when I first started smoking. It seems I have been smoking all of my life. I think I was about eight when I took my first drag and I took to it like a duck to water. Me and my friends used to walk along the gutter picking up all the fag ends we could find and re-roll them in fag papers. I used to sell them to the uvver kids at school – when I was there that is. I would tell them that they were American cigarettes and they never knew the difference. I would roll all sorts of tobacco up in them and I would charge them a penny for five. They never knew if they were smoking black shag or horse-shit. But I can honestly say not one of those kids snuffed it wiv my fags. You could always manage to get a crust round the East End, that's if you were wide enough.

Anuvver little stroke we used to get up to was to go into Woolworth's and nick a paint brush and a tin of black paint. Ya see we nevver paid for anyfing when we could nick it. Well wiv this paint brush and paint we would go round the streets painting knockers. We would knock on the door, and when the lady of the house came out we would say, 'Paint ya knocker lady?'

I knocked at one door and got no answer.

'Knock again Al,' Fred said. So I fawt, *I'll knock a bit louder this time*. Well after a few seconds I heard some old bird shouting, 'All right, I am coming.'

Well, when she opened the door I nearly pissed myself wiv laughing. She was dressed in a big pair of baggy bloomers and a pair of stays and she was about sixteen stone. She yelled when she saw me and Fred standing there.

'What the bleeding hell do you want?'

'Shall I paint ya knocker missus?' I said. Well, she nearly went mad.

'Painzmknocker? Be fucked. Can't ya see I'm trying to have a sodding barf. Piss awf.' And wiv that she slammed the door in our faces.

'All right ya old cow,' I shouted arfter her as she went up the passage, 'don't do ya bloody nut.'

'Did ya see her tits, Al?' said old Fred looking at me.

'Ya,' I said, 'she's got some ain't she. They're to keep her afloat in the barf.' And we went on our way laughing.

I was always called Al by my friends even though my name is Henry. I've walked for miles painting knockers but as long as we earned a few coppers we didn't mind.

In those days we used to take jam jars to get into the dolly mixtures (pictures) and you would have to stand at the back but we didn't mind as long as we got in. The manager would sell the jars and make money. Oh boy, how we loved those old pictures. We would stand at the back eating peanuts and smoking the fag ends we had picked up from the gutter on our way to the pictures.

One night Fred and I were standing at the back watching the film and having a right old time when I said to him, 'The dancers will be on in a minute.'

'Wot bleeding dancers?' he said. Just then, this kid who had been standing in front of us gave out a yell and started to jump all round the bleeding picture house.

'There ya are.' I said to Fred, 'I told ya there were some dancers on the bill didn't I.' Ya see, this kid who was standing in front of us was wearing wellingtons and I dropped a fag down one of his wellies. Boy, he put on a better show than any one of those dancers that was on the pictures. Well Fred nearly pissed himself wiv laughing, and the tears were rolling down his boat-race (face). Everybody was shouting to this kid, 'Shut ya bleeding noise up. We want to hear the picture.' And wiv that the attendant came up and slung the kid out on his ear. I mean the talkies were bad enough in those days without some kid doing the war dance all round the place. Besides, the picture was nothing to do wiv bleeding Indians. The film we went to see was one of the early Tarzan films. Me and old Fred lapped it all up.

On the way home we had to go through the market and one of the shops had left their shade down. 'Look Al,' said Fred, and he made a dive for the shade. One minute he was swinging frew the air, and the next he was on the ground. There was one almighty crash and Fred came down shade and all. *Blimey* I fawt. 'He's pulled the front of the shop down.'

'Fuck me Fred, run.' I said.

'I can't. I've broken me back,' said Fred.

'Don't talk like a berk,' I said helping him to his feet. He managed to get up and we started awf down the road.

'I've done me bottle (arse) in,' Fred said, when we was well out of the danger zone. When we got home to my house I said, 'Let's have a butchers at your bottle.' When he took his strides down he had a bruise on his bottle as big as a dustbin lid and he had torn the arse out of his strides.

'Blimey Fred,' I said. 'You've got a big bruise on ya bottle.'

'Never mind me bottle, Al,' he said. 'Wot am I going to do wiv me trousers? If me old lady sees these she will just about kill me.'

'Don't worry. If ya go straight up to bed when ya get in she won't see them will she,' I said. I could see by his boat race he wasn't happy wiv the idea.

'Can't I mend them in your house?' he asked.

'How can ya? My old lady will be up when I get in and she will know we have been pissing around and then I will get a whacking won't I.'

I fawt for a minute and then I said, 'I know wot we can do.'

'Wot?' he asked.

'We can ask my sister to mend them for ya.'

'Gawd Al, you're a proper mate,' he said.

When we got home I slipped him up to Lil my sister's bedroom and I told her wot had happened. Lil was twelve years old at the time and she shared the bedroom wiv her sister Rene.

'Ya better take the bleeding fings awf while I go and get some cotton,' she said to him. Well old Fred didn't like the idea of taking his trousers awf in my sister's bedroom.

'Don't be a berk.' I said. 'Get them awf or she can't mend them for ya can she?'

Well he ended up taking his trousers awf and he was sitting on the bed in his shirt and socks and plimsoles, trying to cover up his manhood wiv his hands. All of a sudden the door opened and in came the old lady. The look on her face was enough to frighten the devil.

'Ya dirty little barsteds,' she shouted, and before we could tell her wot we was doing she hit my sister one round the ear 'ole and knocked poor old Fred frew the door calling him all the names she could think of.

'Wot's the matter muvver? Ya gawn potty?' I said.

'You, ya little barsted. I am going to have you put away.'

'Leave awf,' I said. 'Ya don't know wot ya talking about.' And wiv that she frew one of her shoes at me and it hit me right in the head. the room went all black and I didn't know any more.

When I woke up I was in the local hospital wiv five stitches in my winny peg (head) and poor old mum was at the bed wiv tears streaming down her cheeks and all she could say was, 'I didn't meant it son.' For the next few weeks I could do as I liked and Fred never tried to do a Tarzan act again.

He was a good old mate, Fred. I remember one night he said, 'I know what Al. How about becoming blood bruvvers like the Indians do on the dolly mixtures?'

'*That sounds OK*, I fawt. And wiv that Fred went in 'is house to get a knife. A few seconds later he came out wiv a bleeding big carving knife.

'Wot the bleeding hell ya going to do wiv that?' I said.

'Well we've got to do it properly ain't we or it won't work will it?' he said. *I don't want him to fink I am scared*, I fawt, so I stuck out my arm.

Before I knew what happened he slashed my Oliver Twist (wrist). Boy was that carving knife sharp! There was blood all over the gaff and all he kept on saying was, 'Join them togevver.'

Well, it looked OK on the pictures but when it came to it it was a different matter. I ended up in the hospital having four stitches put in my wrist. When I got home from the hospital and the old lady saw all my wrist done up in bandage she went potty and banged me one around the ear 'ole.

'Ya silly little barsted. Ya could have cut ya bleeding arm awf!' she said. And then she banged me one wiv the old man's walking-stick.

21

'All right ma,' I shouted, 'don't go fucking mad.' The more I shouted the more she walloped me.

'Go on. Piss awf to bed and ya don't get no bleeding supper ya bleeding little barsted,' she yelled arfter me as I went up the stairs.

'You wait till I see his bleeding mate,' I could hear her saying to my sister, 'I'll give him bleeding blood bruvvers.' When I got into the bedroom my bruvver Albert was in bed.

'Wot's the old lady doing her nut for now?' he said. I told him about it. About twenty minutes later the old lady crept into the room wiv a mug of cocoa and a slice of bread and marg. Wivout saying a word she put it down and walked out of the room. She was like that, my old Mum. One minute she would knock ten buckets of shit out of ya and the next minute she would be cuddling ya. I have that scar on my wrist to this day and every time I look at it, it brings back memories of my unkindest cut of all.

One day the council workmen came down our street to dig up the road. It was made of hard wooden blocks covered in tar and pitch and called tarry blocks. When you burnt them on the fire they would make a lovely blaze. To get hold of these blocks was a rare fing and a great treat, so as soon as the word got out that the workmen were digging up the road, all the kids down the street came out wiv buckets and sacks to pick off the chippings that had broken awf of the blocks. The foreman certainly had his work cut out wiv all those bleeding kids. As soon as the workmen dug up a section the kids would nick the blocks, and the worse fing they did was to knock awf for dinner.

'If we wait until they go to dinner, we can nick the bleeding lot,' I said to Georgi and Fred.

'That's a good idea that, Al,' said Georgi.

'I bet they leave someone there to look arfter them bleeding blocks,' said Fred. 'Don't be bleeding silly,' I said. 'All those geezers want their dinner, don't they?'

'All right we will wait and see,' replied Fred.

By about twelve o'clock the workmen had stacked up a nice pile of tarry blocks.

'I am going to have some of them, me old son,' I told Fred. 'They will burn lovely on my old lady's fire.'

Well, we were all sitting on the pavement watching the workmen digging, when I saw the foreman looking at his watch.

22

'Hi up lads he is going to blow the whistle for dinner,' I said, and just then he did that.

'Righto lads blow up,' he shouted and wiv the next breff he added, 'Charlie, ya better take a late dinner.' Then, looking in our direction, he said, 'We won't have any bleeding blocks left wiv this lot round 'ere.'

'I told ya the old barsted would leave someone behind to look arfter them, didn't I?' Fred said.

'You're like a bleeding witch you are,' Georgi said.

'Fuck it, now we can't get none over that old barsted,' I said.

'Don't worry me old son,' said Georgi. 'Where there's a will there's a way.'

'Wot ya talking about?' I asked. 'It's easy, ain't it,' Georgi said.

'Well, tell us how, and we will bleeding get some,' said Fred.

'All we've got to do is for me and Al to start mucking about on that pile of shit over there wot they have dug out of the ground and while that old geezer is chasing us awf you, Fred, can fill the sacks up.'

Well that was the plan and it worked a treat. Georgi and I started running up and down this big pile of erf frowing lumps at each uvver, while Fred stood by wiv the sacks. Arfter a few minutes, a voice shouted, 'Hi' get ya bleedin arse awf of there.'

'Take no notice of him,' I said to Georgi. 'Make him come over to us.'

I could see Fred out of the corner of my eye, working his way round to the pile of tarry blocks.

'Hey you! Ya bluddy deff or somefing? I told ya to piss awf, didn't I!' the old boy was shouting as he made his way towards us.

'Go and have a good shit ya old ponce,' Georgi shouted back at him.

By this time Fred had vanished behind the tarry blocks and I could see his hands going to work filling up the sacks.

'Didn't I tell ya to piss awf!' the old geezer was shouting. Just then Georgi frew a big lump of clay at him and it caught him right on the forehead. 'Ya little barsted,' he shouted and he began to run up the pile of dirt arfter us.

'Run Al,' Georgi shouted and we bofe ran for our lives as we knew the old boy had no chance in catching us. He chased us 'arf way up the turning and then gave it up as a bad job. Arfter a

23

while we stopped running, and I said to Georgi, 'I wonder if Fred got away wiv the sacks.'

'I don't know how he is going to manage it,' said Georgi. 'He's got free sacks.'

'Well, we watched the old boy return to his post and we made our way back home via the next street. When we got home there was dear old Fred wiv two sacks of tarry blocks, and he was as black as the ace of spades.

'How many did ya get?' asked Georgi.

'Two sacks-full,' replied Fred.

'Only two bleeding sacks full?' shouted Georgi. 'There's bleeding free of us.'

'They were bleeding 'eavy,' said Fred.

'Well, we will have to split them up between us,' I said.

Arfter we had a share-out we all took our day's spoils home. When I got in, my old Mum said, 'And wot ya got in that bleeding dirty sack?'

'It's Tarry blocks for the fire.'

'Tar'y Blocks? Where the hell did ya get them from?'

'Muvver,' I said, 'ask no questions and ya 'ear no lies. As long as we have got a fire for Albert and Dad to come in to, who bleeding cares?'

'I bleeding care. I don't want no bleeding coppers knocking my door,' she said.

'Leave awf, Muvver. They're for free, so we got some.'

'Oh, all right then, stick them in the coal 'ole and we will light a nice fire for tonight.'

That night we had a lovely blazing fire right up the chimney. As I sat there wiv my feet in the fireplace, my old Mum said 'Don't sit there wiv ya feet in the fireplace you will get chillblains.'

'Muvver,' I said, 'I couldn't give two monkeys about chillblains. I am too bleeding warm to move.'

The next day the workmen were back in the street getting ready to fill in the 'ole that they had dug the day before. Laugh – there wasn't enough tarry blocks left to finish the job. They were about about free dozen blocks short. The old foreman was doing his nut and poor old Charlie – that was the guy who was left to look arfter fings while the uvvers went to dinner – got a right old bollocking from the foreman.

Fred said, 'They ain't got enough blocks to fill the 'ole in wiv.'

'Who bleeding cares about them? I don't,' said Georgi.

'I couldn't care less,' I said. 'If I couldn't care about getting bleeding chillblains, I don't bleeding care about their sodding 'ole.' And wiv that we all ran away laughing.

Thursday night was always a giggle, for Fred and me and a few of the uvver boys belonged to the church choir at Saint Gabriel's Church, Poplar, and that night was choir practice night. All the girls would be placed in the front and all the boys at the back. Laugh ... while we was going up and down the scale my hand would be going up the girls' skirt in front of me. There was one little bird there and she was a cracker. I always made sure that I got behind her.

'Gladys, why must you figet so girl?' the old choirmaster would say. Little did he know I was smoothing Gladys's arse. It was no wonder that Gladys would sing awf key. She loved the boys, that Gladys. The more boys she had round her the more she liked it. Arfter choir practice me and Fred used to make a beeline for Gladys. We used to nick her street-door key. She would put the key on the table in the vestry while she was taking off her cassock. It seemed she did it on purpose so as we could get that bloody key. Once outside of the church we wouldn't give her the key back unless she gave us a kiss. If she didn't we would stuff it down her knickers. She loved it. She was eleven years old at the time and she was about four foot ten wiv dark-brown hair and green eyes. She was a cracker.

I fink the old choirmaster, Mr Reed, was glad to get rid of us that night as there had been so much pissing about during choir practice. We used to wear mauve and white cassocks on Sundays. Old Mr Reed was a weedy little man with greying hair and gold-rimmed specks and he spoke wiv a posh accent. He was always blowing his note.

I used to work in the market on a Saturday and I worked wiv a geezer selling toof powder. Laugh ... he used to call himself Doctor Johnson. He was no more of a doctor than I was a cowboy. Well this was our act: I would stand in front of the crowd pretending to watch him and when he got a big edge (crowd) he would say, 'Come here, sonny,' and I would go and stand by him.

'When did you clean your teef last?' he would say and I would give him some patter about not having a toofbrush. He would give the punters a lot of bullshit about how he was going to make my teef shine like ivory, and he would stick this old toofbrush he

25

had in this powder and rub like mad at me teef. Each time he'd scrubbed my teef, he would get a bottle of water and say, 'Rinse your mouth out, sonny.'

Well, we went frew this act about fifteen times a day on a Saturday, and every time he called me out I would fink to meself, *Aye aye, we're awf again.* At the end of the day me me gums were just about knackered. I don't know what was in the powder but I think it was chalk crushed up. I'd help him to pack up his gear, and he would bung me fourpence for the day's work. I'd say, 'See ya next week doc,' and awf I would run as happy as a sandboy, (bleeding gums and all).

Old Doctor Johnson used to work all the markets in the East End. The first time I worked for him was one Saturday morning. I was standing in the crowd watching him, when he got hold of my arm and pulled me to the back of the stall, and told me to clean my teef wiv some of the powder he had put on an old toofbrush. I done as I was told and when the pitch was over he asked me if I would like to work for him every Saturday. 'OK guv,' I said and that's how I started working wiv Doc Johnson. Where he lived I don't know. He just appeared in the market every Saturday morning. I can honestly say that old Doc Johnson's toof powder never done me any harm and I have never had any trouble wiv my Hampstead Heath (teef) until a few years ago when I had to have all my top teef out and that was frew old age.

The name of the market was Chris Street, Poplar. It was a long market wiv stalls each side of the road, and you could buy nearly anyfing there. It was one of the biggest markets in the East End. During the week there would only be a few stalls out, but on Saturdays and at Christmas time it would be full of stalls.

I would go home and give my mum freepence of the money I got from Doc Johnson and keep a penny for myself. Arfter I had a couple of slices of bread and dripping and a cup of tea, I would be back in the market until eight o'clock helping to put the stalls away. I'd cop a few more coppers, and arfter that my time was my own.

I would always meet up wiv the rest of the gang somewhere in the market, and then the fun would start. Someone would start frowing old rotten apples, and that was it. We would sling all sorts of shit at one anuvver and we would have a right old giggle.

The pawn shop used to do a roaring trade in the East End as everyone was skint. In the East End a woman would put her man's suit in pawn on a Monday morning and she would get it out again on a Friday so he could wear it for the weekend, that's if he had a suit – on a Friday night you would see all the geezers dressed up in their best suits. You would see all the old girls lining up outside the pawn shop on a Monday morning waiting to pop (pawn) somefing.

One Saturday night we was all pissing about in the market arfter we had put the stalls away and we were slinging things about and having a right old giggle, when old Bobby Rutter, one of our mates who was a short dumply little sod wiv ginger hair, picked up a big banana trunk and slung it in the air as high as he could. Just as he let it go a geezer came down the road wiv a bird on his arm, and they were both done up like the King and Queen of Limehouse. Well, this banana trunk came down and it hit this geezer right across the head knocking his little bowler flying. Well he was covered in shit. He let out one almighty yell, and ya could have heard him in Australia.

'Ya little barsted. I'll kill ya,' he shouted and started to run after us. Before he knew wot happened he slipped arse over head on some cabbage leaves left by one of the stall owners. His bird was in tears by this time, and all she kept saying was, 'Now we can't go dancing.' Well, this geezer went mad. Picking himself up awf the ground he said to the bird, 'Piss awf and fuck you and ya bleeding dancing.'

I knew wot he was finking to his self, 'I won't get a light on this suit in pawn on Monday morning.' The more he tried to get the shit awf, the worse it got. We didn't wait to see wot happened. Arfter that we was away a bit lively.

Chapter Two
Soliciting at the dock gates

That pawn-shop lark was a right old game. You could always earn a copper or two on a Monday morning by taking fings to pawn for the old birds who didn't like taking the fings themselves. Even the poor have some pride.

There was one old girl who I had as a regular customer. She would come to the door every Monday morning and say to my mum, 'Would your Harryboy like to do a little errand for me?' The old lady would shout up the passage, 'Harryboy, you're wanted!' and I would go to the door. There would be old Ma Long wiv her old shawl around her shoulders. She was a little old lady wiv snow white hair and a fresh complexion.

'Will ya do that little errand for me, son?' she would say to me, and I knew what she meant. I would then go to her house and there on the table would be her old man's suit neatly wrapped up, ready to go to old man Cohen's pawn shop in North Street.

Old Cohen was a little old Yid wiv a shiny bald head. He always wore a pair of specs on the end of his nose, and spoke in broken English.

On Monday morning old Ma Long said to me, 'Do ya fink you could get me seven and sixpence on it this week as I have got the old man bad in bed and I want to get some coal?'

'I'll try,' I said to her, 'but you know what old man Cohen is like. He would skin a turd for a tanner.'

Well I tucked the old suit under my arm and awf I went to the pawn shop.

When I got to the pawn shop there was old man Cohen behind the counter. He was a skinny little Yid and he always seemed like he wanted a wash. He looked at me over the top of his glasses.

'Vot do you vont?' he asked me in broken English. I put the parcel on the counter and he unwrapped it wiv boney fingers.

'How much do ya vonts?' he growled.

'I looked him straight in the eye and said, 'Seven and six this week, guv,' letting him know it had been in pawn before. He looked at the suit to see if it had any mof holes in it.

'How much do ya say ya vont?' he said, looking over the top of his glasses.

'Seven and six, guv,' I replied.

'Vot's it got, gold buttons or somefing? For weeks you have been bringing me dis smutter and I have been giving ya five bobs. Now all of a sudden ya vonts seven shillings.' And holding his head wiv his hands he said, 'Yo, yo, vot a business.'

I told him about the old girl wanting to buy some coal, and arfter some more bartering he said, 'I'll tell ya vot I am going to do. I'll give ya seven bobs if ya come and light my fire for me on Saturday morning for nuffing.' 'OK guv,' I said, 'it's a deal.' And we shook hands on it.

I went back to the old girl and when I gave her the seven shillings she was so pleased that she started to cry.

'Don't cry, missus,' I said. 'There's no shame in being poor.' My dad said God loves the poor people. That's why there is so many.'

'You're a good boy Harryboy,' she said and gave me a penny.

'That's all right, missus,' I said. 'I won't charge ya for going.' And she insisted that I took the penny.

When I got home my old lady said, 'Wot did old Muvver Long want ya for?' I told her I just had to run an errand. I did not say where to as that was our little secret.

We had no barf in our house so we would wash down in the sink or take a bar of soap and have a good scrub down in the canal. It was nuffing to see about a dozen kids on a Friday night in the summer, down in the canal having a scrub up. It was the only time the canal coppers – they were a private force employed by the Port of London Authority – stayed away. I fink they knew it was our barf night. The canal was known locally as The Cut. The barges used to go along it carrying all sorts of fings. The danger of swimming in the canal wiv dirty water and water rats never seemed to worry us. As a matter of fact, we used to chase the water rats across from one side to the uvver.

There was an old brass round our way, called Old Joan, and I used to go and get punters for her. I was only ten years old at that time. I would stand outside the dock gate and when I saw any foreign seamen coming out and I fawt they were likely punters I would run up to him and I would say, 'Ya want a bird Johnny, jigee jig, fuckee fuck?' and if they wanted a bird I would take them to old Joan. She was a big old bird who wore lots of make-up. She had big red lips and red rosie cheeks and a big bosom. She always had the neck of her dress open so ya could see all her tits.

The first time I met her she asked me if I would go and get her a jug of stout. Arfter I got the beer she said, 'If ya would like to get me some seamen from West India Docks and fetch them here to me I will give ya some pennies,' and that's how it all started. The dock gates were in West India Dock Road.

If Joan was in a good mood and she had had a good day she would give me twopence for every customer I got her. Mind you, ya 'ad to know what ya was doing. It was no good taking anuvver customer up to the flat too soon because the first punter could still be on the job and that would never do.

Limehouse in those days was one big cesspit. There was all the crime under the sun going on. There was prostitutes, gangsters, drunks, and all the filth ya could fink of, but we was happy. I've seen many a copper kicked cold, but there was no kid-glove treatment from the law.

I saw two cufflinks (Chinks) having a punch up one night, and one of them had a big brick tied onto the end of a long piece of string. He was swinging it round his head and he was hitting this uvver geezer wiv it. There was blood everywhere. All of a sudden two coppers arrived. Well the geezer wiv the brick ran for his life, so the coppers ended up nicking the uvver Chink. Well this little cufflink couldn't speak English and he was trying to explain to these two coppers. Well the coppers weren't having any of it. They just lifted this little Chink up by the scruff of the neck and they carted him awt to the nick. He was lucky they didn't frogmarch him all the way there.

I've seen many a geezer being frogmarched down to Limehouse nick in West India Dock Road. (In them days it was an old grey stone brick building wiv steps leading up to two big green doors, and hanging over the doors outside was a blue gas-lamp wiv 'Police' on it. It is still there to this day, but they have dressed it up a bit.) One copper would take one arm and one leg each and carry him face down and if the geezer got a bit out of hand they simply dropped him on his boat-race (face).

I shall never forget one week my poor old Dad was ill and he couldn't go out busking. Wot wiv having to pay for the doctor fings was a bit hard. So the old man said to the old lady, 'There's nuffing for it, old girl. You'll have to pawn the concertina to get a few bits for the kids.' Well me and the old lady was on our way to the pawn shop when we saw this big crowd of people and they were all shouting and lord mayoring (swearing) and then we saw them.

There were two coppers and they was trying to frogmarch this geezer and he was struggling like mad. The more he struggled the more they dropped him on his face. All the crowd was shouting, 'Let him go you dirty barsteds,' and someone in the crowd frew a big dirty cabbage and it hit one of the coppers right in the face. The copper let go of this fellow's arm and as he did so this geezer managed to get loose. He done no more, he just kicked the uvver copper right in the balls and the copper went down like a sack of bricks. Someone shouted, 'Run mate,' and the geezer was away like lightning. Those coppers didn't know who to nick next.

'Come on mum,' I said, 'Let's get out of this.' When we came out of the pawn-shop most of the crowd had gawn.

When we got home I fawt I was seeing fings. Standing by the fireplace was this geezer the size of a bleeding house and he was dressed like a cowboy. I fawt my poor old mum was going to have a fit. She screamed 'Oh my lawd!' and they both fell into each uvver's arms. The tears were rolling down the old lady's face and all she could say was, 'Jack! Jack!' *Who the bleeding hell's Jack?* I fawt. Arfter the excitement had died down, I found out it was her bruvver from Australia.

Arfter we had drunk a pot of tea we told him where we had been and he said, 'You can go right back in the morning and get that concertina back. There's one fing I am going to 'ear before I go back to Aussi and that is old Bill playing his concertina.' No, my old man wasn't a copper – that was his name.

That week he was wiv us was like heaven, and boy, did I stick my chest out. When I told my gang that I had an uncle who was a cowboy in Australia and that he was indoors they all laughed at me.

'Leave awf, ya bleeding potty,' said one of them.

'Take no notice of him, he's bleeding potty,' said Billy Jones. 'You don't know what you're talking about, Jonesy,' I said. 'You're like ya old man, you're all bleeding mouf.'

Billy Jones wasn't always wiv the gang. We only let him come along for a giggle. The gang consisted of Bomber Ellis, Gobber

White, Georgi Hunter, Freddy Barker, Frankie Taylor, Tommy Kocker and myself – and wot a load of basteds we were too. We never really formed the gang. It was just that we were always knocking around wiv one anuvver.

'All right then, show him to us and then we will believe ya,' replied Jones. The only way I could do that was to go indoors and ask the old lady if my mates could use the carsey (toilet). When I got in the house the old lady was at the copper washing some fings and my uncle Jack was sitting talking to my dad.

'Can my mates go to the bog?' I said to the old lady.

'Wot's the matter wiv their own bloody lavatories?' she asked.

'Well they don't want to go all the way home do they?' I said.

'Oh all right then,' she replied. Little did she know there was about ten of them outside.

I went out and said, 'OK, ya can all come in.' To get to the toilet we had to go right frew the kitchen and they couldn't be awf of seeing my uncle Jack sitting there talking to my Dad. Just as we all got into the kitchen so Uncle Jack stood up. Ya should have seen their faces. They just stood there wiv their moufs wide open and all Fred could say was, 'Blimey.'

When the old lady saw all of the mob she yelled, 'Wot the bloody hell's all this lark?' Frankie Taylor was the youngest of the gang and he just said, 'Blimey, he's a real cowboy.' Old Uncle Jack tumbled wot it was all about. In his best cowboy voice he said, 'Howdy pards,' and those kids just stood there wiv their moufs open. Uncle Jack told them all about Australia and how he rounded up sheep on a horse. They all stood there wide-eyed and took in every word he said to them. When the old lady finally told them to go, Uncle Jack put his hand in his pocket and gave each kid a penny. I don't fink those kids ever forget that day for a long time arfter they spoke about my Uncle Jack.

One morning my Uncle Jack said to me, 'Are they the only shoes you've got, Harryboy?'

'They ain't shoes, Uncle Jack, them's plimsoles,' I said.

He got up from the chair and put his jacket on and said, 'Come on, let's go and get you a decent pair of shoes.'

'Shoes ain't no good to him, Jack,' the old lady said. 'He'll have them frew in a week. Wot he needs is a good pair of hobnailed boots.'

Well awf we went to the market and arfter trying on a couple of pairs of boots I found the right ones that fitted. The lady in the shop said to my Uncle Jack, 'Shall I put them in a box for you, sir?' Before Uncle Jack could reply I was walking out of the shop wiv the boots on and I never saw them old plimsoles again. I have never forgotten those boots. They had steel tips on the toes and they were covered in steel studs all over the soles. Boy, I looked after those boots as if they were to be the only pair of boots I was ever going to wear. I polished them every time I went out and they shone like glass. When those boots wore out and they could be mended no longer it was as if I had lost a dear friend. The kicking I done wiv those boots was out of this world.

There was a kid round our way and he lived just across the road from us, and every time he saw me he would punch ten buckets of shit out of me. One day the old lady sent me to get some matches at the corner shop. Well, on my way to the shop I saw this kid coming down the street. I fawt *Aye, aye, here comes that barsted Georgi Hunter.* Georgi was a lot bigger than me, and about two years older than me and it seemed he used to pick on me as I was a lot smaller than him.

Well, as he reached me he said, 'I've got ya ain't I, ya little barsted,' and wiv that he got hold of me by the jersey. 'Get awf,' I said and the more I pulled to get away the more he hung onto my jersey. I fawt, *Harryboy, it's now or never. If ya don't stop this geezer from whacking ya, he'll be whacking ya when ya ninety.* So before he could do anyfing else to me, I kicked him right in the knackers with the boots my Uncle Jack had bought me. He dropped like a ton of bricks and he was yelling like a stuck pig. He nearly broke my eardrums. *Right, you barsted*, I fawt, *you're down and that's where you're going to stay*. So for good measure I stuck the boot right in his face. He was on the ground groaning wiv pain.

'Right ya barsted,' I said, 'If ya want more ya can have it.' Just then I looked up and I saw a copper coming down the road. I bent and I said to Georgi Hunter, 'If ya tells the copper I done ya over I'll kill ya,' and wiv that I ran home. When I got in the house, the old lady said, 'Where's the bloody matches I sent ya for?'

'Sod ya matches,' I said. 'I've just had a go at that barsted Georgi Hunter!' My bruvver was at the sink having a wash and he turned round and said, 'It's about time ya had a go at him. Now he won't be so fond at having a go at you any more, will he.'

Just then there was a knock at the door. BANG! BANG!

'Who the bloody hell's that?' said the old lady. When she opened the front door it was old man Hunter and his kid, Georgi. Before the old girl could ask him wot he wanted, he started shouting and bawling.

'Wot ya bleeding shouting ya head awf for?' said the old lady. Old man Hunter was going mad.

'That little barsted Harry of yours 'as nearly killed my Georgi,' he said. 'Hold on,' shouted the old girl, 'who are you calling a barsted? My boy's no barsted.' Old man Hunter kept on shouting and the old lady couldn't get a word in.

All of a sudden he said, 'Where's ya old man? Out cadging I suppose.' Well that done it. My brother was up the passage like the shot of a gun. You see we never cadged in all of our lives and we always put on a good show. I have seen my poor old Dad's hands stiff wiv the cold in winter trying to get a few bob to keep us kids on, but cadge? Never.

As my bruvver Albert got to the street door he hit old man Hunter right in the gut knocking him in the road. My bruvver was standing over him saying, 'Get up ya ponse. I'll kill ya.' By this time the whole street was in an uproar. Old muvver Hunter was jumping on my bruvver's back shouting, 'Leave my Sam alone ya barsted. You're a lot younger than he is.' Albert was only eighteen at the time, but he was young and fit and he gave Sam wot for. Well I mean to say, old man Hunter got all he asked for. Ya see, there's buskers and beggars and we were genuine buskers. We never begged in our lives.

A couple of the neighbours parted my bruvver and old Sam and it was all over. About six o'clock that night there came another knock on the door.

'Harryboy, go and see who that is,' said the old lady. I went out and opened the door, and who do you think it was? Well it was old Sam Hunter and his bleeding kid, Georgi, *The ponce 'as come back for more*, I fawt.

'Muvver, it's old Sam Hunter,' I called out. 'He wants to see ya. The old lady came to the door wiping her hands on her apron wiv my bruvver at her heels.

'Now wot ya want?' the old girl was asking.

'I've come to say I am sorry for wot I said about old Bill. I've known ya for years now Lil and I know he's no cadger.' And wiv that he put his hand out to shake hands wiv my bruvver. Well ya could have knocked me down wiv a fevver.

34

When my dad and sister came in we told the old man all about it.

'That's what I call a man,' he said. 'It takes a good man to say he's sorry.' Well, arfter that me and Georgi was the best of mates, and where you saw me and Fred you could see Georgi.

Sam Hunter used to go away to sea – when he felt like it, that was. Every time he came home he put his old missus in the family way. I once said to Georgi, 'You'll have so many kids in your family your old muvver will be able to start her own football club. When Albert had a punch up wiv old Sam, old Mr Dove and anuvver man parted them. It was old man Dove who told Sam Hunter that he should be ashamed of himself for calling Blind Bill a cadger.

In those days we couldn't afford to have the chimneys cleaned so we had to do it ourselves the best we could. One morning the old lady was burning some old wooden boxes that I had got from the market and the room was full of smoke.

'Blimey muvver,' I said, 'wot ya bleeding doing?'

'It ain't me,' she said. 'It's the sodding chimney. It wants bleeding cleaning.'

'All right,' I said, 'if ya don't light the fire in the morning I'll clean the chimney for ya.'

Well, the next day was Friday and when I got up the old lady had already lit the fire.

'I fawt I told ya not to light the fire, muvver. You know I said I was going to clean the chimney for, I said.

'All right,' she said. 'I'll let the fire out and you can do it for me arfter dinner.'

Well arfter dinner, there I was on my hands and knees, messing about wiv a bundle of rag tied on the end of a long stick and I was poking it up the chimney when in came Fred.

'Wot the bleeding hell ya supposed to be doing, Al?'

'Wot ya fink I am doing?' I said. 'Saying me bleeding prayers? I am cleaning the bleeding chimney, ya berk.'

He watched me for a few seconds and then he said, 'I don't clean my old lady's flue like that.'

'Wot ya do? Put yer hands up her drawers then?' I said wiv a laugh.

'Ha ha, bloody funny that,' said Fred.

35

'All right, then, clever cobblers, how do ya do ya old lady's chimney then?' I asked.

'Easy,' he said. 'I get on the roof and I put a brick in a sack. I tie it to a long piece of string and I drop it down the flue and that way you clean all the flue.' *That's a good idea*, I fawt. *I'll have a go at that.*

Well I managed to get onto the roof all right but once up there it was anuvver matter. There was about six chimney pots all in a row. I said to myself, *Aye aye, Harryboy, wot one is yours me old son?* All this time Fred was looking out of the bedroom window. I shouted across to him, ' 'Eh Fred, there's about six chimney pots up here. Wot one of them is mine?'

'They're all yours ya berk,' he answered back. So I get to work to clean the lot like a good 'un. About five minutes later the street was in an uproar. Being Friday afternoon, the old bird next door was barfing all her kids in front of the fire and they ended up getting smothered in soot. They all went running into the street stark bollock-naked and they looked like a lot of pickaninnies and there they was jumping and dancing all over the street.

You should have heard the language from that old bird. It was enough to make a navvy blush. I was awf that roof like lightning and ya couldn't see my arse for dust. Old Fred was pissing himself wiv laughing.

'You dirty barsted,' I said. 'You nevver told me that some of them chimney pots were hers next door.' But all he could do was laugh.

When we went to the front door I said, 'Wot's up Emmy?' Her full name was Emmy Sanders. She had five kids in all. She was a tall skinny woman and she always wore her hair in paper rollers, and she could swear like a docker.

'Wot's up!' she yelled. 'Some fucker has dropped a sack down my bleeding chimney and they have smothered my bleeding kids in shit.'

'Don't talk darft,' I said. 'How could that happen? There's no one on the roof.'

'If there is, I bet it's that nutcase next door to ya,' said Fred. Well the next fing we knew she was banging on old Ted's door.

I must admit old Ted was a bit of a nutter. He was five foot six and twenty-four years old. His favourite trick was to piss in the horses' trough at the top of the market. He once took off all his togs, and then the coppers came and took him away.

36

Emmy was shouting, 'Come out here ya dirty barsted.' Wiv that, old Ted opened the door. Before he could say a word, she punched him right in the boat race, knocking him flat on his back. Poor old Ted didn't know what it was about. He didn't know wot hit him.

'Wait till my Frank gets home,' Emmy was shouting. 'He'll kill ya.' *I know how much*, I fawt. *Your Frank couldn't punch a hole in a doughnut*. All this time, the little saucepan lids were jumping up and down wivout a stitch on, and screaming their heads awf. I nevver cleaned no more chimneys arfter that.

We had some right old nutters round the East End. There was one geezer we called Silly John and he was always flashing his manhood to the old girls in the market. Johnny the flasher was about five foot four. He always wore a long overcoat, a flat cap, and he had big ears and they seemed to stick out under his cap. He had big rubber lips and he was always dribbling. He was about thirty-one. Everybody knew poor old Johnny and most of the girls knew he meant no harm.

When he used to flash himself to some of the old girls they would say, 'Put it away Johnny, or I will cut it awf for ya,' and all Johnny would do was to laugh. Johnny was a favourite wiv all the costers (people wiv fruit stalls) in the market as he 'ad done a lot of lifting for them.

One day Johnny got himself into a lot of trouble. He went up to this lady in the market who was looking in a shop window, and as usual he got at the flash. At first she tried to ignore him but Johnny wasn't having any. The more she tried to ignore him, the more he exposed himself and the more he kept on grinning.

Well, this bird ended up going and getting a copper. When she came back wiv this copper, Johnny was helping Big Jim to lift some sacks of spuds onto the stall. The copper came up and he grabbed Johnny by the scruff of the neck. Poor old Johnny didn't know wat it was all about and the grin soon left his face and the tears were rolling down his cheeks.

'Wot the bleeding hell ya fink ya doing?' said Big Jim to the copper.

'You mind your own business,' said the copper. Well he must have been new on the patch, as no one spoke to Big Jim like that. Copper or no copper. Before you could say cobblers Big Jim knocked this copper flying. An old bird who had a rabbit stall joined in and started hitting this copper wiv a dirty old rabbit skin. Mind you, this copper was game. He took all they could dish out and he gave some too. Anuvver two coppers arrived on the scene and they soon had fings sorted out. It took free coppers to get Big Jim to the nick. Jim got six months' hard labour and the old bird wiv the rabbit stall got a fine. We nevver saw poor old Johnny arfter that and I found out later that he was in a nut farm. Poor little bugger.

At the top end of the market there used to stand a coffee-stall owned by old Bob and all the cab drivers and costers used to go there for their tea. There was no name on the coffee stall. He had been at the top of the market for a long time before I was born. The stall was like a big box on wheels wiv shafts to pull it wiv. On a Saturday morning I used to take a jug there to get some tea for old Doc Johnson. The geezer who owned it, Bob, was a right old ponce. He would get about five kids to push that bleeding coffee-stall all the way to the pitch at the end of the market, and once they had got it there he would pay a couple of them and then say to the rest, 'Piss awf, I've just paid ya mates.'

He tried it on me, Fred and Georgi once. Mind you, we only started to push it when it was arfway up the market. When we got it there I held out my form (hand) for the poke (money) and he said, 'Piss awf, I've just paid ya mates. I am not paying out any more so ya can all piss awf or I'll frow a bucket of slops over ya.'

'Yeah? I'd like to see ya, ya old barsted,' I said. And wiv that he went to get a bucket of water that was hanging down under the coffee stall.

'Come on Al,' said Fred. 'He ain't werf arguing wiv.'

On our way back through the market I said to Fred, 'We'll get that old barsted for that one of these nights.'

One night we was all messing around the coffee stall when Georgi noticed a lump of rope hanging down from under the stall.

'I dare ya to tie that rope to Charlie's cab,' Georgi said to Fred. Charlie was at that time having his nightly cup of tea and talking to one of the costers. Well Fred didn't want daring twice. He was under the stall before ya could say bang and all was tied nice and secure. Charlie drank up his tea and bid us all goodnight.

'Goodnight Charlie!' we all shouted waiting for the awf. By

now we was all getting excited. As Charlie was getting into his cab he shouted over his shoulder, 'See ya later, Bob.'

'OK Charlie,' was Bob's reply. That's what you fink ya old barsted, I fawt.

Then it happened. The cab and the coffee stall went tearing up the road. Old Bob went arse over head onto the floor of the coffee stall. There was hot dogs, bread rolls, tea leaves, and cups everywhere. There was Bob wiv his legs in the air shouting, 'Ya little barsteds.' Just then Charlie tumbled somefing was wrong and he slammed his brakes and the coffee stall went straight into the back of the cab with a terrible crush. We didn't wait to see what happened after that.

The name of my school was Saint Gabriel's. There must have been about two hundred kids at that school. We had mixed classes of boys and girls. Boy, did we have a laugh wiv some of those girls. The headmaster was Mr Willis. He had a wooden leg and sometimes it would squeak as he walked. Then there was old Gibbo our teacher, and Mrs Hepburn, Miss Edwards, and Mr Croft. They are the ones that stick in my mind most.

Mr Willis was about six foot tall, wiv grey hair and he always smelt of clean soap when ya got near him. Mr Gibbs was stocky built wiv brown hair and blue eyes. He used to walk very fast in his heavy brown shoes. Old Gobbo liked kicking you up the bottle and glass (arse) as ya went frew the door, and he would frow bits of chalk at ya. He was always calling us scum. As for Gibbo's temper, he was like a mad man when he lost it. He would bend the cane about harf a dozen times before he whacked ya wiv it. He used to call us kids all sorts but scum was his favourite.

The school was just around the corner from where I lived and it took me only a few minutes to get there. It was in Violet Road, five hundred yards down from the nick. The stink from some of the factories there was diabolical. The coppers were always coming to the school for one fing or the uvver. They would walk in twos down our way. You never saw one on his own.

I never spent much time at school and when I was there I was let out early free times a week so I could take the old man out busking. I started work busking wiv my Dad at the age of twelve. My Mum cut down a pair of long trousers belonging to my bruvver for me, and I wore a flat cap to make me look older.

When I first worked wiv my Dad all I did was to take him to the pubs wot he wanted to work and I would bottle for him. The bottling bag was made out of a piece of navy blue serge from one of my Mum's old skirts. I remember, on a Friday arfternoon about free o'clock I would put my hand up and the teacher would say, 'All right Hollis, you can go,' and awf I would run. All the uvver kids would say, 'Ya lucky barsted.'

I would get home, have a lump of bread and marg and a cup of tea. I would change into my long trousers and then I would be ready for work. The last fing my old Dad would say to me before we left the house was, 'Have ya got the bottling bag, son?' And I would say, 'Yus Dad.' The bottling bag is a cloth bag to collect the money in.

My Dad was a stickler for work and he would say to me, 'Son, busking is a business.' We would start work at the dog-biscuit factory at about five o'clock. The dog-biscuit factory was in Morris Road, Poplar. It was a big old factory and it looked like a prison from the outside. The smell was like malt. All the workers used to come out wiv flour all over them. Arfter we had done that and caught all the workers coming out we would get a tram over the river and work all the bevvys (public houses) up until 10.20 as we had to get the last tram home. I was fucked at the end of the night.

If there was a beano going round our way, they would always send for Blind Bill (my Dad) to work it. A beano is a day's outing to the seaside. The landlord of the boozer would hire a charabang (coach), and all the customers of that boozer would go on the outing. Sometimes it was an all men outing and sometimes it was for women.

Us kids would like it better when it was all women going on the beano as the old birds were more generous wiv their moldies. Moldies is all the loose change that they would have in their purses. Sometimes the guvner of the boozer would hand out about two pound in pennies and 'apennies. And just as the charabang moved awf, all the kids would shout out, 'Frow out ya moldies,' and the old birds would wind down the windows of the charabang and frow out all the money.

Then there would be one big punch up, I have seen more kids wiv black eyes coming away from a beano than I have had hot dinners. There would be one big shower of pennies and 'apennies

40

and all ya could see was arms and legs everywhere and shouts of 'That's mine ya barsted.'

When my Dad went on these beanos Albert would always go wiv him for the day, and he would be sitting at the back of the charabang playing his old concertina wiv Albert by his side.

It was always the women who would dress up on these occasions. There was two old birds round our way who used to be the life and soul of the party – old Ma Hughes and old Ma Barker. Mrs Hughes was about five foot six, wiv grey hair and blue eyes; Ma Barker was a plumpish woman wiv dark brown hair and brown eyes and she was about five foot seven tall. They were the two most respected women down our street.

Mrs Hughes always wore an old black shawl round her shoulders and a man's flat cap wiv lace-up black boots. She was a lovely old girl and she was always there if someone was in trouble. She lived next door to Mrs Barker, so you can guess they were the best of friends. Like most of our old neighbours we lost touch wiv them when the war came along.

If there was a beano going it was the talk of the street for weeks before it went. All the kids would be up early on the great day and we would make our way to the boozer and wait for the charabang to arrive. This would be some time around 7.30 in the morning. Then the first fing they would do was to load it up wiv crates of beer for the journey down to the seaside.

Outside the boozer the guvner would put a large barrel of beer on a table and as each customer arrived they would help themselves to a (drink of) bevvy and then the party was on. It's a funny fing, but all the old birds seemed to enjoy themselves more than the men on them occasions.

My Dad would sit on a chair and start playing his old concertina, and everyone would start to get into the party mood. Then Ma Hughes and Ma Barker would arrive, all dressed up in some kind of costume. Laugh – on one of these occasions, old muvver Hughes came along the street wiv old Ma Barker, and she had all paint and powder on her face. She was wearing a big pair of baggy red, white and blue drawers and a pair of football socks and hobnail boots. Between her legs, hanging in front of her baggy drawers, was a big carrot and two big onions. They were tied round her waist wiv a lump of string. Her counterpart Ma Barker was dressed up as a man, wiv top hat and tails and football boots.

41

Everybody laughed when they saw old Ma Hughes wiv her carrot between her legs.

'Wot's the bleeding carrot and onions for?' said Fred. 'That's in case she gets hungry on the way to the seaside,' said Georgi. 'She can make herself a bleeding stew.'

Once the charabang arrived everyone would climb aboard ready for the awf. Once on their way the moldies would come flying out of the windows of the charabang. Inside, everyone would be having a good old knees-up to my Dad's music.

As time went by and Albert had learnt to play the accordion he used to do the beanos. At night when they returned you could 'ear them coming down the road wiv them singing for all they were worf. They would all pile out of the charabang and start having a knees-up outside the boozer. Then they would finish awf by singing 'He's a jolly good feller' to the guvner of the boozer. And at last they would all go their separate ways. Everyone would say to my Dad, 'Goodnight Bill, it's been lovely, mate.' For his day's work he would get paid by the guvner of the boozer. On these occasions my Dad would always bring us kids a rock back from the seaside. My mum would cut mine up into lumps and I would share it wiv my mates.

Apart from leaving school early free times a week, I played truant a lot. One lovely summer's morning I fawt to myself, 'I ain't having none of that school lark today. I'll have a day awf.' I saw Fred and Gobber White going to school and I told them what I was going to do.

'I can't do that Al,' said Fred. 'The last time my old man found out I played hookey he nearly broke my bleeding back.'

'Ya dead scared of ya old man, ain't ya?' I said.

'It ain't that, Al, but you know wot he is,' said Fred. 'OK. Wot about you, Gobber?' I said. Old Gobber was game for anyfing.

'I'll come wiv ya, Al,' he said and awf we went.

'Where are we going, Al?' said Gobber.

'Let's go up the market and have a giggle,' I replied.

Incidentally, wot can we say about poor old Gobber, Gawd bless him? If he was here today he would be about sixty-two. He was a small kid wiv ginger hair. Why he always spat arfter every sentence I shall never know. He was always getting good hidings from his muvver. He never seemed to have any decent clothes. Wot he did have were full of 'oles. His old man and his old woman were always fighting, and his old man would sometimes go on the piss for days. When he couldn't get no more beer he would return home and beat up the old lady and Gobber.

His farver never worked. He lived on the dole and thieved all his life. The rent collector was afraid to knock on their door as old man White would go out and punch him one and tell him to fuck awf. Gobber's muvver was a big-breasted woman and she always seemed to wear the same old jumper. And I don't fink she combed her hair from the year dot. She liked her beer as much as old man Gobber did. Gobber never had much of a life. Sometimes he never had anyfing to eat all day.

He used to say to me, 'I wish my old man was like yours, Al.' Gobber would sit at his desk and look up the teacher's skirt. He would say to his mate sitting next to him, 'She's got white ones on today.'

'One of these days she is going to cop you looking up her clouts, Gobber, and Gawd help ya,' Georgi would say. Gobber just laughed and spat on the floor and said, 'She can whack me wiv a pair of her knickers any day.'

'You're mad Gobber and you've got a dirty mind,' I would say.

'Yus, I know but ain't it lovely,' he would say.

He was always in bovver and the more his old man punched him up the more he liked it. I've seen him come to school wiv black eyes and all sorts. The teachers took no notice as they knew it was best to stay out of anyfing like that round our way.

Gobber started feeving at an early age. My old Mum once said that he started feeving the day he was born. 'Leave awf muvver, he was too little,' I said.

There was never a day that passed wivout he didn't bring somefing to school that he had nicked the night before. He was always getting the cane for eating in class. His favourite was black sausage. Ya could guarantee he would nick 'arf a black sausage every time he passed the butcher's stall in the market.

One morning we played truant away from school, and we was messing around in the market.

'I'm getting bleeding hungry, Gobber,' I said.

'Ya know wot Al,' he replied, 'I was just finking the same. If ya like to follow me, me old son, I will get us our breakfast.' So wiv me hands in my pockets and whistling a merry tune I followed behind the great Gobber, as I knew I was certain of getting my breakfast.

43

We made our way to Pick's, the butcher's stall. When we arrived, there was a couple of old girls buying their meat.

'When old Pick goes to the end of the stall to serve one of those old birds,' said Gobber, 'I'll be under that stall before he even knows.'

I stood by for the great robbery, and before I knew wot was happening Gobber had vanished under the stall. Arfter a few moments he appeared wiv his jersey bulging. We walked away as if nuffing had happened.

When we had got out of sight of the stall, Gobber produced a long string of beef sausages. Tearing them in 'arf wiv his grubby hands he said, 'Cop 'arf each.'

'How the fuck are we gong to cook these?' I said.

'Cook 'em be fucked,' replied Gobber. 'We eat the barsted raw.' It was the first time I had eaten raw sausages and they turned out to be the best sausages I had ever tasted.

Anyway, we spent 'arf that morning helping to unload spuds from a horse and cart and having a right old feed-up of speckty (rotten apples) that had fallen from the stalls. Around ten o'clock the old geezer who we was helping asked Gobber if he would take the jug and go and get a jug of tea from the coffee shop. Awf went Gobber wiv the jug and I stayed to carry on unloading. Well, I was working like a goodun when out of the blue appeared the school-board inspector, a tall man wiv black hair and dark brown eyes, who never wore a uniform. I had only seen him in the same old suit all the time I knew him, the old barsted.

'And why are we not in school?' he asked.

'Who do ya fink you are then?' I asked him.

'I am the school-board inspector, that's who I am,' he bawled at me. 'And what school do you go to?'

I told him that I went to Saint Gabriel's and the next fing I knew, he had me by the scruff of the neck and he was saying, 'You're going back to school me lad.'

'Piss awf,' I said, 'I ain't going back to no bleeding school.' And that made him really mad and he started to march me up the road by my jersey collar. *If this ponce gets me back to school*, I fawt to myself, *I'll get a right old whacking awf old Gibbo*. And then I realised he never asked me my name. 'Right you barsted, I fawt. The first chance I get I'll have it away. And then out of the blue he tripped up on the kerb and before he knew wot was wot I wrenched myself away from him and ran like mad.

In the arfternoon we decided to go to Victoria Park and mess around on the swings. On our way to the park we saw a baker's cart. Gobber said, 'Aye, aye, our tea is coming up.' I fawt, *now wot's he up to*? and I was soon to find out.

He walked straight up to the cart, opened the back doors and helped himself to a loaf of bread and about six currant buns.

Just as we were about to leave the cart, the driver came out of a house and he nearly collared Gobber, but Gobber was too farst for him and we was away wiv the wind, wiv the geezer shouting arfter us. I ran so fast I fawt my lungs were going to bust. A harf hour later we were in the park eating dried bread and current buns. Arfterwards we washed it down wiv a drink of water from the gardener's tap and spent the rest of the day lazing in the sun.

I spent the rest of the day in the park. I wasn't going back to the market to find Gobber in case that old inspector was still around. I went home at the usual time we came out of school so as the old lady would fink I had been to school. That way the old girl didn't know the difference.

The next day I went to school and as soon as I got in the classroom old Gibbo, our teacher, said, 'Where were you yesterday, Hollis?'

'I had the guts-ache, sir,' I said.

'How comes you have the guts-ache about free times a week?' he said.

'I don't know. It just comes on.'

'Well the next time you get the guts-ache I want a doctor's certificate from you.'

'Leave awf,' I said. 'I can't afford a doctor's certificate. My old lady ain't got no money to pay no bleeding doctor.' And wiv that he pushed me toward my seat and told me to sit down.

I told Georgi and Fred about the school-board inspector catching me in the market and how I managed to escape from him.

'I wish I had been there, Al,' said Georgi. 'I would have punched his bleeding head in.'

'Leave awf, Georgi. Ya couldn't punch shit, could he Al,' said Fred.

Well around ten o'clock the classroom door opened and in walked the inspector.

'Eyes up Al,' said Fred. 'Look who's here.' And before I could blink he spotted me. I fawt to myself: *Just like the Bible says Your sins will find ya out.*

'Come out here, Hollis,' Old Gibbo was shouting at the top of

45

his voice. Here we go, I fawt. He's got a big mouf that school-board geezer. I was taking me time getting out of my desk when Gibbo came running up the aisle and grabbed me by the ear.

'Come out here, scum,' he screamed at the top of his voice and he pulled me to the front of the class by my ear. 'So you never had the shits yesterday did you?'

Before I could say anyfing he was getting the cane out of his desk drawer and saying 'Hold out your hand.'

'Ya ain't whacking me ya old ponce,' I said. Wiv that he banged, me one round the ear 'ole knocking me flying. As I fell I hit my head on the corner of a desk.

Blood! I fawt he had struck oil. I got up and kicked him right in the balls. By this time the class was in uproar. All the kids was shouting, 'Leave him alone ya old ponce.' The las fing I saw was old Gibbo holding his bollocks and doubled up wiv pain. I didn't wait around for the next round. I just ran straight out of school.

When I got home and the old lady saw all the blood on my jersey she nearly hit the ceiling. I told her what had happened, and how the school-board inspector came copper on me. She said, 'I'll give him bleeding school-board man.' The next fing I knew, her old shawl was round her shoulders and she was out the door wiv me at her heels.

When we got to the school old Gibbo had been sent home by the headmaster on account of me giving him one in the cobblers but the school-board geezer was still in the hall talking to the headmaster. The old lady never said a word. She just picked up a big heavy doormat from the hall doorway and belted the school-board inspector all round the hall wiv it. The poor headmaster was trying his utmost to take the door mat away from the old lady.

By this time all the kids was shouting, 'Go on, missus Hollis, kill the old barsted.' Can you imagine that old geezer? He was smothered in shit from head to foot. As I said before, the old lady was only five foot nothing, but she was as strong as a horse. The headmaster ended up calling the law and the nick was only round the corner so the scarps were there in no time at all.

Well, we all ended up in the headmaster's office and when the copper saw all the blood on my jersey he pulled the headmaster to one side and they started to whisper to each uvver. The old school-board man was saying to my Mum, 'What about my coat? Who's going to pay to have it cleaned?'

'Sod ya bleeding old coat,' she replied. 'If ya touch my boy again you'll get more than that.'

Just then the copper came over and said to the school inspector, 'If I was you sir, I would forget it.' Well it was all smoothed over and that old inspector never bothered me again. Arfter that I just went to school as I liked. I fink I must have spent about five years at school altogevver.

Every Saturday morning before I done anyfing else I had to go to the local council borough cleansing station to get free bottles of disinfectant and dustbin powder for the old lady. The council would provide us wiv disinfectant to keep the stink down. They also gave us powder to put in the dustbins. Every Saturday morning before I went out wiv the old man I would have to go round Morris Road to the council yard and line up wiv the uvver kids to get the disinfectant and dustbin powder. I had to be up at 7.30 so as I could get a place in the queue. There would sometimes be about forty to fifty kids all getting disinfectant for their muvvers. The council used to give it away free to keep down the vermin but no matter wot ya done it was no use. Arfter I'd got the powder and disinfectant I would go home and have somefing to eat before going out to earn a few coppers.

To have fish and chips for supper was somefing really special. Even if we wanted an apple we would have to nick it awf one of the stalls in the market. So me and Fred devised a way of getting chips for our supper. We would wait outside Sam's the fish shop in Chris Street (where the market was) for the kids to come out wiv their chips. Fred would be on one side of the door and I would be on the uvver and as the kids came frew the door wiv their chips we would nick a handful and run. If one of us missed, the uvver one was sure to get some.

One day Georgi pinched a 'arf box of apples awf a stall and we ate them between us. Fred said he had never had so many apples in all his life. The next day we ended up wiv the guts ache.

It was a long time before we could go to Bob's coffee-stall so we had to find a new fish shop nearly every night as we had to get our supper somehow. All our sweets we would nick from old Fanny Hoskins. She used to make home-made sweets and sell them from her house. We would get one of the kids to go round the back of her house and kick hell out of her back door, and

47

when she went to open the back door we would nip in the front and nick a handful of toffee.

The story was that Fanny Hoskins's old man went down on the Titanic and it left her a bit potty. She was a fin, frail old lady wiv grey hair and grey eyes. She used to talk wiv a middle-class accent. Her little house was at the beginning of Chris Street. It was a dark-looking old dump, and she used to make sweets out in the back room. The sweet we nicked from her was nobody's business. When old Gobber went into her house to ask her the time he always came out wiv a tray of toffee. Poor old Fanny lost more sweets like that than she knew about. One day, they found her dead in the shit-house wiv her bloomers round her ankles. Before she was cold all the kids was in that house nicking all the sweets. We all had a right old feed up all down to old Fanny. Poor old Fanny. She must have been a lonely old girl.

Chapter Three
Old Kate in the drink

There was plenty of lonely birds like Fanny. Like old Kate for instance. Poor old Kate. How can you describe her? She must have been a lonely old woman. Her hair was matted togevver and she always stunk of piss. Her stockings were as black as the ace of spades and the coat she wore was supposed to have been cream in colour but there was so much grease on it that it could have stood up on its own. Her hair was at one time fair but there was so much dirt in it you could have grown spuds there. Where she came from no one knew. She used to come and go like the tide. She drank methylated spirits, and she stunk to high 'eaven. She was a loner and a mystery. All we knew was she was always drunk. Whenever ya saw old Kate ya could bet ya shilling she would be sozzled.

Well one day we was all swimming down in the canal and Benny Swails had caught a water rat and we tied its back legs to the canal railings and we was frowing bricks at it, when along the footparf came old Kate and she was singing at the top of her voice, as drunk as a sailor. All of a sudden she fell arse over head in the drink.

'The silly old cow's drowning,' Benny Swails shouted. Wiv that we all dived in arfter her and it took free of us to pull her out. We got her out and laid her on the footparf.

The silly old cow 'as blown it out,' Fred said, meaning she was dead. By this time all of us was crowded round her in our birfday suits.

'Don't be bleeding darft, Fred,' I said. 'She's still breeving.'

Before we knew it, up came a canal copper. No one saw him coming. Some of the kids picked up their gear and scarpered. The canal coppers were different from the coppers in the street. They wore a uniform wiv PLA (Port of London Authority) on the collar and a peaked cap.

'Wot the bloody hell have ya got there?' he said. When he saw old Kate lying on the footparf, he said, 'One of ya had better go and get a copper.' Well I done no more. I was frew the fence

49

wivout a stitch on and I ran all the way to the nick. I ran into the nick and you should have seen the look on the sergeant's face behind the counter when he saw me.

'Wot do you want, me lad, dressed like that?' he said. Well I mean, how can ya be dressed when ya ain't got nuffing on? Between panting for breff, I told him about old Kate falling in the canal and arfter five minutes he sent me back to the canal wiv two coppers. We must have looked a right old sight wiv me between those two coppers wiv nuffink on.

When we got back to the canal all the kids were standing Around and there was old Kate still laying on the towparf shaking like a prostitute's tit and the canal copper was trying to cover her up wiv his jacket.

'Wot happened?' asked one of the coppers.

'Well as far as I know, she fell in and this lot pulled her out,' said the canal copper. By this time the uvver copper was bending down over old Kate. He looked up and said to his mate, 'She's pissed.'

'He's a right old berk,' I said to Fred. 'Anyone can see she's pissed. Ya can smell her in Australia.'

Just then old kate came round.

'Wot's ya name, luv?' one of the coppers said. *He must be new on the plot if he don't know old Kate*, I fawt.

'Her name's Kate,' said one of the kids, 'and she sleeps round the back of the boiler house on some sacks in the bone-yard.'

The smell of that bone-yard was out of this world, and the rats were as big as cats. The back of the boney was in Orchard Place. What a lovely name for such a stink 'ole.

Anyway, the copper who had been bending over her said, 'Blimey, she stinks of meffs.' Well we all knew old Kate drank methylated spirits so it didn't take a Sherlock Holmes to sort that out All of a sudden old Kate went out like a light again.

'She's had it this time,' George said.

'Leave awf, she's still breeving,' said Fred.

The copper who had been bending over her looked up at his mate and said 'I think we'd better have an ambulance, Jim,' and wiv that his mate went for an ambulance. While we were all waiting for the ambulance to arrive the uvver copper said, 'Right, let's have ya names and addresses.'

'What ya want our names for, guv?' asked Georgi.

'So I can get ya all a medal from the King,' said the copper. Wiv that all the kids started to give their names.

50

'PIss awf,' said Georgi. 'We pulled the old cow out.' And before we knew where we were there was a punch up and all the kids were shouting at one anuvver.

The copper ended up doing his nut and he shouted, 'If I don't get all your names, I'll run you all in.' Well, as soon as the uvver kids heard that, they didn't want to know and they all seemed to fade in the background.

'Right, what's your name?' he asked Georgi who gave him his name and address. Then the copper said to me, 'Now lad, what's yours,' looking me straight in the face.

'I ain't done nuffing guvnor,' I said.

'You was the one that came to the station wasn't you?'

I ended up giving my name then Fred said, 'Do ya want my name, guvnor? I helped Georgi to pull the old cow out of the drink.'

As the copper was taking Fred's name, up came the meat wagon. When the ambulance men saw old Kate one of them said, 'Oh no, not her again. We only dried her out last week.'

'She must have fallen in the drink last week as well,' I said to Fred. The copper smiled, and said, 'He means she was in the hospital having treatment.'

Well, they put old Kate on a stretcher and took her away. When I got home I was telling the old lady all about it, and how we pulled old Kate out of the canal.

'Leave awf,' my bruvver Albert said. 'It's all bleeding lies.'

'No it ain't,' I said. 'If she was bevvied and she fell in the drink then she would have drowned,' he said.

'No, she never drowned,' I said. 'She's in hospital.'

'All right son,' the old lady said. 'Eat ya bread. I believe ya. '*Ya!* I fawt, *I know none of ya believe me.*

The old man had been sitting there taking it all in. He said, 'He could be right, ya know. I knew a bloke once that fell in the dock drunk and he never drowned.'

I said to my bruvver, 'See, ya don't know everyfing.'

The old man was like that. He never liked to 'ear us kids argue. if we did have an argument he would say, 'That's enough. You are a family. Bruvvers and sisters don't argue.' Yus, he had some good ways, my Dad. Like when we was out busking on a winter's night he would say, 'Are ya cold son?'

'Yus Dad, I'd reply, 'it's me feet that's the coldest.'

51

'Wait until we have done the next bevvy (public house) and I'll get ya two nice hot spuds from old Tony.'

He was a smashing geezer, old Tony. He had a hot-chestnut barrow and he fawt the world of the old man. My Dad had known him for a long time and the old man told me once that he had known Tony when he was a young man when he first came to England. Ya see, Tony was an Italian and he came to England before I was born. While the old man and Tony would be talking, Tony would give me two hot baked spuds and when we left he would give me two more small ones and I would put them in my jacket pocket to keep my hands warm. The last thing Tony would say to me before we left was, 'Keep ya chest done up, Harryboy and keep ya self warm,' and awf we would go to finish awf the last few boozers.

If we earned two shillings it meant we'd had a good night but I can't ever remember earning more than one shilling and sixpence. On our way home we would stop at the pie shop and I would go inside and get four pies in a bag to take home to my muvver and two sisters. The pie shop was in the market and the name of it was Manzie's. It was well known in the East End. The pies cost fruppence and they were full of meat. If ya had pie and mash wiv licker it would cost ya fourpence. Licker is a fick green gravy made of parsley. Nearly all the cockneys were brought up on pie and mash. I haven't met one who doesn't like it.

Saturday was always a long day for me and the old man. We would leave home at ten in the morning, get frew Blackwall Tunnel, and start work over in North Woolwich. We would work all the bevvies we could up until two o'clock wivout having a bite to eat, and then we would get the football crowds at West Ham before they went into the grounds. The punters in those days never had a lot of money, but they were as generous as their pockets allowed.

Arfter about free tunes I would leave the old man and go round wiv the bottling bag. This was in case the crowd started to go into the ground. Arfter they had all gawn in we would go to old Flo's coffee shop which was my favourite.

Old Flo was a big old bird wiv big breasts and blonde hair. She always wore a pinney behind the counter. Her bread pudding was out of this world. She had rosie cheeks and blue eyes and she kept looking at herself in the mirror behind the counter. Old Tom was a lot smaller than her, and all the cab drivers used to pull his leg and say to him, 'Did ya have it last night, Tom?' They also used to say, 'He ties his name on his boots when he 'as anyfing to do wiv old Flo in case he falls in.' Flo would look up and say, 'Leave awf, he ain't got it in him now.'

Tom was about five foot two wiv a round face and blue eyes and dark brown hair. He always wore a white apron behind the counter. He never wore boots when he was working, just house slippers. He wasn't a bad boy, old Tom. He always gave me large teas for small ones and he would cut me a big lump of bread pudding.

Old Flo made the best bread pudding in the East End. The old man would say, 'Do ya fink we could 'ave anuvver lump of bread puddin' between us?' and I would look in the bottling bag and say, 'Yus, I fink we could afford a bit more, Dad.' We would end up having a pint mug of tea each and that had to last us until we got home at night.

We would always sit at the back of the coffee shop on our own. The reason for this was that the old man always liked to count the takings 'arfway frew the day. Arfter we had finished our tea he would say, 'Oh well son, let's count the medzers (money).'

As I told you at the beginning, we buskers have our own language and when we was counting money or talking about our work we would always use this language and this is called the palaree. It was very handy when you didn't want anyone to know wot you was talking about. It was handed down from farver to son. I don't know of any busker today who knows this language.

The take for a Saturday morning was about a beong dooey saltie (1s 2d – about 6p today). If you were lucky it could be a beonk sa (1s 6d – 7½p). For a full day's work on a Saturday you could earn a tray beonk sa (3s 6d – 17½p), and that was from ten in the morning to eleven at night.

Arfter we came out of Flo's coffee shop we would go to the market and fly pitch. The old man would stand in the gutter and I would stand on the pavement and bottle. Around five we would make our way back to West Ham FC to catch the crowds on their way out. We would then start work on the boozers again until closing time, bevvies like the Foresters, the Black Horse, the Bell, the Anchor, and many more. We had to go frew Blackwall tunnel to work them. Lewisham was about six miles from our house. We would work the music-hall and picture-hall queues as well, especially the Hippodrome in East India Dock Road and the Pavilion in East India Dock Road. They were about five minutes' walk from each uvver. The music hall was the Queen's

53

in Poplar High Street. When we done them we went onto the boozers. The old man would play a few tunes. Then I would bottle before the crowd went in.

I shall never forget one winter's night we missed the last bus home and we had to walk all the way frew Blackwall tunnel, a journey of six long miles. When I got home I was knackered. I was so tired I slipped my old plimsoles awf and got into bed wiv all my clothes on. I slept in my old jersey, my long trousers, and socks. All the way home the old man kept saying, 'It ain't far now, son.' I made sure we never missed that bloody bus arfter that.

On Sundays we only worked during teatime, and then we done the slangs (picture queues). Sunday morning, winter and summer, I would take the old man over to Bethnal Green to see his farver. Old Grandfarver Hollis was a tough old bird. He started busking at the age of eight and he wasn't as lucky as me. He wasn't lucky enough to have plimsoles. He went around bare-footed, all the year round.

Old Grandfarver Hollis was a right old barsted but we all loved him. He was a tall man for the East End, about five foot nine, wiv a bald head and a white moustache. He had rosy cheeks and a red bulbous nose which showed he liked his beer. He lived in Bethnal Green but I can't remember the name of the street. The name of the boozer where him and my Dad would go to on a Sunday was called the Rose.

The woman he was living wiv was not his wife. There was talk about his real wife being dead. He used to call the woman Nelson on account that she had a funny eye. I fink it was his farver that started him busking. I must have been thirteen when he died and I fink he died of old age. I can remember he was very patriotic. He used to have two big Union Jacks standing in the corner of his bedroom, and he would hang them out of the window on any occasion to do wiv the Royal Family. Everyone around Bethnal Green knew him, and he was always helping someone out. Him and my Dad would talk the buskers' language when they were togevver in the boozer.

'You kids don't know you're born wiv ya fancy shoes,' he would say to me.

'Ya don't know wot ya talking about grandfarver,' I said to him once. 'Them ain't shoes. Them's plimsoles.' And before I knew it he gave me one round the ear 'ole.

'Never anser ya Grandfarver back, son' my Dad said. 'His word is law.'

I shall never forget the Sunday I showed him the boots that my Uncle Jack had bought me.

'Ya want to get the bloody fings in pawn so ya muvver can get ya some grub wiv the bloody money,' he growled.

'She ain't going to do that.' I said, forgetting wot my Dad had told me about his word being law, and I ended up getting a good hiding wiv a walking stick.

'Ya want to teach that little barsted some manners,' he said to my dad.

'Say you are sorry to ya Grandfarver,' said my Dad.

'I am sorry, Grandfarver,' I said and I ended up sitting on the boozer doorstep wiv a penny arrowroot biscuit. I would watch what I said every Sunday arfter that.

When Grandfarver Hollis died, his coffin and the carriages were covered in flowers. I can remember the old lady taking all of us kids into the front room so as we could all kiss him goodbye in his coffin. I shall never forget the feel of his forehead as I was lifted up by my eldest bruvver to kiss him goodbye. It was cold and hard and it felt like stone. My baby sister was last to be held over the coffin to kiss him and she was too young to understand that he was dead. She thought he was still alive. She held out her hands and in her baby way she was saying, 'Farver, Farver' – that is what she always called him – and she pulled the front of his hair and as my muvver tried to pull her away she pulled and his head seemed to go to one side as if he was looking at me.

I remember going by his favourite boozer, the Rose. The carriages stopped and all the people was standing outside the boozer. The men were standing there wiv their caps in their hands and a few of the old ladies was crying. he was very well known round the East End and wiv all his tough ways he would always be helping people out if they were in trouble.

For my week's work I would get twopence so wiv my uvver fiddles I could earn up to sixpence a week. That ain't bad, I fawt. The rate I am going I could end up being a millionaire by the time I am ninety.

I shall never forget the time my bruvver Albert tried to learn me to play the spoons. First I tried to play a pair of big, old dinner spoons.

'They ain't no good, son,' said my Dad. 'Ya have to have a pair of dessert spoons and they have to be made of alloy or they will have a ring to them.'

'Where will I get a pair of spoons like that?' I said.

'In the pie shop,' said my bruvver Albert who was sitting at the table.

'How will I get them?'

'Pinch 'em ya silly sod, how else?'

'Don't you start telling him fings like that,' said Dad.

'I was only kidding him,' said my bruvver, making gestures to me that the old man couldn't see, indicating for me to go outside.

When we got outside my bruvver said. 'All ya got to do is to go in the pie shop and get yaself some mash in a bowl and just walk out wiv the spoons.'

'I can't do that,' I said. 'The old man will kill me if he finds out.'

'Well ya want to be a star, don't ya? Besides, that's the only place to get the kind of spoons ya want,' he said.

All the next day I fawt about those spoons and I told Georgi and Fred wot I had in mind.

'That's easy,' Georgi said. 'All we got to do is to go in the pie shop and get some mash and licker each and when the old bird ain't piping (looking) we walk out wiv the spoons.'

Well, the great spoon robbery was a great success, and I ended up wiv free spoons instead of two.

'That's all right,' said Fred. 'Ya can keep the uvver one wiv ya in case ya wear one out.' I knocked myself potty wiv those spoons and I was black and blue all over wiv practising. Ya don't just stand there. Ya have to put on a bit of a show wiv them, like running them up and down ya arms and round ya head.

Arfter about free weeks of practising I finally slung them in the canal in rage. By the way, Dad never did find out about the stolen spoons. It was a good job too or he would have made me take them back.

My bruvver Albert worked on his own in them days and he used to play the portable harmonium. That's a little organ that closed down into a small box and ya could carry it on ya back. It was worked by pumping the bellows wiv ya feet. Albert did his own bottling and he worked anywhere he could. He would work boozers, theatres, markets, and anywhere he could earn a crust.

Before we all left home in the morning to go out to graft (work) we would let one anuvver know where we was going. This

56

was so we didn't invade each uvver's round. If you was working and anuvver busker came up and started work near you this was known as topping and he would get blacked out by the uvver buskers and sometimes there would be a fight over a pitch and that sort of thing got ya a bad name. But a proper busker would never dream of doing that.

One Saturday we was in Flo's coffee shop when in came Albert.

'How's the mezzers ya jaggs?' (How's business, mate?) asked the old man.

'Bold ya jaggs,' (bad, mate) replied Albert. So arfter we had our tea we decided to join up wiv each uvver. We made our way to the local market and after a few tunes we had a nice little edge (crowd).

'All bona ya jaggs (Very good mate)', Albert said to me.

I bottled while the old man and Albert carried on playing. Well, when we had finished one of the stall-holders came over to the old man and slipped a tray saltie (threepence) in his hand and said, 'Bill, it's better than the bleeding Albert Hall.'

'Fanks mate,' said the old man. 'Them's my two boys.' I could tell by the tone of his voice that he was proud of us.

Arfter that we became a regular sight in the market every Saturday. I got anuvver rise and I was in the big time. I was now earning fourpence a week. Boy, did I earn that fourpence. We was out in winter, summer, rain, fog, snow and all kinds of wevver that God sent but it was an honest living and the old man was proud of his two boys.

When I wasn't out busking, my favourite pastime was swimming in the canal wiv the rest of the gang in our birfday suits. The water was dirty but I don't fink it was dangerous. If it was, it didn't 'arm any of us kids. The canal coppers would chase us but they never had much success in catching us. All we had to do was dive in the drink and swim to the uvver side of the canal. Once on the uvver side we would call the coppers all kinds of names.

It was about two weeks arfter we had pulled poor old Kate out of the canal we was all larking about as usual when my bruvver Billy appeared.

'Wotcha kid. Wot do ya want?' I asked him.

'Ya better get ya arse home. The coppers have been round the house for ya,' he said.

57

'Wot do ya mean? I ain't done nuffing.'

'And they want ya two mates, too,' he went on to say.

'Piss awf,' said Fred. 'I ain't done nuffing. Nor 'as Georgi, have we, Georgi?'

'I don't know wot it's all about but ya all better get ya arses home out of it,' he said.

We all got dressed and made our way home. As soon as I got indoors the old lady said, 'Wot have you been up to. Bullnose Hanley 'as been 'ere for ya.' Bullnose Hanley was a police sergeant from the local nick and he was a right old barsted. Every time there was a punch up they would send Bullnose out to sort it out.

Blimey, Bullnose! I fawt. *I wonder what he wants.*

Bullnose must have been about fifty-five. All the kids called him Bullnose on account of his hooter. He was about six foot two and built like a house. He was stationed at Poplar nick up the road from where I lived.

Well, the old man didn't say a word as he already knew wot it was all about. All he said was, 'We won't be going out tonight, son, as they are coming back for you.'

'And they want your bloody mates too,' said the old lady.

'Well muvver, I don't know wot they want us for as we haven't been up to anyfing,' I said. Well, I don't mind telling ya, I was shitting myself.

It was about five o'clock when there was a big bang on the front door.

'That's them,' said the old lady, and wiv that she went to open the front door.

'Well, is he in?' a voice said. The old lady called up the passage, 'Harryboy, come out here.'

I went to the front door and there he was, Bullnose himself. *Blimey* I fawt, *it must be a dodge for them to send this old barsted round.*

He looked at me and said, 'Is your name Harry Hollis?'

'You know it is,' I said. 'I used to go and get your tea for ya when I worked in Jones's Cafe washing up and you used to creep in the back for a crafty cup of tea.'

A little grin came on his face and he said wiv a little cough, 'Well, you'd better come wiv me, my lad,' and the next fing I knew I was being pushed into the hurry-up wagon.

When I got into the wagon, I could 'ear Fred saying, 'Wot's it all about?'

'How the bleeding hell do I know?' I said.

'It's all a frame up,' Georgi was saying. When we got to the nick the van drove in the back way and stopped outside the back door. The doors of the van opened and a copper said, 'Right you lot, inside,' and he pointed to the door. Once inside he took us to the charge room, told us to sit down and went out, shutting the door behind him.

'Don't say nuffing and out of nuffing they can't get nuffing,' I said to the uvver two.

'We ain't got nuffing to tell them, Al,' said Fred.

'It's all a frame up,' said Georgi. Arfter a few minutes the door opened and there stood Bullnose.

'Come on you three,' he said. 'Follow me.' Awf we all went and he took us to a big room.

When we got inside there was an inspector and anuvver geezer in plain clothes. Up goes Bullnose to the inspector and he comes to attention and salutes him and says, 'There they are sir. I've got all three of them.'

Cor, I fawt, *They've got an inspector on the job and that geezer in plain clothes must be from Scotland Yard so it must be a big job*. Old Fred, he's giving me the nudge, and whispers, 'Wot do ya fink Al?'

'I told ya before,' I said, 'say nuffink. Wotever they do, say nuffink.'

'Right sergeant, take them through to the uvver room and I'll be along in a minute,' said the inspector.

'Yes sir,' said Bullnose coming to attention, and wiv the next breff he said, 'Right you three, follow me,' and we all followed him down the corridor to a room at the end.

'Wot we having, Bullnose, a grand tour of the nick?' said Fred.

'Not so much of the Bullnose, sunny Jim,' said Bullnose, and we ended up in anuvver small room wiv a door in the corner. In this room there was two lady coppers wearing white aprons. I fawt, *Aye aye, the old ferd degree treatment. They're going to give us the old rubber truncheon lark and them old birds have got them aprons on so the blood don't splash their uniforms.*

'Listen,' I said to Fred and Georgi, 'if they start to pull their truncheons, fight like mad. No matter wot they do go down fighting.'

'We'll do old Bullnose first and then we do the two birds arfter,' said Georgie.

59

'Yus, I fancy some of that. I fink I'll have the dark one,' said Fred.

'Why must you always have a dirty mind?' Georgi said to Fred.

Righto, no talking,' said Bullnose, and he indicated to a long wooden bench. 'Sit down there like three good little boys.'

'He must be joking,' said Georgi. All free of us sat down on this wooden bench awaiting our fate. Arfter a few seconds the door opened and in came the inspector wiv the geezer in plain clothes.

'Right sergeant, you and the ladies can fetch them along now. Everything is ready.'

All this time the geezer in the plain clothes ain't said a dicky bird. *He must be the head man*, I fawt. *He will do all the charging*.

'Don't forget, Georgi boy,' I said, 'stay stoom (say nothing).'

'There's one thing, Al,' said Fred. 'We've had a tour of the nick.'

'I ain't interested in the bleeding nick,' I said. 'I want to know wot we are here for.'

'Right this way,' said Bullnose, and we followed him frew the door into the uvver room wiv the inspector and the rest of the gang following us. When we got into this room there was a table all laid out wiv grub. I'd never seen so much grub in all me life. The inspector was the first to speak.

'Right lads, sit down and get stuck in.'

I fawt I was going potty and that I was 'earing fings, and then it all came to light. The geezer in the plain clothes started to give a speech and he was saying somefing about pulling old Kate out of the canal. In the meantime the two lady coppers were pouring out lemonade and putting bread and jam on plates for us. Georgi and Fred were just looking at all the grub and Bullnose was standing by the door wiv a big grin right across his boat race, and he was like a dog wiv two cocks.

The geezer in the plain clothes was still rabbiting on but we was too busy getting stuck into all that lovely grub. The lady coppers was still ducking and diving all over the gaff and the inspector was sitting at the end of the table helping himself to a glass of lemonade.

All of a sudden the inspector started to clap and we all followed. I couldn't tell ya from that day wot that geezer was talking about. All we wanted to do was to get stuck into that lovely grub. Bullnose was saying somefing about 'Good lads, keep up the good work, there's no telling wot you will get next.'

None of us was listening. We was too busy filling our faces. We was told afterwards that someone at the hospital had told the Town Hall how we had pulled old Kate out of the drink and that was our reward.

When I got home I told the old lady all about the lovely party we had had, and all about the lovely grub. I put my hand in my pocket and said to her, 'I didn't forget ya. I got ya a lovely cream cake,' and wiv that I produced a cream cake from my pocket. It was a little squashed but to her that cream cake was worth all the gold in the world. It was a present to my mum.

The old man just sat there smiling to himself.

'Ya know what, farver,' I said, 'I fink ya knew about that party all the time.' He just smiled and said, 'Yus son, I knew. I said to ya mum, "I won't go out tonight, muvver, we will let the little feller have his party." Did ya enjoy it then, son?'

'I am not kidding dad,' I replied. 'I never ate so much grub in all my life, and I fink I will go to bed 'cos I feel a bit sick.' Awf I went to bed wiv a full belly and I slept the whole night frew.

The next night when we went down to the canal we told the uvver kids all about the party we had in the nick.

'Piss awf,' said Gobber White, 'that's a load of lies,' and wiv that he dived in the canal.

'Ya only jealous, Whitey, ya old ponce,' Georgi shouted after him.

'Don't worry about him, Georgi, we know it's true,' said Fred.

About a year later poor old Kate died. The nightwatchman of the boiler house found her dead on a pile of sacks round the back of the boiler house at the bone factory where she used to sleep. They buried her in a pauper's grave. A pauper's grave is a grave that they bury tramps in. She lived a pauper and she died a pauper.

One day we was all messing around in the market and arfter a while we got fed up, as kids do.

'I know,' I said to Georgi, 'let's go over the cemetery and see old Kate.'

'How the fuck can we see the old cow if they've buried her?' said Fred.

'Don't talk bleeding silly,' said Georgi to Fred, 'we know they've buried her don't we,' and awf we went to the cemetery. When we got there, there was thousands of graves.

'How are we going to find her in this bleeding lot?' Fred said.

'Ask that old geezer there, digging that grave,' said Georgi. 'He should know where we can find her.'

' 'Ey mate, where did ya bury old Kate?' I said to the geezer.

'Who's old Kate?' he asked.

'You know,' said Georgi. 'The old bird who used to drink meffs. They have buried her somewhere in this cemetery.'

The old man lifted up his cap and scratched his head and said, 'Ya better go over to the office by the gate and ask in there. They will know where she is buried.'

'Fanks mate,' I said and awf we all went to the office. I opened the door and we all marched in. There was an old geezer sitting behind a desk. He must have been ninety if he was a day. He had a pair of gold-rimmed glasses on the end of his note. He looked up and in a posh voice said, 'Can I help you?'

'Yus guvner,' I said. 'Where's old Kate buried?'

'Who is this person known as old Kate?' he said. *Anuvver geezer who don't know old Kate*, I fawt. Well Georgi told him who she was and how they found her dead at the back of the boiler house.

Arfter we had told him the story he said, 'How long ago was this?' We told him and then he said, 'When was she interned?' Well, we all looked at one anuvver.

'Buried I mean,' he said. 'You see, I will have to look it up in the register.'

'Blimey,' said Fred. 'It's like being at school. They put ya bleeding name down in a book.'

The old geezer took no notice of Fred's remark. He just looked over his shoulder and said, 'How long did you say?'

'I never did say, guv, but it was about four weeks ago,' I said. He then got a bloody great book awf of the shelf and started to look frew it. Arfter a while he said, 'Ha, there was only one Kathleen interned here four weeks ago.'

'No guv, her name was Kate,' said Fred.

'Kate is short for Kathleen,' said the old geezer.

'Oh, I see,' said Fred.

'As I was saying,' went on the old geezer, 'her name was Kathleen Goodfeller.'

'Gawd blimey, that's a posh name ain't it, Al,' said Georgi.

'Yus,' I said. 'Was she any relation to Longfeller?'

'Who the bleeding hell is this geezer called Longfeller?' said Fred.

'I don't know but old Gibbo was talking about him in school the uvver day,' I told him.

The old geezer told us where to go to find old Kate's grave arfter writing down a number on a slip of paper.

Well we looked and we still couldn't find it so Fred said, 'Give us that slip of paper Al. I'll go and ask that old grave digger again.' Fred was soon back.

'It's up here,' he said, and me and Georgi followed him. Well, we found old Kate's grave and all there was was a big pile of dirt. There was no flowers on it. Just a pile of old shit.

The free of us just stood there, free little snotty nosed urchins wiv dirty faces, torn jersies, no socks, and our toes sticking frew our plimsoles. I said to Fred and Georgi, 'We should have bought her some flowers.'

'I'll go and get her some,' said Georgie, and he was away down the parf. Me and old Fred just stood there looking at this bloody great pile of dirt. A few minutes later, Georgi came back wiv the biggest bunch of flowers I have ever seen.

'Cor, Georgi, where ya get the money to buy them wiv?' asked Fred.

He laughed and said, 'I didn't buy 'em. I nicked 'em awf that grave over there. They only buried the old geezer yesterday. Besides, he had plenty and he ain't going to tell anyone is he?'

Those flowers looked lovely on old Kate's grave. We all stood there for a while just looking. Not one of us said a Word. It was as though we was all saying a prayer for old Kate.

'Oh well, let's go,' said Fred, and we all walked away in silence.

It's a funny fing none of us was laughing anymore.

They've built a big block of flats there now where old Kate's grave used to be. It must be the only address she ever had. No one knew where she came from. She could have been someone posh wiv a name like Goodfellow. Oh well, who knows?

Chapter Four
Me and Gladys on the towpath

I shall never forget the first time I saw the sea. It was on a trip organised by the school, to Southend and it indirectly resulted in my first experience of sex, and it took place on the towpath wiv Gladys.

When old Gibbo our teacher, first told us about that Southend trip and it would cost a shilling a head, I fawt, *How the bleeding hell am I going to get a sodding shilling?*' I knew the old lady wouldn't have a shilling to spare so I had to get the old brain-box working. Arfter old Gibbo had finished telling us about the trip he said, 'Any questions, scum?' Bomber Ellis stuck up his hand and said, 'I've got a question, sir.'

'Wot is it?' asked Gibbo.

'How am I going to get a shilling, sir?'

'That's not a question, Ellis. That's a puzzle. So don't ask me, you bloody moron. If you haven't got a shilling then you damn well don't go, do you,' Gibbo replied.

'No sir, but I was just finking,' said Bomber.

'Well don't think boy or you will get a nose bleed won't you,' and wiv that Bomber sat down, saying somefing like, 'A bob is a lot of money to me, ya old ponce.'

I looked at Fred and said, 'Have ya got a fucking shilling, Fred?'

'No, but we have got free weeks to get it in, ain't we,' replied Fred.

That's true, I fawt to myself. Gibbo went on to say that we would all be going by train to Southend, 'that's all those who have the money to go.' He was looking at Bomber wiv a twisted smile as he said it.

As we all left school that day we was all talking about the trip to the seaside.

'I'll never get the money to go,' said Bomber. 'I can't ask me old man for it as he would kick ten buckets of shit out of me before he'd give me a bob.'

'Why don't ya nick it out of ya old man's pocket when he's pissed?' asked Georgi.

'Ah, that's a bleeding joke that is,' said Bomber. 'By the time he's pissed he ain't even got the price of a packet of fag papers left, the old barsted.'

'How are you going to get your bob?' I asked Fred.

'I'll just have to put in a bit more time up the market, won't I,' he said.

'I suppose so,' I replied.

'Why can't you graft up the market, Bomber?' asked Georgi.

'Leave awf. If I ain't indoors when my old man gets in for his tea there would be murders,' replied Bomber.

'Oh well, ya know wot old Gibbo said. If ya ain't got a bob ya can't go can ya,' I told Bomber.

'I know where I can get a bob from,' said Gobber.

'Where?' asked Bomber.

'I'll nick it out of my old lady's purse when she ain't looking.'

'You're nuffing but a no good barsted, Gobber, nicking from ya own muvver,' I told him, but like wiv everyfing else, he just spat on the ground and laughed and said, 'I'd nick it from bleeding Jesus Christ himself if I had to. Besides, I've never been to the seaside. Fink of all the girls showing awf their knickers when they go in paddling.'

'You're a dirty barsted, Gobber,' said Georgi, 'that's all you fink about.'

'Oh bollocks,' said Gobber as he ran awf home.

When I got home, I was full of the trip to the seaside and I was telling my Mum and Dad about it and how much it would cost. The old man had been listening and arfter a while he said, 'A beonk (shilling) is a lot of money son, but I suppose we will make it somehow for ya even if it means doing a few extra boozers one week.' I felt a lump come to my froat as I fawt, good old Dad, you are always there when one of us kids needs you. Mum looked up and said, 'It's going to cost more than a bloody shilling for that day's outing.'

'Wot ya talking about, muvver?' I asked.

'Well, for a start you'll want a new pair of plimsoles so there's anuvver tanner there. And then you will want some grub to take wiv ya. So I reckon wiv the grub and the plimsoles, you'll want at least free bob.'

'Never mind about the plimsoles muvver. We ain't walking there. We are going by bloody train,' I said.

65

'Don't talk bloody silly, ya silly little sod. Them ya got on there are nearly awf ya bleeding feet now. How do ya fink ya can go in them? By free weeks ya will be walking on bluddy skin,' she shouted at me. I knew she was right as she always was, God bless her.

'Don't worry, son,' said the old man. 'We will find it from somewhere.'

'Bleeding free bob,' said my bruvver Albert. 'It would take me two weeks to earn that.'

'If ya was to stop pissing around Bob's coffee-stall you would earn it, wouldn't ya?' I said. Wiv that, Albert gave me a look as to say, 'Shut ya big mouf ya prat.'

'Ya will like Southend, son,' said the old man.

'Have ya been there, Dad?'

'Yus, many a time. That's where we go when I go on the "Beano" from the Anchor pub in a Charabang.'

'We're going by train,' I told him.

'Oh, bloody posh that is,' said the old lady as she was cutting me a slice of bread the fickness of a doorstep awf of a loaf of bread. 'Now eat ya tea and don't say no more about it or ya won't go.'

'Yus, mum,' I replied, stuffing my mouf wiv bread and marg.

All I could fink of for the next free weeks that followed was that trip to Southend. Then the great day arrived and wot a day it was. It rained from the time we got on the train to go there until the time we had to come back again. But to be honest, we didn't give two monkeys. By the way, Bomber Ellis got his trip to Southend viv the help of old Gibbo – he wasn't all bad – and one of the uvver teachers. It was one big giggle on the train. Half the girls got touched up and the uvver 'arf got jealous, but in the long run a good time was 'ad by all. When we got there we could see the sea from the train window.

'Look,' shouted one of the girls, 'there's the sea,' and we all dived to the windows to look out.

'Blimey, wot a stink,' said Bomber. 'That ain't no stink, Bomber, that's fresh air,' I said.

We all got out of the train at the station and heard old Gibbo say to one of the uvver teachers, 'I think we best let this scum all find their way around and all meet back here later in the day.' Then he gathered us all around him on the platform.

'Right, quiet everybody,' Gibbo was shouting. Arfter a while he got silence. 'Now this what we propose to do,' he said. 'You can all go your own ways but you must be back here at this station by five o'clock and no later. Is that understood?' A few of the kids said, 'Yus, sir,' while some of us said, 'Cobblers.'

Well, we all made our way out of the station to the sea front and all the time the rain kept on coming down in buckets but we didn't have a care in the world. We was at the seaside and that was all that mattered. My new plimsoles began to squelch wiv the wet, but who cared?

We found our way onto the sea front and found the beach was covered wiv pebbles. Some of the kids screamed wiv delight as it was the first time any of us had seen the sea. All our old gang went running down to the water's edge. Awf came our plimsoles and in we went.

'Blimey, ain't it fucking cold,' shouted Gobber. 'The bleeding canal is warmer than this.' He never said a truer word. The water was like ice.

'Come in Gladys,' Gobber was shouting, 'show us yer drawers.'

'Leave her alone, Gobber,' I said. 'She's ours. We have a right old go at her at choir practice.

'Ya know wot, Al,' said Gobber, 'I have always fancied that Gladys.'

'Leave awf Gobber,' I said, 'she won't have anyfing to do wiv a ponce like you.'

Well by four o'clock we looked like a lot of drowning rats. We were soaked to the skin. Georgi, Fred and I took a stroll along the water's edge and we all stopped to look out to sea. There wasn't much to see as it was all overcast. All we saw was a grey mist.

'Ain't that lovely, Al,' said Georgi.

'Yus, but I can't see no boats,' I said.

'They're out there somewhere, Al,' said Fred. There we were, water dripping from our soaked nuts. To me it was the most wonderful experience in all the world.

By five o'clock we were all back at the station, ready to board the train. Going home was just as big a giggle as it was on our way there. All the girls were laughing and some of them were screaming. And that old Gladys started shouting as Gobber made a grab for her knickers. 'Piss awf, Gobber, ya dirty sod. All ya bleeding hands are wet.'

'Ya know wot, Fred,' I said to Fred. 'One of these days that Gobber is going to get done for a bunch of grapes (rape).'

Fred laughed and said, 'I wouldn't mind some of that meself wiv Gladys.'

When we got to our home station we all left to make our way home. When I got home, the old lady said, 'You're all wet ya silly little sod.'

'I know,' I said. 'Wot do ya expect? I've been to the seaside.'

'Ya mean, ya went in the water wiv ya clothes on?' asked the old lady.

'No, don't be silly, muvver. It's been raining all bleeding day ain't it,' I said.

'Well it ain't been raining here all day, 'as it, Dad?'

Me old Dad smiled and said, 'Well Soufend is firty miles away from here muvver. Anyway, have ya had a nice time, son?'.

'Ya sure I have, Dad, it was lovely.'

'How the bleeding hell can it have been lovely if it's been sodding raining all day?' said the old lady.

'It was lovely to me, Mum,' I replied.

'Well, ya better get those fings awf and get to bed and I will bring ya in a hot drink and get these fings dry for ya in the morning.' The trip to the seaside was lovely but I was now home safe and sound wiv my old Mum and Dad.

That trip 'as lived in my memory all these years and it was the best day of my life. To get the money for my trip to the seaside I had to work longer hours wiv the old man. It meant that we had to work four nights extra, rain or shine, and it was more bloody rain than shine.

It's a funny fing but I have always loved the sea even though it was later to be very cruel to me. But more of that later.

The next day when we all went back to school everyone was talking about the trip.

'Wasn't it lovely, Al,' said Bomber and he went on to say about how old Gibbo was the best teacher in the world for putting up the money for him to make the trip.

'You're nuffing but a bleeding hypocrite, Bomber,' said Gobber. 'It was only the uvver day that you called him an old ponce when ya fawt ya wasn't going.'

'Well, I fawt it was good of him to do that for Bomber,' said Georgi.

'I din't see you complaining Gobber,' said Fred. 'You was having a good time wiv that bleeding Gladys on the way home.'

'Leave awf, Fred. I wasn't doing anyfing,' replied Gobber.

68

'Oh, not much,' said Fred. 'How come she was leaving the train stuffing her drawers down her frock then?'

'Perhaps she was hot, I don't know,' Gobber replied.

'That's a fucking joke that is,' I said, 'bleeding hot? It was freezing cold, pissing down wiv rain, and you've got the cheek to say she was hot.'

'On bleeding 'eat more like it,' said Fred.

'Ya knows wot, Al, I fink you're bleeding jealous,' said Gobber.

'Piss awf. I ain't jealous of you. I can beat your time wiv her any day, can't I Fred?'

'Ya ain't got a chance wiv her, Al,' replied Fred.

'All right then, prove it,' said Gobber.

'Now how the bloody hell can I prove it to ya?'

'Easy, ya make a date wiv her, and we will all follow ya round the boney (bone yard) and watch ya wiv her,' said Gobber. *Blimey*, I fawt, *wot have I let myself in for here? I wish I had kept my big mouf shut.* Then I fawt, *well, I don't know. She's not a bad little palone* (girl) *that Gladys.*

By this time all the boys were saying, 'Go on, Al. Prove it to him.'

'OK you're on. When she comes out in the playground I will make a date wiv her.'

At 10.15 we all filed out of the classroom to get our free milk and cod-liver oil.

'Look out, Al,' said Gobber. 'Here comes Gladys.'

'All right Gobber,' I said. 'There's no bleeding rush.'

'Ya turned bleeding yeller ya ponce,' he said.

I grabbed him by his old ragged jersey and yelled, 'Don't you fucking say I'm yeller, ya barsted,' and before I knew it we were on the hall floor punching fuck out of one anuvver. Then I felt someone grab me by the scruff of the neck and lift me in the air. It was old Gibbo.

'You scum. You both get yourselves along to the headmaster's room and wait for me there,' he screamed. Awf we went to face the great man himself and we knew only too well wot was in store for us. Along came Gibbo, his face as red as a virgin's bum.

'Right, get yourselves in here,' he said as he opened the door to the headmaster's office.

In we marched as the headmaster looked up from a book he was marking.

'And what's all this, Mr Gibbs,' he asked.

'These two urchins were having a free for all, sir.'

The headmaster looked at Gobber and said sternly, 'White, if I have told you once about fighting, I have told you a thousand times, and I will not have it.' All the time he was laying down the law he was pulling the cane out of the desk and lovingly fingering it.' 'Now what was you fighting about?' he asked.

'We wasn't fighting, sir. We was playing,' I volunteered.

'Playing? Playing? Look at the state of your nose, Hollis. It's bleeding.'

I fawt, *it's less than that barsted Gobber is going to get when I get out of this office.*

'I've never heard anyfing so stupid in all my life. Right, get them up, White,' he thundered ominously as he swung the cane in the air. Gobber stuck out his two hands and the headmaster swung the cane down as hard as he could. He gave Gobber the best six handers he could wish for.

When he had finished wiv Gobber he said, 'Right Hollis, you as well.'

Wiping my hand across my bleeding nose I stuck out my two hands and winced as the cane crashed down on them.

'Now get back to the playground and I don't want to see you in this office again,' he shouted, and wiv that we both marched out of the office to the playground wiv our stinging hands tucked under our armpits. We both tried to hold back the tears, and it was very hard.

When we got to the playground, all the gang came round us.

'Wot happened, Al?' asked Fred.

'We got a bleeding whacking, didn't we,' I replied.

'That old ponce of a headmaster wants fucking,' said Gobber.

'It's all your bleeding fault, Gobber,' said Fred.

'I didn't mean nuffing,' retorted Gobber waving his hands in the air to cool awf the pain from the caning.

'I wouldn't mind but I've missed me cod-liver oil and malt over you, ya barsted,' I said.

'I'm sorry, Al,' said Gobber. 'Let's forget all about it, and you can have my cod-liver oil and malt tomorrow morning.' I fawt, *two lots of cod-liver oil and malt is better than having a punch up.*

'Right, you're on,' and that was the end of that.

At lunch-time we were in the playground and Georgi said, 'Hi up, Al. Here comes Gladys. Now's ya chance to ask her for that date.'

70

'Go on, Al,' Fred chipped in. 'Don't fuck about. Get in. This is ya big chance.'

'Wot was ya fighting over, Al?' asked Gladys.

'Old Gobber called him yeller,' said Fred.

'Ya want to be careful of that Gobber,' she said. He will try and get 'is own back on ya.'

'Leave awf,' I said. The only way he will get his own back is if he pisses in the wind.'

We all laughed and Georgi said, 'Go on, Al, ask her then.'

'Ask me wot?' inquired Gladys.

'He wants to meet ya tonight to take ya for a walk,' said Georgi.

'I don't go out wiv boys,' she replied. 'Besides, I have got to do some housework for my muvver.'

'Well if that's the bleeding case, I won't ask ya then,' I said angrily. She looked a bit taken aback at my straightness.

'Maybe I could come out arfter I have done the work,' she said sheepishly, looking at the ground wiv a couldn't-care-less look.

'Wot time will that be then?' I said. 'About nine o'clock,' she said. I fawt, *that's good. It will be nearly dark by then*.

'OK nine o'clock then by Stink House Bridge.'

'You've cracked it, Al, me old mate,' Fred said triumphantly.

'It's all right for you but I don't want any fucking about when I take her round the boney,' I said.

All that arfternoon I was finking of wot I was going to say to Gladys and wot we was going to do. In the end I fawt, *bollocks, I'll let nature take its course.*

That night arfter I had my tea I was about to have a wash in the kitchen sink when the old lady said, 'I hope ya don't fink ya going out yet. I want that bloody yard washed down before you sod awf.' *There she goes*, I fawt, *more bleeding work. I fink she's trying to work me to bloody death.*

Well, I knew it was no good arguing wiv the old lady so wiv bucket and broom I set about cleaning down the backyard. I fawt, I'll soon finish this barsted awf. It only took me about twenty minutes to finish the job.

I went back indoors to report to the old lady that all was well.

'Here ya are muvver, all done.'

'Right,' she said, 'now ya can go and get me some bread from the shop.'

'Why do ya have to wait until I get home from school? Why didn't ya get the bleeding bread this morning?' I said cheekily.

71

'Don't have so much mouf and get that sodding loaf, ya little sod,' and wiv that she frew the money for the bread on the table. I snatched it up quick awf of the table and ran out of the door to the shop. I knew if I said anuvver word she would have belted me one.

The yard washed down, the bread fetched from the shop, I fawt, *there can't be any more jobs*. But how wrong can ya be?

'Now, ya can go and get ya feet washed in that bloody sink,' she said.

'Wot for? Me bleeding feet ain't all that dirty.'

'Do as yer bloody told or ya won't go out of this house tonight me lad.'

Fuck that, I fawt. *I've got to meet that Gladys*. So wivout a word I whipped awf me plimsoles and did just as I was told. While in the process of washing my feet who should come in but Fred.

'Wot ya doing,' Al,' he asked.

'Walking a bleeding tightrope. Wot ya fink?' I replied. 'I am washing my bleeding feet, ain't I?'

'Well, now I've seen everyfing,' said Fred. 'You mean ya washing ya feet to see Gladys?'

'No, it was the old lady's idea.'

'I fawt it was funny,' said Fred, 'ya don't shag a bird wiv ya feet do ya?'

'What makes ya fink I'm going to shag her then, clever cobblers?'

'Leave awf, Al. It's a racing certainty wiv that bird.'

'How do you know, Fred. Ya haven't had her have yer?' I asked him.

'No, but Gobber wasn't playing pissing football on the train back from Soufend wiv her was he?' *That's true*, I fawt. By this time I was ready to put my plimsoles back on and I shouted to the old lady, 'Have ya got a pair of clean socks for me to put on, muvver?'

'You will have to wait until I sew the 'oles up in these,' she answered back from the kitchen door.

'Wot time are ya going to meet that bird, Al?' Fred was asking.

'About nine o'clock,' I replied. Just then the old lady shouted from the front room, 'Harryboy, go to that bleeding street door and tell those sodding mates of yours to piss awf.' By now quite a crowd had gathered in the street.

'How can I go to the door? I'm drying my feet, ain't I.'

'Tell Fred to get his arse out there then,' she shouted back.

'Do me a favour, Fred. Go out and see wot the bloody lot wants,' I asked Fred. Arfter a few moments Fred returned to tell me that all the boys were waiting for me at the street door.

'Wot the bleeding hell do they all want?' I asked him.

'They said that they all want to watch ya perform wiv Gladys,' Fred replied.

'Oh, do they? Go and tell them all to piss awf.'

'You can't do that, Al,' replied Fred.

'Why can't I?' I asked him.

'Well ya had a bet wiv Gobber that ya could do anyfing ya liked wiv Gladys,' said Fred.

'I'll soon fix that bleeding lot when I get out there,' I said. 'I'll tell them all to piss awf.'

But it was like frowing sawdust to the wind, to talk to that lot. Arfter some discussion at the front door, I agreed to let the gang follow me at some distance, but before we left to meet Gladys I made it clear that I wanted no fucking about from any of them.

'That's my SOS' I laughed.

Ten minutes later I was out on the street minus my clean socks. As my old lady said she couldn't mend the clean ones as they were too far gawn.

'Don't worry, son. I'll get you a penny bundle of socks awf of the secondhand stall in the market on Saturday,' she promised.

I made my way towards Stink House Bridge. Everybody called it Stink House Bridge as the stink from the waste of the chemical factory came up there in the canal, and, believe me, it didn't smell like roses. The gang had gawn ahead round to the boney as that was where I'd planned to take Gladys.

As I approached the bridge, there she was sitting on the wall of the bridge looking as clean as a new pin. *She's not bad, that girl*, I fawt. *I'll have some of that tonight, no mistake about it.*

'You're late,' she said impatiently as I approached her.

There she goes, I fawt, *just like all the uvver birds. She finks she owns ya just 'cos I say I'm taking her out for the night.*

'Only ten minutes,' I replied.

'Ten minutes is long enough. Anyway, where are we going?' she asked.

'Let's walk along the canal for a bit,' I suggested.

'Bit of wot?' she said wiv a grin. *Aye aye, Harryboy*, I fawt, *you've cracked it here.*

'All right,' she said, 'but I don't like walking along that canal when it's dark. There's too many rats.'

73

'Leave awf,' I said bravely, 'they won't 'urt ya. We play about wiv them when we go swimming in there.' Well, I finally persuaded her to walk down the towpath of the canal. I knew wot I was about, as the towparf led to the boney.

Going along, I made small-talk between intervals of frowing stones into the canal.

'Do you like my frock, Al?' she said.

'It looks smashing,' I said. 'Then I took a deep breath and wiv a larf I added, 'Have ya got any drawers to go wiv it?'

Ya know wot? That little bird didn't even blush. She lifted up her frock to reveal a pair of snow-white knickers, and said, 'Of course I have, clever dick.'

'Leave awf Gladys,' I said. 'Someone will see ya.' 'Don't be silly,' she said. 'Who's going to see us down her?' *That's true*, I fawt. *There ain't a soul in sight.*

By this time we were 'arfway down the towparf to the boney.

'Well, when are ya going to kiss me then?' she asked, pouting her cupid-like lips. At that, I stopped and got hold of her to kiss her. She smelt and felt so soft and lovely and I wanted more. We took no notice of time. We just went on kissing and cuddling each uvver.

Boy, was that little bird hot. She was like a bleeding house on fire, and she wasn't the only fing that was on fire.

By this time my hands were in places I'd never dreamt of. Arfter a few minutes she said, 'Wait a minute. Let me take my knickers off.' And wiv that she lifted her frock and took them right awf. Goodness knows wot I was going to do. I hadn't the faintest idea. All I knew was fings were happening that I didn't understand. I had only heard about them from the uvver kids at school. Wiv her knickers removed she said, 'Well, go on then, do it.'

'Do wot?' I asked.

'You know, put yours in mine.' Before I knew it, she was opening the flies of my trousers and putting her hand inside. I jumped about six feet in the air when she got hold of my manhood, if that's wot ya could call it. It was then the size of 'arf a pencil. I jumped again when she exposed it to the night air. She was just about to show me where to put it and wot to do wiv it, when it happened. We heard urgent footsteps on the gravel of the towparf, and we saw a torch flashing along the wall.

'Blimey, it's a canal copper. Let's run,' I said. And we were

74

awf like the wind, wiv me trying to put back all I'd got, and Gladys stuffing her knickers down the collar of her frock.

I stopped for a second just to put my shaft back in its hiding place.

'Come on,' shouted Gladys, 'he will get us if we don't get a move on.'

'It's all right for you,' I said breathlessly, 'but I ain't running over Stink House Bridge wiv my cock flowing in the wind for no barsted.'

'Wow, that was close,' Gladys said, when we got onto the main road.

'Fuck him,' I said, 'he nearly had us, the barsted.'

Then when it was all over we both started laughing. 'I wonder what time it is, Glad?'

'How the bleeding hell do I know?' Jus then a copper came along on his bike.

'Wot time is it, guv?' I asked him.

He took his watch out from out of his tunic pocket and said, 'Ten to eleven, and it's high time you were both in bed.'

'Fanks guv,' I said as we ran on our way.

'Bleeding ten to eleven,' I said to Gladys. 'My old lady will kill me when I get in. Wot will your muvver say?'

'Nuffing, she goes to bed early,' she replied. 'Let's go back down the canal. That copper must be gawn by now,' she said.

'Leave awf, I can't. My old lady will go mad when I get in.'

By this time I was really stepping it out.

'I'm not coming out wiv you no more if ya can't stay out,' she was saying as she breathlessly tried to keep up wiv me.

'I don't give a fuck about you,' I said, 'I've got to get home,' and awf I ran.

I looked back and saw her putting her knickers back on. I fawt, *that's the end of that, Harryboy, me old son*. And then it hit me. I had forgotten all about the gang waiting round the boney. *I will have to tell them some story in the morning*, I fawt.

When I got in, the old lady started laying down the law about the time.

'Leave awf muvver,' I said. 'I ain't been up to nuffing.'

'It's a bloody good job too. I don't want the coppers knocking at the door 'cos you've been up to ya bleeding tricks.' Muvver, if ya only knew. Ya would go hairless.

At eight o'clock the next morning Fred was knocking on the door. The old lady went out to see who it was and I heard her say, 'You're early this morning, Fred.' He muttered somefing as he came frew the door and as he entered the kitchen I said, 'Wot the bleeding hell do you want at this time of the morning?'

'I fawt I'd come early to see wot happened last night,' he said.

'Nuffing happened last night.'

He seemed shocked.

'We all waited round the boney for ya,' he said.

'Well hard luck, ain't it,' I said.

'Gobber was doing his nut 'cause you didn't turn up wiv that bird,' he said. 'Anyway, Gobber 'as won the bet.'

'Wot fucking bet?' I asked.

'Ya had a bet with Gobber that ya could beat his time wiv that Gladys.'

'I didn't bet him anyfing. Besides, I have nuffing to bet wiv, I told him.

'Well, when we get to school Gobber will want to know wot happened, won't he,' Fred was saying.

'Well, for your information, mate, I ain't going to school today, am I.'

'Ya got to go to school, Al, or Gobber will fink ya are yeller.'

'I don't give two monkeys wot he finks. I just don't feel like going to school.'

Just then, my old mum opened the kitchen door and yelled, 'You can get your bleeding arse to school and don't you forget it.'

'All right muvver, don't do ya nut. I am going to the bleeding school, ain't I.'

As we got to the school gates we came face to face wiv Gobber and Bomber.

'Wotcha Gobber,' said Fred.

Gobber wasn't taking any notice of Fred. He just looked past him and said to me, 'Well, where did you get to last night wiv that bird?'

'Mind ya own bleeding business. It's nuffing to do wiv you,' I told him.

'You said you were going to take Gladys round the boney.' Turning to Bomber he added, 'Didn't he, Bomb?'

'Yus, that's right, Gobb,' replied Bomber.

'Well I did, didn't I?'

'Well, where did ya take her and wot happened then?' asked Gobber.

'We went down the canal and nuffing happened 'cos a copper came along the towparf and we ran.'

'Ya mean to tell me, nuffing happened?' he asked me once more.

'Look, Gobber. I told ya nuffing happened, so leave it at that, unless ya want to make somefing of it,' I told him looking him straight in the eye.

'If ya ask me, I don't fink he knows wot to do wiv birds,' said Bomber.

'No one is asking you, clever cobblers,' I told him.

Spitting on the ground, Gobber said, 'If I had that little bird round the boney, I'd show ya wot to do. I would be in like a shot from a gun.'

'If ya fink ya can make it, Gobber, why don't ya take her out then?' I said.

'OK then.'

'You ask her for a date at playtime and let's see how you get on then.'

'I'll ask her for a date and Gawd help her if she comes out wiv me,' said Bomber.

'Don't make me laugh, Bomber,' said Fred. 'You stink. How do ya fink a bird like her would go out wiv a stink bomb like you?'

'That's right, Bomber,' said Gobber. 'Look at the state your jersey's in. You've got so many 'oles in it, it looks like a gorgonzola cheese.'

'What the fuck is a gorgonzola cheese?' asked Bomber.

'If ya don't know, I'm not going to tell ya,' replied Gobber. Then the bell went and we all piled into school.

Gobber never did get the chance to take Gladys out as she told him to piss awf when he tried to make a date wiv her. As for yours truly, the furver away from her I was, the better.

Chapter Five
Monkey business

Christmas time was always a hard time for us buskers as all the punters were hard at it, saving for Christmas and in them days every penny counted.

I shall never forget one Christmas. It was freezing cold and we had just reached the first pub we were going to work, The Bell in Curry Street, Limehouse. When we got to the door, it was closed.

'It's shut, Dad,' I said to the old man.

'Don't be silly,' he said. It can't be shut on Christmas Eve.'

'But it is, Dad,' I said, and tried pushing the door again. Just as we was about to walk away the old landlady of the pub, Ada Bennett, came to the door. As she opened the door, she said, 'Oh, it's you, Bill.'

'Wot's up missus?' said the old man. 'Sold out of beer?'

'No Bill,' she said. I'm sorry to say my husband Bob dropped dead last night.'

'Gaw blimey,' said the old man, 'that's a bit of a rum do.'

'We was only talking to him last week,' I said.

'You'd better come in,' she said. 'Don't stand out there in the cold, and I'll make ya a nice hot cup of tea.'

I led the old man up the passage to the back room where we found her daughter, Ruth, and son-in-law.

'Yus,' said the old landlady, 'he was be'ind the counter pulling a pint and he just went wallop. He fell down and that was it.'

The daughter started to cry and said, between tears, 'It ain't going to be much of a Christmas for us, this year.'

'That's true,' said Ada, 'and I got all that grub in too.'

I looked up and said, 'You're better awf than us. We've only got a rabbit for our dinner on Christmas day.'

'Ah, God bless ya, son,' said the old bird. 'I tell ya wot, hang on here a minute,' and she vanished into the next room. A few seconds later she came back carrying the biggest bleeding chicken I had ever seen. She then got a big lump of brown paper and she started to wrap this chick up.

'There ya are, son,' she said. 'You take that home to ya muvver.'

Well, I couldn't speak and me winny pegs went like jelly. But the old man never did like charity.

'No,' he said, 'that's all right missus. We're all right for Christmas. As the boy said, we've got a rabbit and as long as me kids eat I am OK.'

But the old landlady insisted and said, 'Now you look here, Bill. You take that bird home to ya missus and give them kids a good feed up for Christmas.'

By this time, the daughter had made us a cup of tea and was putting it down on the table. I gave the old man his tea and we was drinking it when the old landlady started to talk about how old Bob died. All of a sudden she said to me, 'Would you like to see him, son? He is laying upstairs.'

Well, I didn't know wot to do. I was glued to the floor. The old man was holding my arm all this time and he gave my arm a little squeeze.

'Go on son,' he said. 'Pay ya last respects to the guvner.'

I mean, wot do I know about paying respects to anyone, but as long as I had that bloody chicken I would carry the old barsted to the grave on my back. The old man let go of my arm and I followed the old bird upstairs to the front room and there on the bed, covered wiv a white sheet, was old Bob.

'Shssh, don't make a sound,' said the old bird, putting a finger to her mouth. She's potty, I fawt. That old barsted can't 'ear us.

And with that, she whipped back the bleeding sheet and there he was laid out on the kip, his bald head shining like a billiard ball. The bandage was tied round under his chin and over the top of his head. When I asked the old man wot it was for, he told me that it was to stop his mouf from falling open. He must have hit his head when he fell, as he had a big bruise on the side of his head. He looked like a bleeding easter egg. I stood there looking down at him.

'He looks well, don't he?' said the old bird. I mean how can a geezer look well if he's dead?'

I looked at him again and said, 'Yus missus, he do look well, don't he? *The sooner we get out of here the better*, I was finking.

'Come on son let him rest,' she said. 'Gawd bless him.' And wiv that, we went downstairs.

The chicken was still on the table and I made a beeline for it.

As I was tucking it under my arm, I said, to the old man, 'Come on Dad, we have got a lot of walking to do.'

He fanked the landlady for the monster chicken and we left to go on our rounds. I held on to that chicken wiv all my life and when we got to the pubs that we had to work, I put it on the floor between me legs. No barsted was going to get that chicken from me. One of the landlords in one of the boozers that we worked said to the old man, 'Did ya 'ear about old Bob snuffing it, Bill?' *We sure did*, I fawt. *We've got his bleeding dinner*.

I couldn't get home fast enough that night. When we got home, the old lady was in the kitchen skinning the rabbit.

'Never mind about that, muvver,' I said. 'Look wot we've got.' Well her poor old eyes nearly came out of her head.

'Where on erf did ya get that from, boy?' she said. Well, I told her about how old Bob was dead and that I saw him wiv all his head done up in this bandage. All the time she was looking at the chicken and saying, 'Ah, Gawd rest his soul.'

'Never mind his bleeding soul, muvver,' I said. 'We've got this bleeding chicken. Let's get it in the bleeding oven.'

'I can't put it in the oven until I've stuffed it,' she said.

'Never mind about stuffing it,' I said. 'Let's get it eaten.'

By this time it was about twelve o'clock at night and it was Christmas Eve. The stalls in the market was out till about four in the morning so it was our job to go and help the costers to put the stalls away and we would get paid a couple of coppers and a bit of fruit. I said to the old lady, 'I am awf up the market and I'll see ya in the morning,' and out I went. When I got to the market all the gang was sitting round a coke fire that was burning in a dustbin.

'Watchya Al,' said Fred. 'Have ya just finished work wi ya old man?'

'Yus,' I said. I fawt to myself, *wait till I tell ya about the chicken*.

'Bleeding cold, ain't it, Al,' said Georgi.

'I won't care how bleeding cold it is tomorrow.'

'Why's that?' asked Fred.

'Well we've got a chicken for tomorrow's dinner, ain't we.'

All the kids looked up togevver.

'You're a fucking liar, Hollis,' said Franky Bowman, a kid who lived about free streets away from me, who fawt he knew everything.

'Who are you calling a liar Bowman?', and wiv that I gave him one round the ear'ole and we started to have a punch up.

'Don't fight, Al,' Georgi said. 'It's Christmas.'

'I'll fucking kill you one of these days, Bowman,' I said. And it was all over before it started.

Arfter we all settled down again round the fire, Fred said, 'Have ya really got a chicken, Al?'

'It's no good of me telling ya 'cause that barsted Bowman don't believe me,' I said.

'All right then, where did ya get it from?' asked Frankie Bowman.

I told them the story and how I saw old Bob lying still on the bed.

'Ah, that's a load of old cobblers,' said Georgi. 'It ain't, Georgi,' I said. 'We're going to have it for tomorrow's dinner.'

The rest of the night we sat around the fire until it was time to help put the stalls away and around five in the morning we was all on our way home wiv the little bits of fruit and the few coppers we had earned. Some was carrying a few old wooden boxes so they could have a fire for Christmas Day.

I was well pleased wiv the perks I got for my night's work as I knew I had chicken for dinner that day. And I was finking to myself, *I'll give that chicken a right old belting at dinner time.*

'If you've got a chicken for dinner, Hollis, wot about letting us see it?' said Frankie Bowman.

'Leave awf. How can I take you all indoors at this time of the morning?'

'There ya are, I told ya it was all lies,' said Bowman.

'All right I'll go in and I'll bring it out and show ya,' I said.

When we reached my house I said, 'Right, you wait here and I'll go and get it and show ya and then we will see if I'm lying, Bowman.'

Well, there they all were waiting for me to bring out the bleeding chicken. I found it in the oven where the old lady had left it. As I got to the street door wiv this bleeding chicken in a baking tin there was one roar of excitement.

'Gaw,' they all exclaimed.

'Wot a whopper,' said Georgi. Poor old Fred. He just stood there wiv his mouf wide open. The excitement woke up the old lady and I could 'ear 'er coming down the stairs.

'Wot's bloody going on out there?' she was shouting.

'I am only showing the boys the chicken, mum,' I yelled back.

'Tell them all to piss awf and get yaself to bed or ya won't get up in the morning,' she yelled back.

81

As I turned to go in I said, 'There ya are, Bowman. I told ya we had a chicken, didn't I?'

'Gaw, ya are lucky, Al,' said Fred.

As they was all leaving, I called Fred back.

'Come in Fred,' I said, 'and I'll make a cup of tea.'

When we got into the kitchen, the old lady was putting the kettle on for a cup of tea.

'I fawt you went back to bed, muvver,' I said. 'How the bloody hell do ya fink I can sleep wiv that bloody lot at the door?'

'Sorry about that, mum, but that ponce Bowman didn't believe we had a chicken for dinner.'

Fred looked up and said, 'It's a lovely chicken ain't it, Mrs Hollis? It's the biggest chicken I've ever seen.'

Beautiful ain't it, Fred,' I said.

'It's lovely,' he replied.

'I tell you wot I'll do,' I said. 'We'll save ya a bit, won't we mum. We'll give him a bit of our chicken, won't we, mum.'

'Gaw, that will be lovely,' said Fred.

'Wot ya got for dinner, Fred?' the old lady said as she was setting the two teas down on the table.

'I don't know but I heard my old lady say she was going to get some bacon bones to make us a stew wiv,' said Fred.

I will never forget that Christmas as long as I live. Arfter dinner I was sitting looking out of the window and I saw Fred coming down the street. *Aye aye*, I fawt, *he is coming for a bit of chicken*. I lifted the window and shouted, 'I dodgee cobblers, wot do you want, a bit of bloody chicken?' Fred was smiling all over his boat race.

'No,' he said. 'I fawt I'd come and see if ya were coming out.'

'Well, if ya did come for a bit of chicken we ain't got none. We have scoffed it all.'

You should have seen his face. I fawt he was going to cry.

'Al,' he said, 'you're a dirty barsted. You said you was going to save me a bit.' And I could see the tears coming to his eyes.

'Leave awf,' I said. 'I was only kidding ya. How could we eat all that in one go? You saw how big it was. Come in and I'll get the old lady to cut ya a lump awf.'

When he got in the house I said to the old lady, 'Fred's come for his bit of chicken we promised him, Mum.' The old lady got the rest of the chicken out of the oven, and as she was cutting Fred awf a nice big slice, she said, 'Ya want a bit of bubby (bread) wiv it, Fred?'

'If ya like, Mrs Hollis.' But before the old lady could cut him a slice of bread, he was stuffing it in his norf and souf and he was giving it a right old chew up.

'Ya know wot, Al,' he said, wiv his mouf full of chicken. 'That's the best bit of chicken I have ever tasted.'

'Leave awf, when did you ever taste chicken before?' I said.

'I ain't ever tasted chicken before, but that is the best I have ever tasted,' he said.

'Come on, you're as darft as arse 'oles. How can it be the best ya ever tasted if ya never had it before?' I said.

Taking the slice of bread awf of the table that the old lady had cut for him, he said, 'It's still the best.'

As we was going out the door so Georgi was about to bang on the door.

'Wotcher Georgi,' said Fred. 'I've just had a lovely lump of chicken awf of Al's mum.'

'You're a dodgy barsted, Fred,' said Georgi. 'You only came for Al so you could get a bit of chicken. *Aye aye*, I fawt. *I've got to give Georgi a bit. The way fings are going I'll have to give the whole bleeding gang a bit of that bloody chicken.*

Arfter I got Georgi his bit of chicken, he said, 'That was lovely Al. You're the best pal anyone could have.

'Tell us about the old boy who was laying on the bed, dead,' said Fred.

'Never mind about him,' said Georgi. 'All I know is we had a lump of his bleeding chicken.'

I told them about old Bob and how he was laid out on the bed.

'That's nuffink,' said Georgi. 'I saw my old grandmuvver when she was dead. We had her laying in her box in the front room.'

'Did ya sleep there, Georgi?' I said.

'Where the bleeding hell do ya fink I slept?'

'I wouldn't like to sleep in the same house,' said Fred. 'Was ya scared, Georgi?' I asked.

'Not really. But every time I had to go by the front room I used to run by the door for my bleeding life. My mum said, "She won't hurt ya Georgi. She's dead." But I wasn't taking any chances. I knew wot an old barsted she was when she was alive so I would scarper by that door a bit lively.'

Things was always tight after Christmas. The old man used to call January and February starvation months because everybody was brasic lint (skint). They had spent wot money they had at Christmas. That was when the busking game was really hard. We would walk miles trying to get a few coppers but we seemed to manage somehow.

It was on a winter's night when Charlie Beckett had his ear bit awf by a rat. Those rats must have been hungry, 'cos Charlie was always pissing himself and he always stunk. His muvver told my Mum that he was sound asleep when he woke up screaming.

'He woke the 'ole of the bloody house up,' she said, and when she went in the bedroom and put the light on there was this bloody great rat hanging onto Charlie's ear 'ole. Poor old Charlie. They took him to the hospital and cut the rest of his ear awf. We used to call him Luggs.

Arfter he came out of the hospital he had all his head done up in bandages and he looked a right old mess. One night, one of the kids said, 'Take the bandage awf, Charlie, and show us ya ear.' Well he done just that. When he took the bandage awf, all the kids laughed and one of them said, ' 'Ey look, he's only got one lugg,' and that name stuck to him. Everyone called him Luggs arfter that.

Every Friday morning, Nitty Nora used to come to the school. Nitty Nora was a nurse employed by the council to go round the schools to look in the kids' heads for lice. She was a big, fat old bird. She used to love to get the boys between her legs, as she was looking frew their hair. She would run a small toof comb frew ya hair and if she found any nits or fleas she would send ya to the school clinic in East India Dock Road and they would shave all ya hair awf.

One Friday she came to the school and arfter she was finished, Georgi said, 'Ya know wot, Al. That old Nitty Nora loves putting us boys between her legs. She gets a frill out of it.'

Old Bomber was always going to the clinic for one fing or the uvver. Ya see, he had no muvver. She ran away and left Bomber and his two sisters to his old man. His old man was a right old barsted. He used to come home drunk and belt Bomber wiv the broom. Poor old Bomber used to come to the school black and blue where his old man had belted him wiv the broom when he was pissed.

'One of these days,' Bomber would say, 'I am going to run away to sea and then I will come back and give him the biggest hiding of his bleeding life.'

Bomber got his name because he always stunk and he only had

one set of clothes to put on. He was about four feet two wiv blond hair and blue eyes. He never combed his hair, and the only time his body saw water was when he went swimming in the canal. His farver was a barsted to him and his sister and his muvver walked out on them when they were about seven and she went on the game down West India Dock Road, Limehouse.

It was the same winter that Charlie got his ear bit awf when Georgi broke his leg. It was a long time arfter we sent old Bob and his coffee stall for a ride tied behind a cab. Somehow we managed to worm our way back to Bob's coffee stall to have a giggle wiv the costers and the cab drivers.

On this very cold day we was helping to push Bob's coffee stall to the pitch and it had been snowing the night before and all the road was iced up. Georgi was in the shafts pulling, and me and Fred and Gobber White was pushing at the back. Bob was walking by the side wiv the oil lamp.

Well, we was goin' like good 'uns when all of a sudden the coffee stall started to go towards the kerb and the next fing we knew there was a terrible scream.

'O, me leg, me leg!' yelled Georgi and the bleeding coffee stall ended up on the pavement. The next fing I saw was Georgi under the coffee stall screaming his bleeding head awf. Wot happened was, Georgi had slipped on the ice and went arse over head and ended up wiv the coffee stall running over his right winney peg. I ran up and said, 'Wot's up, Georgi?'

'Me bleeding leg's cut awf,' he yelled.

'Don't talk bloody darft,' I said.

'Wot's going on?' said old Bob. 'Look at me bleeding coffee stall. All the cups have come awf of the shelf.' I told ya old Bob was a right old barsted. He didn't care as long as he got that coffee stall at its pitch. There was poor old Georgi laying on the ground screaming his bloody head awf and all that old barsted could fink of was his bloody old coffee stall.

By this time there was a big crowd of people. Four costers came over and lifted the coffee stall awf of Georgi's leg and, as they did so, there was a big crash from the inside of the coffee stall. It was the rest of the mugs coming awf of the shelves.

'Blimey,' said one of the costers. 'I don't like the look of that. Someone better go and get an ambulance. I fink he's done his leg in.' By this time poor old Georgi was rolling about wiv pain.

'Don't worry, Georgi,' I said. 'The ambulance will soon be here.'

'I ain't going to no bleeding hospital. They will want to cut me bleeding leg awf.'

'Don't worry son,' said one of the costers. 'You'll be okay.'

A few minutes later up came the ambulance. Out jumped one of the geezers who came over to Georgi and said, 'Now wot have you been up to, my lad?' and wiv that he got hold of Georgi's leg to have a look. Georgi let out a yell, calling him all the names he could fink of. The ambulance man looked at Georgi's leg and said, 'Don't worry, son, we'll soon have you fixed up.'

Just then his mate came up wiv a sort of chair, lifted Georgi onto it and put him in the ambulance. The geezer in the back of the ambulance was just about to shut the door when I said, 'Hold on, guvner, that's our mate.'

'You'd better come with him, then,' he said. As me, Fred, and Bomber was getting into the ambulance, old Bob was shouting, 'Wot about me coffee stall? How am I going to get it to me pitch?'

'Never mind about ya bleeding coffee stall,' said Fred. 'We're going for a bleeding ride.'

All the way to the hospital, poor old Georgi was moaning wiv pain and saying, 'Sod old Bob's coffee stall.' He kept repeating it.

When we got to the hospital – the Poplar hospital in East India Dock Road – they took Georgi in in a wheelchair, and the nurse said to us, 'You can sit over there.' While we was waiting, in a cream and green room, Fred said, 'I tell ya wot, Al. I bet they cut his bleeding leg awf.'

'That will be a bleeding lark,' said Bomber. 'Then he won't be able to go to school.'

'Ya, and if he don't go to school I am going to have his bleeding milk,' said Fred.

'Ya, and I'll end up having his cod-liver oil and malt.'

That was the only fing I ever went to school for. They used to give it to all the kids that was underweight and I used to love it. It was like fick brown toffee and it was 'ansom. Nearly all the kids got free milk but only a few got cod-liver oil and malt and they were the small skinny kids like yours truly.

I looked at Fred and I said, 'I hope they do cut his bleeding leg awf Fred, 'cos me an you will be all right.'

'Yus,' said Fred, 'we will be laughing.'

We hung around that hospital for about two hours and all the time we could 'ear Georgi bawling his head awf.

86

'You know wot, lads,' I said, 'that Georgi might be a big fucker but he's nuffink but a bleeding cry baby. 'Ark at him screaming his bloody head awf. The way he's performing in there those nurses will fink we're a load of queers.'

'I wouldn't like to have my leg awf,' said Bomber.

'Why's that, Bomber?' asked Fred.

'Well, I wouldn't be able to run away from my old man when he's whacking me wiv his broom, would I?'

Well, it wasn't very long arfter that when a nurse came out wiv a pale-looking Georgi in a wheelchair.

'There you are,' she said. 'Have you got to go far?'

'Not far,' said Bomber.

'As he got to go to school, miss?' asked Fred.

'Of course not. How can he go to school like that?' *Aye aye*, I fawt, *that barsted Fred is finking of that bloody milk.*

We came out of the hospital and we was pushing Georgi along the road.

'It's my turn to push him now,' said Bomber, and wiv that, Fred let go of the wheelchair and it rolled awf of the curb and Georgi came out on his boat race and ended up wiv a bloody nose. He was calling us all the names under the sun.

'Shut ya bloody mouf, Georgi, or we will leave ya here to roast,' I said.

We had the time of our lives wiv that wheelchair. On our way frew the market we saw one of the costers that helped to put Georgi in the ambulance.

'Wotcher son,' he said. 'How did ya get on?'

'He's broke his leg, guvner,' I said.

'Never mind, ya'll soon get over that,' and wiv that he dived his fork in his bin (pocket) and gave Georgi a penny saying, 'There ya are son. That's for being a brave boy.'

'This could be a good fing if we work it right,' I said to Fred and Bomber.

Well, we ended up taking him round to all the stall-owners and telling them wot a brave boy he had been when they was putting the plaster on. Little did they know, the ponce was screaming his head awf. We ended up wiv fourpence so I said, 'All right Georgi, let's have a share out.'

'Piss awf,' said Georgi. 'It's my money and I am not sharing it wiv you free.'

'I'll tell ya wot, Georgi,' Fred said. 'If ya don't share that poke wiv us we will tip ya out of this chair and bloody well leave ya.'

'Well, it's my leg that's broke,' said Georgi.

'Yus, and it will be ya bleeding back that will be broke if ya don't hurry up and have a share out,' said Bomber.

'Come on ya ponce. Share out the poke or I'll nick the bleeding lot,' I told him. He finally agreed to share out the fourpence and we ended up pushing him home frew the market.

When we got him home his muvver went potty when she saw him in the wheelchair.

'Oh my good Lord,' she said, 'wot the bloody hell's he done?'

'Well, we told her wot had happened and she said, 'It's always the same when he is wiv you free. He always gets into bovver.'

'Leave awf missus,' said Fred. 'It's his own fault. He wasn't doing his job properly.'

Georgi looked up and said, 'Don't tell fucking lies. You put me in the shafts and told me to pull and you free was at the back, pissing about.'

Well, his muvver banged him round the ear'ole and said, 'You ain't going out wiv them free any more.'

'Oh piss awf muvver,' said Georgi. 'Ya don't know wot ya talking about.'

When we finally took that wheelchair back to the hospital, it only had two wheels. Georgi's muvver took him back to the hospital arfter free days and they fitted him up wiv a pair of crutches and the only time he used the wheelchair was if anyone mentioned about him going to school.

One day we was wiv him in the market and we had the wheelchair wiv us as we went to get a load of empty boxes on it so we could sell them as firewood. There was a geezer in the marking selling flowers.

'I'll give ya a tanner for them wheels ya got on that wheelchair,' he said.

'I can't sell ya them,' said Georgi. 'The fing 'as got to go back to the hospital.'

'Make it ninepence guv and ya can have the whole bleeding lot,' I said.

'Right,' he said. 'I'll give ya ninepence, but I only want the two back wheels.'

'We can't do that, Al,' said Georgi. 'I'll get into bovver.'

'Don't worry Georgi,' I said. 'Wot we can do is take it back to the hospital and tell the nurse that ya left it outside ya house all night and some dirty barsted nicked the wheels awf of it.'

'Just fink of it, Georgi,' said Fred. 'We can have freepence each.'

Well, Georgi fawt about it for a while and he agreed to the transaction so there and then we took the wheels awf of the wheelchair. The following week we helped Georgi to take the wheelchair back to the hospital and when we got to the hospital gates we let go of the wheelchair and I said, 'Right Georgi, you go in and tell the nurse someone 'as nicked the wheels.'

'Georgi went in like a good 'un. A few minutes later he came out wiv two porters. One of them said, 'The barsteds will nick anyfing round here.'

'That's the easiest ninepence we ever earned,' I said to Fred.

'I'll get anuvver wheelchair next week and we can sell the bleeding lot,' said Georgi.

'Leave awf, Georgi,' I said. 'That's taking liberties.'

Georgi got on like a house on fire wiv those crutches. He was the fastest bloke I knew on one leg. We had some right old larks while he was on those crutches. The only fing that made him mad was that he couldn't go swimming wiv us in the canal.

We was down at the canal one day and Georgi got a bit cheeky, so Fred got hold of his crutches and slung them in the canal. Georgi went mad and he called us all the names he could lay his tongue to.

'Behave ya bleeding self or we will make ya hop all the bleeding way home,' said Fred. Georgi agreed to behave and Fred dived in and got his crutches for him.

'You're a dirty barsted, Freddy,' said Georgi. 'I've got to take them back to the hospital when I'm done wiv them.'

'Not if we sell them first,' I said.

'Who the bleeding hell wants to buy them?' asked Georgi.

'I don't know but we might find a punter for them.'

'How much do ya fink we could get for them, Al?' asked Fred.

'Well they must worf at least a tanner.'

'Piss awf,' said Georgi. And wiv that we went along the towparf to where the rest of the gang was.

The same old gang was there except for a new kid.

'Who's the saveloy?' said Georgi.

'He's my cousin,' said Arfer Cocker.

'I don't care if he is Old King Cole,' said Georgi. 'He is not in our gang and he is not following us about.'

Gobber White was there.

'You should see his sister, Al,' he said. 'She's a little cracker. I'd love to give her one.'

This new kid looked at Gobber and said, 'I'll punch ya in the bleeding nose. That's my sister ya talking about.'

Gobber spat in the canal and said, 'Piss awf.'

'Leave awf,' I said. 'We don't want any punch ups here.' *Who is this little bird Gobber is talking about?* I was finking.

'Wot's ya name?' I said to the kid.

'Tommy,' he replied.

'OK Tommy,' I said. 'You can be in our gang if ya like.'

'No he can't 'cos he ain't big enuff,' said Fred.

'Shut ya bloody mouf,' I said.

I am the biggest here and I've got the biggest cock,' said Georgi. 'Al's next and Fred is arfter him, and that bloody Gobber, he ain't got no cock at all 'cos we've seen it, ain't we Al?'

'Ya,' I said.

All Gobber done was spit in the drink and laugh 'cos he was scared of Georgi even though he was on crutches. We all ended up having a good old giggle and I got on like a house on fire wiv Tommy and he turned out to be a good mate. Tommy was about four foot free tall wiv black hair and brown eyes. He always seemed to have nice fings to wear as his dad was always in good work. They wasn't posh, but they was always clean.

I shall never forget the first time I saw Tommy's sister. I knocked on his house one Saturday morning to take him wiv me up to Whitechapel, fire lighting for the Yids.

'Come in, Al,' he said. 'The old lady's gawn up the market, shopping.'

I followed him up the passage to the back room and there standing at the sink having a wash in her vest and knickers was his lovely sister. I fawt, *if Gobber White was here now he would go potty*. She had lovely long black hair and her eyes were dark and wonderful.

She turned round from the sink and looked at me as if I was dirt. She looked at Tommy and said, 'Where do you fink you're going, then?'

'I am going wiv Al up to Whitechapel to light fires.'

'Oh no you're not. You know mum said you were going to help me tidy up.'

'Are you coming or not, Tommy?' I said. 'If we don't get up there soon we won't earn nuffing.'

'Wot do we want?' said Tommy.

'I've got the paper and wood and all we need is some matches,' I said.

'We've got some in the cupboard,' he said.

By this time his sister had got dressed and she looked even lovelier in her white pinney.

'You're not to take them and you're not going,' she said.

'Leave awf,' he said. 'I tell you wot I'll do. If ya don't say nuffing to the old lady I'll give ya 'arf of wot I get.'

Well, like all the birds, she fawt to herself, *there's wages on the end of this*, so she agreed to let Tommy go. I looked at her and I fawt to myself, *you can have all I am going to earn today, darling*.

When we got outside I said, 'Wot's ya sister's name, Tommy.'

'Diana,' he replied, 'but we call her Di. *Wot a darling that Diana is*, I fawt.

Diana was her proper name but I called her Dian. Or sometimes I would call her Di. She was beautiful. She was about four foot two wiv long black hair and big brown eyes. Her eyes always seemed to be laughing. She was full of life. Her teef were as white as snow, and she looked like a small Sophia Loren. She was so lovely.

Well, Tommy and I got to Whitechapel and I told him wot to do. He ended up wiv freepence and I got a tanner. When we got back to Tommy's house there was Diane on her hands and knees whitening the doorstep. She looked a picture in her white pinney over a worn dress and old plimsoles. She had no socks as Tommy's muvver couldn't afford them. *There she is*, I fawt. *A real Cinderella*. She looked up from the doorstep.

'Well, how much did ya get?' she asked, looking at me. I held out my hand and showed her the six pennies I had earned.

'How come you've got a tanner and he's only got fruppence?'

'Well, Al had done it before,' said Tommy. And wiv that he gave her a penny. She turned the penny over in her small white hand and at the same time she looked at me. Her piercing clear eyes seemed to say, 'Come on, wot about yours?'

I took two pence from my pocket and said, 'Here, you can have this.'

She took the money from my hand and her fingers touched mine and I knew that I was in love wiv her. She looked at the twopence and said, 'Fanks, now I will be able to go to the pictures.'

Before I knew it I was saying, 'I'll come.'

She looked at me and said, 'All right then.'

That night I couldn't get our farst enough. But first I managed to get a handful of marg to hold my hair down plus a clean jersey. Then I was all ready for the awf.

When we got to the cinema I ended up paying for the two of us. She held on to her money but I didn't care and the biggest larf of all was when we got inside we had to sit in separate seats. She was over one side and I was over the uvver.

That bird was over the moon wiv that twopence I gave her and she never left me alone arfter that. I was only twelve years old at the time. She would follow me everywhere and the boys would say, 'Tell her to piss awf, Al. We don't want her wiv us.' Georgi was still on his crutches so if we went anywhere he would hang behind wiv me and Di. The rest of the gang soon got used to her being wiv us and she became one of the gang.

The last time I took her out was at the beginning of the war when Mum, Dad, and the girls were sent to Scarborough, and at the time I was nearly eighteen. I was waiting to go in the Navy but I still can't remember the name of the film. At that age I was too busy cuddling her in the back row. I fink I really loved her.

On a Saturday we would send Georgi in to the pictures and when they put the lights out he would let us all in frew the side door. One Saturday there were about five of us and Fred said to Georgi, 'Now don't forget to open the doors as soon as the glims go out.'

Well, Georgi done as he was told all right. Wot we didn't know was that the manager and the attendant was waiting for us in the toilet. We all pushed our way in as soon as Georgi opened the doors and once we was all inside the manager and the attendant pounced from the toilet.

The triumphant manager put out his arms and said, 'I've got ya ya little barsteds,' and he shouted to the attendant to call the law.

Gobber didn't hang about. He just pushed the manager on his bottle and glass. We all ran away and Georgi was going like the clappers on his crutches.

All of a sudden it happened. Georgi done a somersault arse over head and he hit the tobby (ground) wiv a wallop.

'I've got ya,' said the attendant. 'Oh me head, oh me head,' Georgi was screaming.

By the time we got back to see if Georgi was all right there was blood all over the pavement.

When the attendant saw the blood he said, 'Wot the bloody hell ya done, son?'

'You done it ya dirty barsted,' Georgi said, and the poor old attendant didn't know wot to do. An old bird that had come out of a house across the road was taking her apron awf and putting it round Georgi's winney peg.

'Someone had better go and get an ambulance,' she said. Oh no, I fawt. Not again. His old lady will 'it the roof when she 'ears about this lot.

'Al,' said Fred, 'it looks like anuvver hospital job.'

'Get up Georgi,' I said. 'Anybody would fink ya was dead.'

But Georgi wasn't listening. He just lay there wiv his eyes closed.

'That's fucked it,' said Gobber. 'He's dead.'

Just then a geezer pulled up in a big car and asked wot the trouble was. He said somefing about being a doctor.

'I saw his slip and hit his head on the pavement,' said the old bird.

Well, this geezer pulled a little torch out of his pocket and started to look in Georgi's eyes.

'Wot's he looking for, Al?' said Fred.

'How the bleeding hell do I know?' I said.

'He's looking to see if his brains are still there,' said Tommy.

Just then this geezer looked up and said to the attendant, 'You'd better go and get an ambulance.'

Awf goes the attendant. Just then Georgi opened his eyes and tried to get up.

'Lay there, son, you'll be all right soon,' said the geezer and wiv that he pushed Georgi back down onto the pavement.

'Piss awf,' said Georgi, 'I want to go home.'

'Now don't be silly,' said the geezer. We have got to get you to the hospital. You have had a nasty fall.'

'I ain't going to no bleeding hospital,' said Georgi and wiv that he went out like a light again. The geezer opened Georgi's jersey and he started to rub his chest.

'Does anyone know where he lives?' he asked.

'Yus guv, he's our mate,' said Gobber.

Before the geezer could ask any more questions the ambulance arrived and this geezer starts to talk to one of the ambulance men.

'I'll see to that, doctor,' I heard the ambulance man say. As they was putting Georgi into the ambulance he came round again.

'Is anyone wiv the lad, doctor?' one of the ambulance men said.

'Yes guv, we are,' said Fred.

'You'd better come along with him, then,' said the ambulance man. And wiv that five snotty nosed little sods scrambled into the ambulance.

'Blimey,' said the ambulance man. 'How many is there?'

'We're all wiv him, guv,' I said.

'Well, I am afraid you all can't come wiv him.' So of course we booted the uvvers out of the ambulance.

All the way to the hospital, Georgi was moaning and the ambulance man was saying, 'Don't worry, son, we will soon be there.' When we got to the hospital, the nurse said to Georgi, 'Now lad, what have you been up to?'

'He slipped on his crutches miss and he's split his nut open,' I told her.

She took Georgi into anuvver room and told Fred and me to sit down and wait for him.

'Who's going to tell his muvver, Al? I bleeding ain't and that's for sure,' said Fred.

'You know what she said before when he done his leg in,' I said. 'She blamed us for that.'

We had been sitting down for about twenty minutes when the nurse came out.

'Is he all right miss?' Fred asked.

'Yes, we are just going to put some stitches in his head. He had a nasty fall, you know.' *You're telling me*, I fawt. *Ya can say that again missus. He bounced like a rubber ball.*

Arfter about half an hour Georgi came hopping out. Laugh . . . he was in a right state wot wiv the bandage on his head and the plaster on his leg. He was a mess.

'Blimey, Georgi,' I said, ''ou look like a wounded soldier.'

'He looks more like a bleeding snowdrop,' said Fred wiv a laugh.

'It's all right for you two. Wot about my old lady? She will go awf her bleeding nut when she sees this lot.'

'Don't worry about your old lady. We will soon sort her out, won't we Al,' said Fred. I fawt, *you can tell her, Fred, cause I ain't.*

94

All the way home Georgi kept on about his old lady and wot she would do wiv him when she saw him.

'If she finds out we was bunking in the dolly mixtures she will give me a bleeding good hiding.'

'Well, that won't be nuffink new will it. You're always getting punched up by her, ain't yer,' said Fred.

'I ain't arf got a headache,' Georgi kept on saying. *That ain't all your going to have*, I fawt. *You wait till you get in.*

'Wot am I going to tell me old lady?' asked Georgi.

'Don't worry. We will tell her you slipped on ya crutches down the railway steps, won't we Al,' said Fred.

'I don't know wot ya worrying about, Georgi, you'll be all right by the morning,' I told him.

When we got to the corner, I fawt, *his old lady will kill him. When she sees him she will cut our bleeding heads awf.*

Georgi was a little way in front of us so he couldn't 'ear wot I was saying to Fred.

'Eh Fred,' I said. 'I ain't having none of it wiv his old lady. I am going to scarper.'

'Funny fing Al, I was finking the same fing,' Fred said.

As we got a little way on, I said, 'O well, Georgi, I've got to leave ya here.'

'Wot ya mean?' asked Georgi.

'Well I've got to take the old man out to get the bread money, ain't I?' And wiv that I scarpered.

Just then I heard Fred say, 'I'll see ya tomorrow, Georgi.' Well, you should have heard that Georgi. He said words that wasn't in the English language. All the way up the street he was shouting, 'Ya dirty pair of barsteds. I am not coming round for ya in the morning.' *I know ya not coming round for us tomorrow*, I fawt. *Your old lady will just about finish ya off when ya get home.*

When I got indoors my old muvver said, 'Where the bleeding hell have you been?'

'Muvver,' I said, 'I've been up to the hospital.'

'Wot the bloody hell for?' she screamed.

'Well, Georgi slipped on his crutches and he split all his nut open so we took him to the hospital,' I told her.

'Ah, that poor lad,' she said, 'he's properly in the wars, ain't he?'

'Muvver, you should see him' I said. 'That boy looks like a wounded soldier and should get a medal.'

'Ya sure ya ain't been up to ya bloody tricks again?' she bawled at me.

'Leave awf muvver, I told ya wot he done, ain't I?'

I was just about to sit down to eat some bread and dripping when there was a banging at the door. The old lady went out to open it and I heard Georgi's muvver saying, 'Is you Harryboy there, Lil?' *Aye aye*, I fawt, *it's Georgi's old lady.* Before ya could piss frew the eye of a needle, my old lady was shouting, 'Harryboy, come out here.'

When I went to the door, Georgi's muvver said, 'Wot happened to my Georgi's head?' Well, I told her the story we made up about him falling down the steps and how we took him to the hospital.

'That bleeding boy of mine will be the sodding death of me,' she said. 'It's a good job his farver is still away at sea.'

Incidentally, when Georgi went to hospital he never paid any money. The hospital did send a bill to his farver but the Board of Guardians paid it. That is like our Social Security of today.

Well, Georgi's muvver seemed satisfied wiv the fanny we had given her and she went on talking about Georgi's old man being away at sea and how he would be coming home in a few weeks time. *I wonder wot he will bring home this time?* I fawt, as Georgi's old man used to bring home all sorts from sea.

He brought a monkey home once. The fings we did wiv that monkey was enough to turn its hair green. When we first saw it Fred said, 'Wot's its name, Georgi?'

'He ain't got one,' said Georgi.

'I know, let's call him Kong,' said Tommy.

'Yus that's a good name,' I said.

'No, we can't call him that,' said Georgi, ' 'cos my old man calls him Shits.'

'Wot's he call him that for?' asked Gobber.

'Well, he keeps shitting himself,' said Georgi.

'Well, if that's wot ya old man calls him we will have to call him the same name or the poor little barsted won't know wot his real name is,' I said.

Arfter Georgi had had Shits for about a week the monkey started to bite its own tail, and it bit all the end awf.

'Georgi,' I said, 'that poor little barsted's hungry or he wouldn't bite his tail like that. Look, it's red raw.'

'Leave awf. He can't be hungry. I gave him a dish full of dog

96

biscuits that I nicked out of the pet shop on Saturday,' said Georgi.

'Why don't ya take him to the dog hospital to see wot's wrong wiv him?' said Diana.

'If ya keep on giving him dog biscuits the poor little barsted will start barking one of these mornings, won't he Al?' said Fred.

'I fink we should take him to the RSPCA doctor to see wot's wrong wiv him.'

'There's nuffink wrong wiv him,' said Georgi.

'Don't talk bloody darft. There must be somefing wrong wiv him or he wouldn't bite his tail like that, would he?' said Gobber.

Well, we took him to the RSPCA shop to see the geezer and Georgi had him on a piece of string under his coat.

'Why don't ya let him out, Georgi,' said Diana, 'so he can get some air?'

There was about free uvvers in the waiting-room wiv their dogs and we all sat down to wait our turn. The door opened and in came some old bird wiv a big black cat and she sat next to Georgi.

'Ya want to give him some air, Georgi,' said Diane once more.

'OK' said Georgi and he took the monkey out from under his coat, and sat him on his lap. The big black cat went mad and tried to get away from the old bird when it saw the monkey.

Just then, one of the dogs saw it and he went just about crazy. He made one dive for the poor old monkey pulling his owner wiv him. Well the dog pulled its owner flat on his face. This started all the uvver dogs awf. There were chairs all over the place. By this time the poor old monkey jumped on Georgi's head and shitted itself wiv fright. Laugh . . . there was shit all running down Georgi's face and he was smothered in it. The old vet came out of the surgery to see wot all the fuss was about. One young girl sitting holding a puppy ran out of the shop screaming her head awf. Poor Georgi was trying to clean the shit awf of his face. The old geezer whose dog had pulled him on his face was trying to untangle the dog lead.

Well, we got Georgi cleaned up after tearing a bit awf of Fred's shirt.

'You'd better come in first as I don't want any more trouble,' said the old vet to Georgi, who took the old monkey into the surgery. Arfter about ten minutes he came out carrying the monkey under his coat.

'Wot did he say, Georgi?' we all asked.

97

'He 'as given me some cream to put on 'is tail,' said Georgi.

'It looks as though ya want something on ya bleeding head,' said Fred. 'You've got all shit in ya ear'ole.' On our way home we washed Georgi's head in a horse's trough.

It took free of us to hold that monkey down to put the bloody cream on his tail and each time we put it on so he licked it awf.

'There's only one way, Georgi,' I said. 'We will have to put his tail in a bandage.' So we got hold of him on Georgi's kitchen table and put on a fresh lot of cream and tied a rag round his tail.

Arfter I tied the knot, I said, 'Right Georgi, let him go.' Well that little monkey went mad. He ran up the wall trying to get the bandage awf of his tail and he ended up on top of the cupboard in Georgi's kitchen still trying to get the bandage awf.

'If ya get that bandage awf, ya little barsted, I'll get a bleeding chopper and cut ya fucking tail awf,' Georgi shouted at him.

'Georgi,' I said, 'you're nuffing but a cruel barsted, talking to that poor little monkey like that.' Just then the monkey took one jump and landed in the sink full of dirty water. The poor little sod looked like a drowned rat when we pulled him out.

We put that cream on his tail for about two weeks and still there was no difference.

'I don't know wot I am going to do,' Georgi said. 'He won't stop biting 'is bleeding tail.'

'Why don't we take him round to see old Perry?' I said. 'He should know wot to do as he comes from the jungle.'

'That's a good idea,' said Gobber. So awf we all went to see old Perry, who lived two streets away and came from the West Indies. He was as black as the night. He used to go away to sea a lot but he got too old so he lived on money provided by the Board of Guardians.

When we got to his house I banged on the door and, arfter a while, out comes old Perry's white wife.

'Wot the bleeding hell do you lot want wiv that bloody fing?' she said, looking at the monkey.

'We want to see Perry,' said Fred. Just then a voice shouted from the back room:

'Who's dat dere, mudder?'

'It's us, Perry,' I said as he came up the passage. He was a long skinny man wiv hair like grey cotton wool and his skin was as black as ebony. It seemed as though his nose went right across his black face and the whites of his eyes were like organ stops.

'Wot dus you want dar?' he asked.

'We want ya to have a look at Georgi's monkey,' said Gobber.

'Monkey? Wot monkey?' asked Perry.

'This monkey,' said Georgi, holding the petrified monkey up by the scruff of the neck wiv one hand and holding its tail wiv the uvver.

'Look,' he said, 'he keeps biting his tail.'

'You better bring dat dar monkey into de house,' said Perry and we all followed him and his wife up the passage to the back room. It was a tidy little room wiv well-worn furniture. Mrs Perry closed the door arfter us once we was all inside.

Fred was the first to break the silence. 'We want ya to tell us how to stop him from biting his tail.'

'Wot makes ya fink dat I knows wot to do wid him?'

'Can't ya tell us wot to put on his tail to stop him from biting it?' said Georgi.

'Man I can tell ya all sorts to do wid him.'

'We fawt you would know seeing as you lived in the jungle when you was a little boy,' I said.

Perry gave a little smile and looked at his wife and said, 'Wot do you fink, mudder?'

'Wot the bleeding hell does she know?' I said to Fred. 'She's like us. She's never lived in the jungle.'

Mrs Perry smiled and said, 'Why don't you give him some Black Magic medicine? That will stop him from biting his tail.'

Well, we all stood there wide-eyed waiting for Perry to do a war dance or sumfing, but all he did was to go to the cupboard and bring out a tin of mustard and wiv his finger he put some on the monkey's tail.

'Dar you is. He won't bite his tail any more,' said Perry wiv a smile.

'Well I be fucked, why didn't I fink of that?' said Georgi.

The poor old monkey didn't know wot it was all about so he got hold of his tail and he bunged it in his mouf and he got a mouf full of mustard. He went mad and he slung all kinds of somersaults and the tears was running down his cheeks.

'The poor little sod is crying,' I said to Georgi. Wipe his eyes wiv this damp rag,' said Mrs Perry and handed Georgi the rag to wipe his eyes wiv.

'Ya want to be careful, Georgi, or he will have bad eyes and then he will have to have glasses,' said Gobber.

'Piss awf. How can a monkey have glasses?' said Georgi.

We fanked old Perry for his services and went on our way. It

99

took a month before that monkey stopped biting his tail and then the poor little sod went and hung himself. Georgi couldn't afford a collar for him so when we took him out he would tie a piece of string round his bushel and peck (neck) and he would sit on Georgi's shoulder and Georgi would tie the uvver end to the buttonhole of his coat.

One night we had the old monkey wiv us and saw the rest of the gang swinging on a rope tied to a lamp post.

'Georgi,' I said, 'do ya self a favour and tie that old monkey to the railing over there and we can keep our eye on him and we can all have a giggle.'

'That's a good idea,' said Georgi, and he tied the monkey up to the six-foot-high railings.

We was all messing about, swinging on the rope when Tommy shouted, ' 'Ey, Georgi, there's sumfing wrong wiv ya bleeding monkey. He's laying on the ground.'

Well, we all ran over to see wot was wrong wiv the old monkey and there he was, his eyes popping out of his head. All the string was round his neck and his tongue was hanging out the side of his mouth.

'He's not breeving,' I said to Georgi. 'He's hung his bleeding self wiv the string. He's dead.'

'Don't say that, Al. My old man finks the world of that little barsted,' said Georgi.

'If he finks the world of that monkey he will bleeding kill you when he comes home from sea,' said Gobber.

'Wot am I going to tell me muvver?' Georgi was saying.

'It ain't ya muvver you've got to worry about. It's that old man of yours,' I told him.

Well, we untangled the poor little monkey from the string and we got him awf the railings.

'Ya better tell ya old man wot happened,' said Fred.

When Georgi got home he told his muvver what had happened to the old monkey.

'It's a bleeding good job ya farver is away or he would have bloody killed ya,' said his muvver. 'The best fing we can tell him is that the bloody fing scarpered and we couldn't get him.'

The next day when I saw Georgi, I said, ' 'Ey Georgi, wot have ya done wiv the old monkey?'

'He's still under the stairs in a cardboard box,' he said.

'Ya can't leave him there,' I said. 'Ya got to get him buried or he will stink the house out. I know, let's bury him in your yard. We can go and get the rest of the gang and give him a funeral.'

'OK then,' said Georgi, 'and we can put him in a wooden box.'

We told Fred and the rest of the kids wot we were going to do and Gobber got a lovely little wooden box which was an old kipper box that came from the market.

'We can put him in this and nail him down,' said Gobber.

'Wot ya want to nail him down for?' asked Fred.

'So he don't get out, ya berk,' Georgi said.

'That's wot they did to old Bob when he died. They put big nails in his box,' I said.

'Ya, they done that to my old grandmuvver too,' said Georgi.

On our way back to Georgi's house we saw Tommy and Diane.

'Ya want to see a funeral, Tommy?' asked Fred.

'Whose bleeding funeral?' asked Tommy.

'The old monkey's. We are going to bury him in Georgi's backyard,' Gobber told him.

'Yus, we'll come, won't we Di,' said Tommy.

We all went in Georgi's house and his muvver said, 'Wot the bloody hell do you lot want?'

'We're going to bury the monkey,' Georgi told his muvver.

'Ya want to do sumfing wiv the barsted fing before it starts stinking,' she said.

'That's just wot I told him, Mrs Hunter,' I said and wiv that Georgi went to the cupboard and lifted the monkey out by its tail.

'Ah, don't do that wiv the poor little fing,' said Diane.

'Why not?' asked Tommy. 'He can't feel anyfing.'

'Let's get him in the box and get him nailed up,' said Fred.

'Put him in, Georgi,' said Gobber and he held out the box wiv the lid awf.

'Ya want to wrap him up in sumfing,' said Diane.

'Wot the bleeding hell for?' asked Georgi. 'He can't get colder than he is, can he?'

Well, we put the monkey in the box and nailed the lid down and took it out to the backyard. Old man Farmer, a next-door neighbour of Georgi's was out in his backyard feeding the pigeons when he saw us digging the hole.

'Wot ya burying, Georgi boy?' he said.

'It's the monkey, Mister Farmer,' said Tommy.

'When did he die?' asked Mr Farmer.

'he didn't die, he hung himself,' said Georgi.

101

'Is that deep enough?' Georgi asked Gobber, pointing to the hole.

'Yus, that will do,' said Georgi.

'Frow the barsted in then,' said Tommy.

'No, don't frow him in,' said Diane, 'put him in properly.' So Georgi put the poor old monkey down in the hole and we covered him over in dirt.

'Stamp it down,' said Fred.

'Wot for?' said old Mr Farmer. 'He ain't going to get out.'

'That's true,' I said.

'That's that,' said Georgi, and we all started to go out of the yard.

'Ya want to put a little cross on that,' said Mister Farmer, 'or ya won't know where ya have buried him.'

'That's a good idea. Let's make him a little cross,' I said.

'How can ya do that? If Georgi's farver comes home and sees a cross there, he will say, "Who's that buried under there?" and ya will give the game away,' said Fred.

'Blimey, we didn't fink of that did we, Al?' said Georgi, and that was that.

'Ya know wot, Fred, we are going to miss that old monkey,' I said.

'Ya, we sure had some laughs wiv him, didn't we Al,' replied Fred.

Chapter Six
A Murder on the manor

That night we all met as usual and we was bored with nuffing to do.

'I wish the old monkey was here, don't you, Al?' said Fred.

'Yus, we would be having a giggle now, wouldn't we?' I said. 'Why don't we have a game of knock-knock?'

It was a right old laugh. What ya did was to get a reel of cotton, tie it to a knocker, go to the uvver side of the road and pull the cotton. When the old bird came to the door there would be no one there and she couldn't see the cotton. Once she went back inside, you pulled the cotton once more and out she'd come again.

Well this old bird came to the door four times. It was a laugh to see the old bird's face every time she came to the door and found no one there. Well, it was Gorgi's turn to pull the cotton and Fred was saying, 'Go on Georgi, pull it.'

Georgi was just about to pull the cotton again when this old geezer hit Georgi right round the ear'ole. Georgi gave out such a yell, you could have heard him in China.

'Hold that ya little barsted,' the old boy was shouting. 'Run!' Fred shouted.

Well, we didn't want a second telling and we was away like lightning.

When we got round the corner, Georgi was saying, 'How did that old barsted know it was us?'

'He must have crept out of the back and come round the uvver turning,' I said.

'Anyway, that will teach ya to play knock-knock, won't it,' said Gobber.

It was a funny fing but Georgi always came awf worse out of the four of us.

Arfter that, we went up to Bob's coffee stall to have a giggle wiv the cab drivers. When we got there the first fing Bob said to us was, 'Right you lot, piss awf. I can do wivout you lot pissing about here.'

'Piss awf yaself,' said Tommy, 'we ain't 'urting no one and besides it's a free country.' Bob ignored Tommy and went on pouring out a mug of tea for one of the cab drivers.

I had twopence in my pocket that I had earned that morning.

'Give us a hot dog roll, Bob,' I said.

'I told ya to piss awf, didn't I?' he said.

Old Frank, one of the cab drivers looked up and said, 'Ya must be a rich man, Bob, to refuse money like that.' We all laughed and jeered at old Bob.

'I ain't bleeding rich, but if I serve him before the night is out I'll be sorry,' he said.

'Ya never said that when our mate Georgi nearly got his bleeding leg cut awf wiv ya stinking old coffee stall, did ya?'

'That was his own fault for pissing about,' Bob replied. 'He wasn't doing the job properly.'

'By the way, Bob, ya didn't pay us for that,' said Georgi.

'Ya never finished the job properly, did ya?' was Bob's reply.

'You're a hard man,' I said.

'I've got to be wiv you little barsteds,' and wiv that he handed me the hot-dog roll I had asked for.

'Give us a bit, Al,' said one of the uvver kids.

'Piss awf, get ya own,' I told him.

I saw Fred and Georgi whispering and I knew they were up to sumfing. I walked over and said, 'Wot's it all about?' Just then old Bob started spitting and coughing all over place and the coffee stall was full of smoke. While he had been arguing wiv me wevver to serve me or not, old Fred had climbed up the side of the coffee stall and blocked the chimney up wiv old paper.

'Ya want to clean that chimney, Bob,' said old Charlie, the cab driver.

'It was all right when I lit it,' said Bob.

Well, it was getting worse and old Bob was spitting all over the gaff. All of a sudden he tumbled wot was up and he went stark raving mad and he frew a soup ladle and an empty tin full of tea-leaves at us.

'Ya little barsteds,' he was screaming at the top of his voice. 'I knew ya was up to sumfing.' Old Charlie and the rest of the cab drivers couldn't stop laughing, and ya couldn't see old Bob for smoke.

Well, we departed from there as farst as our legs could carry us. We said goodnight to Georgi as he had to get home to his muvver. Me and Fred decided to go down the docks to see old Joan, the brass I told you about earlier.

When we got there, she was sitting on her doorstep and as we approached her, she took a pinch of snuff out of an old tin box.

'Hallo, darlings,' she said as she was bunging snuff up her nose.

'Wotcher, Joan. How's fings?' asked Fred.

'It's quieter than the bleeding grave,' she replied. 'Ya know wot? I ain't had a bleeding geezer all sodding day. I must make a few bob tonight,' she said.

'Do ya want us to go and get ya a jug of stout?' I asked her.

'Gawd bless ya. I'll go and get ya me old jug,' and wiv that she vanished inside. A few seconds later she was back out wiv the jug.

'Here ya are. Get me a jug of stout and you two can have an arrowroot biscuit each.' Awf we went to the boozer, the Blue Post, which was known locally as Charlie Brown's. They did have bottled beer in them days but Joan liked draft stout straight from the barrel.

'She ain't a bad old bird, is she, Al?' said Fred.

'I bet she's worf a few bob,' I said.

'How come?' said Fred.

'Well that's all shit about her not having a punter all day. Ya work it out. If she 'as four punters a day at ten bob each that is two nicker a day. That's fourteen pounds a week.'

'Fuck me. That's a fortune, ain't it, Al,' said Fred.

We got the stout and we both 'ad a swig out of the jug before we got back to her.

'Here y'are, Joan. Do ya want us to go to the docks and get ya some punters?' asked Fred.

'Gawd bless ya. You're two good boys to old Joany,' she said. And as we was going away she shouted arfter us, 'Don't forget to look out for Old Bill, and don't forget – no blacks.'

'Wot's the difference from a black cock to a white one?' Fred asked.

'Ya knows I don't like blacks,' she called arfter us.

'OK Joan, no blacks,' we shouted back and awf we went to the docks.

We wasn't there long before we saw two swarthy geezers coming out of the gates.

'Ya want a bird?' I asked them.

'Me no understand, me Polish,' said one of them.

'Ask him if he wants jigger jig,' I said to Fred.

'Ya want jigger jig,' asked Fred.

'Ha, jigger jig,' said one of them and he turned to his friend and said sumfing in Polish and they both laughed.

'Ten bob each,' I said.

'OK you take,' one of them said and awf we went to old Joan. She saw us coming down the street wiv the two geezers.

'Here ya are, Joan. We got two customers for ya,' said Fred.

'Hallow darlings,' she said as she tried to get awf her fat arse where she was sitting on the steps and wiv the next breff she said, 'I can't take the two of ya at once and it's ten bob each, money in advance.'

The two geezers was talking in their own language to each uvver. I fink they were discussing who was going first. Arfter they had made up their minds who it was going to be, Joan went inside wiv one of the men. Fred, the uvver geezer and me, sat on the doorstep.

'Do ya speak English?' asked Fred.

'No English, no much,' he said.

'Ask him if he's got any snout (cigarettes), Al,' said Fred.

'Have ya got any snout, Johnny?' I asked him and I made a gesture wiv my hand as if I was smoking.

'Ha, smoke,' he said, and he gave us both a Polish fag.

Arfter we had all lit up and was smoking well, Fred said, 'Wot the bleeding hell's in this fag? It tastes like horses' shit and tram tickets.'

'Leave awf,' I said, 'they're good for ya. Don't ya know that all Polish fags are strong?'

'How comes they are stronger than ours?' asked Fred.

'Well, they pack the backer tighter and that makes them strong,' I said.

'Well, I fink they have burnt this barsted,' said Fred. Just then, Joan comes out wiv the geezer.

'Blimey, that was quick,' said Fred.

'Well, he's been away to sea for a long time and he had a lot of dirty water to get off his chest,' said Joan.

Fred looked up and said, 'If I smoke any more of this bleeding fag I'll have bleeding soot on mine.' And wiv that he frew the fag away.

Joan had gone in the house wiv the uvver geezer.

'Did ya like jigger jig, Johnny?' Fred said, and the geezer said, 'Ya, very good.'

106

'He's a dirty barsted, ain't he, Fred?' I said and wiv that the uvver geezer laughed all over his face.

It wasn't long before Joan came out wiv the uvver geezer. She was smiling to herself.

'You're very good boys to ya old Joan,' she said.

'Bung us a tanner, then,' I said.

'There ya are, 'arf a tanner each,' she said.

'We have got to get home now Joan,' said Fred, 'it's getting late and if I am in too late, my old man will punch me up.'

'All right, me lovelies. See ya again.'

And wiv that we went running awf home, satisfied wiv the night's work. Little did we know that night, that Joan had only four more weeks on this 'erf. One of the uvver brasses found her dead one morning wiv a stocking around her froat and she was as stiff as a poker. She had been strangled wiv one of her own stockings. Old Bill said she had been strangled by persons unknown. The police questioned about a dozen seamen and all the uvver brasses that lived in the same house as Joan.

There were about six of them: Millie, Annie, Dot, Brenda, Rita and Lil. They were all near enough the same in age. Some had dyed their hair blonde and some were dark. They all used plenty of make-up on their faces. We only worked for Joan but when she got knocked off we worked for Milly. Rita opened her big mouf and told Old Bill about me and Fred. She told us later that one of the plain-clothes detectives told her that they already knew about the two boys that used to get punters for Joan. Well ya can guess wot happened next. The rozzers came round my house arfter me. They already had Fred down at the nick. I was indoors trying to stick a patch on one of my plimsoles when there came a knock on the door.

'Who the bleeding hell's that?' asked the old lady.

'Muvver, how the hell do I know? I can't see frew the wall, can I,' and she went to the door to find out who was knocking. I heard a voice say, 'Is your son in? We would like to have a word with him.'

'Wot son? I have free of them,' I heard the old lady say.

When they explained the old lady said, 'It's my Harryboy you want,' and wiv that she said, 'Harryboy, get yaself out here. There's some men who want to talk to ya.'

I hopped up the passage wiv one plimsole awf. As I got to the door the old lady said, 'These two men want to see ya.'

'Wot ya want, guv?' I asked.

107

'We are police officers,' said the taller one, 'and we would like to ask you some questions.'

'Wot for? I ain't done nuffing,' I said.

'We know you haven't son, but we need your help.' *Blimey, I fawt, there could be anuvver tea party at the end of this.* 'OK, wot ya want to know then, guv?'

'Do you know one of the ladies down at the West India Dock Road by the name of Joan?'

'Yus, guv. She's a brass.'

'Oh my Gawd. He's mixed up wiv whores,' the old lady said.

'Why don't ya shut ya mouf, muvver? Ya don't know nuffink about it.' And wiv that, she clipped me round the ear'ole.

'It's all right, muvver. He hasn't done anyfing,' said the copper. He then went on to tell us about poor old Joan being found strangled. Then he asked me about Fred and wot we used to do for Old Joan, and I told him we used to go and get punters for her. The old lady gave me anuvver bang round the ear'ole and shouted at me, 'Fancy getting mixed up wiv whores like that.' The copper could see he wasn't getting nowhere wiv the old girl keeping banging me round the ear'ole.

'We would like you to come wiv us to the police station if it's all right wiv you, Mrs,' he said, looking at the old lady.

'Ya want to take the little barsted there and keep him there, for wot good he is,' she said. 'Go and get ya uvver shoe and go wiv these two gentlemen.' I went in to get me uvver plimsole on to go down the nick wiv the two coppers.

While I was getting me uvver plimsole on, the old lady was saying, 'Fancy getting mixed up wiv whores. Ya wait till ya farver 'ears about this. He'll give ya a bloody good hiding.'

'Leave awf, muvver,' I said. 'You will get me life the way you're carrying on.'

When we got to the nick, I saw Fred sitting on a seat and there was a plain-clothes man writing down all he had to say. When he saw me his face lit up.

'Wotcher, Al. Have ya heard about old Joan getting done up?' I fawt, *bleeding big mouf. Trust him to let Old Bill know about everyfing.*

'Of course I know about it. Wot ya fink I am doing here? Waiting for a bleeding tram or sumfing?'

'Right lad,' said one of the coppers. 'Sit down and I'll be wiv you in a moment.' I sat down next to Fred and the copper who was taking down Fred's statement got up and went into a room.

'Wot ya been telling them?' I asked Fred.

'I ain't said nuffing, Al,' he said.

'Well wot have they been asking ya then?' I asked.

'They asked me when I saw Joan last and they asked me if I took any geezers to her last night.'

'And wot did ya say?' I asked him.

'I told them that we wasn't down the docks last night,' he replied. 'I bet the geezer who done it is soon got because these coppers are from Scotland.'

'Who said they was from Scotland?' I asked him.

'Well, that big geezer who brought you in said he was from Scotland Yard and that's in Scotland ain't it, Al?' asked Fred.

'Don't be a berk. Don't ya know anyfing?' I said to him. Just then one geezer who had come for me came out of the room and came across to where I was sitting.

'Now then, Harryboy, tell me wot you know about this lady called Joan.' I fawt, *Aye aye. We are on first names are we, ya crafty barsted.*

'Right, guv,' I said, 'wot ya want to know?'

'Tell me when you saw her last and who you took to her last night,' he said. I fawt, *He's trying to catch me out. He knows we wasn't down the docks last night.*

I looked him straight in the eye and said, 'Come awf it, guv. Ya know me and me mate wasn't down the docks last night.'

'I know that,' he said, 'but I want to know who you took to Joan last.'

'The last time we saw Joan was a few days ago,' I told him. He asked me a lot more questions and arfter about ten minutes the big geezer came back to join us.

'Right, Sergeant. How are you making out?'

'Well, this is wot I've got so far, sir,' and he handed him the paper he had been writing on.

The big feller read it and all of a sudden he said, 'I tell ya wot, sergeant. You go down to the canteen and get these two young men a nice glass of lemonade each. You'd like that, wouldn't you?' he said wiv a smile.

'Not 'arf, guvner,' I said. And wiv that, awf went the uvver geezer to the canteen.

'Is that right, you and your mates come from Scotland, guvner?'

'No, we don't come from Scotland son, we come from Scotland Yard,' he replied.

'Well that's in Scotland, ain't it?' asked Fred.

'Hardly, it's in Westminster.'

'Where the bleeding hell is that, Al?' Fred was asking me.

'How the bloody hell do I know?'

Well they kept us in the nick for about two hours and all the time the big geezer kept asking us questions.

'It wasn't us, guv,' Fred said.

'I know that, son, but I must ask you all about her and wot you used to do for her,' he said. Just then the uvver geezer came back in the room wiv two glasses of lemonade.

'Ha, that's a good fellow, sergeant,' said the big geezer. 'Now drink up lads and you can tell me all about it.' I fawt *this geezer must be awf his head. He 'as already asked us about her. Now he wants to know more.*

'When did you first meet this lady?' he asked.

'You mean Old Joan, guv?' asked Fred.

'Well, yes, old Joan as you call her.'

'Oh, we have known her for a long time now,' I said.

'Yus, a long time,' said Fred, taking a swig of his lemonade.

'And wot did she ask you to do for her?' he said, and this time he was looking at Fred.

'We got geezers for her and we used to take them back to her ken (house) for her,' said Fred.

'You mean, you used to take seamen to her house for her?'

'Yus, that's right, guv,' I said. Just then he looked round at the uvver copper.

'And wot did they do, these men when they got there?' he asked.

'Well they used to get on the bed wiv her.'

'How do you know this?' asked the uvver copper.

'Well, we've seen them, ain't we, Fred?' I said.

'Yus, we used to look frew the burnt cinder (winder) and have a laugh at the geezer jumping on top on her,' said Fred as he drained the last drops of pop from his glass.

'When did you take a man to her last?'

'Oh, about free weeks ago now,' I told him.

'Would you know any of these men if you saw them again?' asked the uvver copper.

'I don't know. All I know is it can't be a black feller that done her in.'

'Why is that?' asked the big geezer.

'Because old Joan wouldn't have any blacks, would she, Fred?' I said.

'The last geezer we took to her gave us a fag, didn't he, Al?' said Fred.

'I never had no fag,' I said. I fawt, *This Fred's got a big mouf telling them we have been smoking.*

'Yus ya did. It was that Polish geezer that gave us the fag.'

'All right, so we've been smoking.' He went on to say somefing when the door opened and a young copper came in.

'Excuse me, sir, but there are two women at the door inquiring arfter the two lads.'

'Tell them to wait a minute, constable, we are nearly frew,' and the young copper vanished as farst as he came in.

Well, the big geezer asked us a few more questions and then said, 'Well, I won't keep you any longer.' I fawt, *Fank Gawd for that, he's going to let us go.* And then he started to lay the law down.

'Now you two young men listen to me and take note of what I am telling you. If I ever see you hanging around the dock gates again, I'll have you both locked up, and I don't want to catch you smoking or you will both go away for a long time.' And wiv the next breff he said, 'Right, you can go.' As we went frew the door he warned, 'I know where to find you if I want you.'

When we got outside the old lady and Fred's muvver was waiting for us.

'Can I have a few words wiv you two ladies?' said the big geezer and we was made to sit down while he took my muvver and Fred's muvver into the room. Well I don't know wot he said to my old lady and I have never found out to this day, but as we was coming out of the nick my old lady kicked me right up the bottle and glass, and sent me flying down the nick steps. As she sent me flying she shouted, 'You keep away from those whores, ya barsted.' All Fred's muvver kept saying was, 'Well I never, well I never. If ya farver 'ears about this, 'e'll kill ya.'

'Oh leave awf, muvver. I ain't done nuffing,' said Fred, and his old lady belted right round the ear'ole.

It didn't do us much good as we were back down the docks by the next night.

They never found the geezer who done old Joan in. 'They will never get the geezer who done it,' my bruvver said, 'as there was seamen coming and going all the time, and he could be thousands of miles away.' Mind you, we did miss old Joan for the copper or

111

two we could 'ave awf her. I bet she's making a fortune wherever she is.

We soon found anuvver brass to take the place of Old Joan and we was back down the docks waiting for the seamen to come out so we could take them to our new employer. Milly was her name. Milly was about five foot two tall wiv brown hair and brown eyes. Her hair was cut short and bobbed. She was about thirty years old and she had a nice figure and as she walked she would wobble her bum. There was only one fing wrong wiv Milly. She loved the old gin bottle. She would polish awf about six punters and she would send us for a bottle of gin and she would drink the bleeding lot. Her room was a small room wiv a bed in the corner hidden by a curtain that went across the room on string. There was a small gas-ring on top of the sideboard and there was a small fireplace wiv a mirror hanging above the top. Also in the room was a small table and four chairs. There was anuvver small table in the corner near the window, and on this stood a wash basin and jug.

I shall never forget one Friday night after she had had a good night. Fred and me took her four punters – that was apart from the punters she had got herself.

'I fink it's about time ya old Milly had a drink,' she said to me and she gave us the money to go to the pub for her bottle of gin. When we returned to her wiv the bottle she held it up to the light and said, 'Ah, that's lovely,' and she pulled the cork and started to knock it back.

'She's awf,' I said to Fred. 'We might as well piss awf as she ain't going to work anymore tonight.'

'All right,' said Fred, 'we might as well go. We're going now, Milly,' he said to her.

'Oh, don't go and leave ya old Milly,' she said. 'Sit down and I'll make you a nice supper.'

Thinking of the supper we said, 'OK then, we will stay for a little while,' and we both sat down at the table. It was the first time we had been to Milly's little flat. I pointed to the bedroom and said to Fred, 'That's where it all happens in there me old son.' Fred laughed and rubbed his hands as he always did when he got excited. In between swigs of the gin bottle Milly set about cutting us some bread and cheese.

'I'll make ya a nice cup of cocoa,' she said, putting the kettle

112

on the small gas-ring that stood on top of the sideboard. We started to get stuck in to the bread and cheese that Milly had put on the table for us.

'Ya had a good night, Milly?' Fred asked as she was coming towards the table wiv two steaming hot mugs of cocoa.

'Ya would never believe this boys, but I've had twelve punters today all told and they have all been good-uns and straightforward. None of this kinky lark,' said Milly.

'Blimey Milly, ya must have taken six nicker today at least,' I said.

'Never mind how much I took. Ya get on wiv ya bleeding supper,' she said, giving me a friendly tap round the ear'ole while she took anuvver swig of the gin bottle.

'I don't know how you can drink that stuff,' said Fred to her.

'Wot do you bleeding know about it? It's good for ya and it puts hairs on ya chest. Look,' she said, opening her blouse and flashing all her bosom. We all laughed and Fred said, 'Some chest, eh Milly.'

Arfter we had finished our supper we sat talking to Milly and we could see she was getting real merry as she was 'arfway down the bottle.

'Where did ya live before ya come to Limehouse, Milly?' Fred asked.

'In bloody Liverpool,' she replied.

'Whereabouts is that, then?' I asked her.

'That's up in Scotland, ain't it, Milly,' said Fred.

'Up in Scotland my arse,' she said, taking anuvver swig, and wiv a swallow she said, 'It's a bloody long way from here.' Then she started to tell us about Liverpool and about the docks. 'It must be like round here then if it's got docks,' I said.

'I suppose so,' said Milly. 'Anyway, I don't want to talk about Liverpool,' she said. 'Let's drink up and be merry.' And she offered the bottle to Fred.

'Go on, have a swig,' I said to him and he took a deep swig out of the bottle. Ya should have seen his boat race. He went red, white and blue, in that order. I couldn't stop laughing.

'That ain't pissing clever,' Fred said. 'You have a swig.' 'E pushed the bottle in my direction.

'Leave awf, I ain't drinking that shit,' I said, pushing the bottle away. Milly laughed and picked up the bottle.

'Ha, that's lovely, me darlings.' By this time Milly was well away and she was saying how hot it was in the room wiv the gas

113

fire on and wiv that she took off her blouse and she was showing all her Bristol Cities.

'Gaw, ain't she got some, Fred,' I said. 'Look at those.'

'Do ya like 'em,' Milly said, and she lifted her breasts up in her two hands. Old Fred's eyes nearly came out of his head.

'Gaw Blimey. Wot a pair of bristols you got, Milly.'

'Do ya fink so?' asked Milly.

'Not 'arf,' replied Fred.

Arfter a while, Milly began to take off her stays and she just stood there wiv her gigantic breasts completely naked.

'Come and touch them. They won't bite ya,' she said, offering those huge mountains to us.

That was our first introduction to Milly's world. At the age of twelve ya wonder wot it's all about. Arfter about an hour of messing around wiv Milly's bristols we got fed up and went home leaving Milly asleep on the bed.

When we told Georgi the next day he said wiv a laugh, 'Ya want to take old Gobber wiv you the next time ya go. He'll go potty if she flashes her bristols at him.'

We saw Milly a lot arfter that night and she turned out to be a good'un. She sometimes gave us sixpence a customer. We liked running for Milly and she was always good for a laugh, especially when she was drunk.

One night arfter we had taken her a punter and she had done wiv him she said, 'Ya old Milly's got a surprise for ya pair of sods. Come in.' *Aye aye*, I fawt, *it's show time again*, and we marched in the house after her.

'I wonder wot the surprise is, Fred,' I said.

'Maybe she's going to strip right off for us tonight,' he replied wiv a grin.

When we got into the room, Milly said, 'I've got a lovely supper for you two tonight,' and she produced from the oven the biggest bleeding meat pie I had ever seen.

'Blimey, Milly. Where did ya nick that from?' asked Fred.

Milly said somefing about having it wiv the butcher and she never nicked it.

'Ya mean to say ya had it awf wiv the butcher and the old barsted paid ya wiv a meat pie?' I said.

'That's right, dearie,' she replied.

Arfter we all had our supper I said, 'That was 'ansom, Milly.'

'It ought to be. That barsted knocked the living daylights out of me,' she said.

114

There was no strip act from Milly that night as one of the uvver brasses had asked her to go out for a drink at Charlie Brown's, a boozer in West India Dock Road which all the seamen used.

'I'll see ya tomorrow, boys,' Milly said as she was putting on her coat.

'Yus, try and get us anuvver pie,' said Fred. 'That was 'ansom.'

'Piss awf,' Milly said. 'If you two had ya bleeding way I would be shagging for meat pies only.'

One night poor old Milly had a miscarriage and it nearly killed her. Me and Fred went down the docks to try and get some punters for her and arfter a while Fred said, 'Let's go and see Milly. She may have some pie for supper.'

We got to Milly's room and banged on the door but we got no answer. I opened the door and called out, 'Are ya there, Milly?' All we heard was Milly moaning.

'Blimey,' said Fred. 'Wot's the matter wiv her?' We stood looking at her on the bed.

'Wot's up, Milly? Someone done ya over?' I asked and she said somefing about calling Peggy. (She was anuvver brass who lived along the landing from Milly, a little fing wiv blonde hair and blue eyes who wore a lot of make-up on her face).

'Go and get Peggy,' she kept on saying.

'You go and get Peggy and I'll stay wiv her,' said Fred.

So awf I went to Peggy's room and banged on the door and shouted, 'Are ya there, Peggy?'

Peggy came to the door and said, 'Piss awf. Can't I have a bloody rest? It's too early for me to go to work yet.'

'Come quickly,' I said. 'There's somefing wrong wiv Milly.' As we was making our way to Milly's room Peggy was muttering somefing about the old cow being pissed again.

'She ain't pissed. She is really ill,' I said.

Well, when we got back in the room, Milly said, 'Peg, I am losing the barsted. Get old Ma Taylor. She knows wot to do.'

'Wot's up wiv her, Peg?' Fred asked.

'Never you mind. You two go and get old Ma Taylor and hurry,' said Peggy.

Awf we went to old Ma Taylor's house, only a few doors away from Milly. Ma Taylor was a big-breasted woman in her fifties and she used to do fings for the prostitutes when they became pregnant.

115

When she came to the door and saw us she said, 'Piss awf, I don't want any.'

'We ain't selling anyfing, Ma,' said Fred. 'It's Milly. Peggy sent us for you and she said ya got to come right away as Milly is ill.'

'Ill me bloody arse. Pissed more like it,' bawled old Ma Taylor.

But she still agreed to come and when we got back to Milly's place Peggy said somefing about losing farst. Old Ma Taylor done no more. She pulled the bed clothes right back and said, 'Let's have a look,' not realising we was still in the room. There was blood all over the bed sheets. I looked at Fred and he looked at me and we just stood there wiv our moufs open.

'Right, Peg. Get some hot water on and let's get this mess cleared up,' Ma Taylor was saying.

Poor old Milly was in a right old mess. She was crying out and saying all sorts of fings even my ears were not used to hearing. Ma Taylor soon set about getting fings done. She turned round and saw me and Fred.

'Outside you two, and sit on that bloody doorstep and don't move in case I need ya to go and get somefing for me,' she ordered.

Out we went to sit on the doorstep as Ma Taylor had instructed.

'Wot ya fink is wrong wiv Milly?' Fred asked me.

'I don't know,' I replied, 'but I don't like the look of all that blood.' Just then Peggy came out and sent us for a 'arf bottle of gin from the pub on the corner. We got the gin and took it back to Peggy.

When we got back, Ma Taylor was saying how we should have to get old Doc Kelly in to have a look at Milly. Everyone used to say he was a quack as he was always pissed on Scotch.

'He won't come out this time of night,' Peggy was saying.

'He bloody will if he knows I want him,' said Ma Taylor. 'If he don't come I'll go round and drag the barsted here. Someone 'as got to see her as sure as God made apples,' she went on to say.

'Here ya are, Peg,' I said, putting the gin on the table.

'There's a good boy,' said Peggy as she was taking the cork from the bottle. She poured some out into a glass and took it over to the bed where Milly was laying.

Putting one arm around Milly's shoulders she said, 'Here, love. Take a swig of that. It will do ya the world of good.' But Milly just pushed the glass away from her lips and sank back onto the pillow. I fawt, *Blimey, she doesn't want a drink of gin.*

116

Old Ma Taylor was bending over Milly and she was saying, 'Now listen, love. I am sending for old Doc Kelly. He'll help ya, love, so just lie back and don't worry.' Poor Milly looked terrible.

'Don't worry, love,' Peggy was saying. 'We will look arfter ya.'

'Ya, we will look arfter ya, Milly,' said Fred.

Milly gave us a weak smile and I could see tears in her eyes.

'Now, listen you two. Ya knows where old Doctor Kelly lives, don't ya?' old Ma Taylor was saying to us.

'Yus Ma, round the corner by that Chinese gaff,' I said.

'Well, I want ya to go round and tell him that Ma Taylor wants him and don't come back here wivout him, even if ya have to drag him here. If he says he ain't coming tell him that old Ma Taylor said it's a miscarriage. Now go on and hurry ya bloody self,' she said as she was pushing us frew the door.

Doc Kelly lived about five streets away from Peggy. We ran all the way to his house. On the way, Fred said, 'What's a miscarriage?'

'Oh, it's somefing to do wiv ya legs when ya can't carry nuffing,' I said.

'How come's that?' he said.

'Well ya legs break and ya can't walk and that's wot Milly's got,' I told him.

'Is that why Milly's got her legs up?'

'Ya, I suppose so.'

Well we worked it out and that was that. By this time, we was at Doc Kelly's door and Fred was ringing the doorbell. Arfter a few minutes Doc Kelly staggered to the door. He was a big man wiv a big red face and a big Derby Kelly (belly) wiv a watch-chain stretching from one waistcoat pocket to the uvver.

'Wot the bloody hell do ya what at this time of night?' he bellowed at us. Me and Fred both stood there, wide-eyed. It was Fred who spoke arfter a little shove from me.

'Ma Taylor sent us, sir,' Fred stammered.

'Well speak up, lad. Don't just stand there,' bellowed old Kelly.

'Well, it's Milly. Her legs have all gawn wrong and there is a lot of blood on the bed sheets and she can't carry nuffink,' said Fred.

'Her legs? What the hell is wrong wiv her legs,' yelled old Doc Kelly.

'They're missing carriage,' I told him.

He looked at me and said, 'You'd better hang on there. No,

you'd better come inside and wait.' We followed him in the large house and he said, 'Wait in there,' and he showed us into a big room.

It was the biggest room I have ever seen. It had lovely wallpaper and a nice big clock on the mantelpiece and it smelt like wax polish. I said to Fred, 'We'd better not sit down. We might dirty the chairs.' So we stood there, frightened to move. Arfter a while old Doc Kelly appeared in the doorway.

'Come on, let's go,' he said, and we followed him frew the door. All the way up the street me and Fred was trying to keep up wiv the old Doc as he was taking one stride to our two. When we turned the corner and we was approaching Milly's place, we saw old Ma Taylor waiting on the doorstep.

'It's about time,' she was saying to the doctor as we got to the street door. 'I don't know wot all the fuss is about, calling me over a broken leg. She could have gone straight to the hospital,' the doctor was saying.

'Broken leg, me arse. The girl's having a miscarriage,' said old Ma Taylor as the doctor followed her up the passage and into Milly's room. Then Doc Kelly was saying somefing about the brasses and french letters.

'Who writes to Milly from France?' I said to Fred. 'How the bleeding hell do I know?' was Fred's reply.

Ma Taylor turned round and was pushing us through the door.

'Outside you two. This is no place for little boys.' And before we knew it, we was out on the doorstep.

'Well, the old cow. Wot ya know about that arfter us doing the dirty work,' said Fred.

'Well, they can't have all of us in that little room,' I said.

'Do ya fink old Kelly will cut Milly's leg awf?' Fred was asking.

'I hope not. We won't be able to earn any more out of her if he does that, will we?'

'How comes that then, Al?' Fred asked.

'Well, who wants a bird wiv no winny pegs? She will be 'arf a woman. Besides, she won't be able to jump in and out of the bed, will she?' I said to him.

'Well, if he do cut her legs awf she will only have to charge 'arf price as she will only be 'arf a bird, won't she?' said Fred wiv a laugh.

'Sometimes I fink ya potty,' I said. Arfter a while Peggy came to the door. Wiping her forehead wiv a towel, she said, 'Fank goodness that's all over.'

118

'Wot's it all about, Peg?' Fred asked.

'Oh, she is going to be all right now, fank Gawd,' said Peggy.

'Fank the Lord for that,' I said. 'We fawt he was going to cut her legs awf.' Peggy laughed and then she told us wot it was all about and we sat there listening wiv our eyes wide open.

Arfter she had finished explaining to us wot a miscarriage was, Fred said, 'Blimey, I wouldn't like to go frew that.'

'Don't worry, dearie,' said Peggy wiv a laugh, 'you've no fear of that.'

The next night I took Georgi to see Milly and when we got there she was sitting up in bed. I banged on the door and Milly shouted, 'Who is it?'

'It's me, Milly,' I shouted back.

'Oh, come in,' she replied and in we went.

'How ya feeling now, Milly?' I asked.

'Oh, I'm okay now, fanks to you and your old mate,' she said.

'Ya don't look so bad now, Milly,' I was saying as the door opened and in came Ma Taylor.

'Wot do you two sods want?' she asked.

'We came to see Milly,' I told her and she seemed to be satisfied wiv that.

'Now ya here ya can do a few errands for me,' she said.

'OK, Ma. Wot ya want?' She then produced a pencil from her apron pocket and started to write out a shopping list.

'Do ya want a drink of gin?' I asked Milly.

'No fanks dear, but I'll have a nice cup of tea when ya come back from the shops,' she replied. By this time, Ma Taylor had finished writing the shopping list.

'There ya are. Go and get this and don't forget I want the change,' she said, handing me five shillings and a paper carrier-bag.

And as we went frew the door, she shouted arfter us, 'And don't take all bleeding day.'

On our return, Milly was sitting up in bed wiv a cup of tea that old Ma Taylor had made for her. I put the fings on the table in the carrier bag.

'Here ya are, Ma,' I said.

'How much bloody change have ya got me out of five bob?' I opened my hand and counted out the change. There was exactly one shilling and sixpence.

'One and six,' I said, putting it on the Cain and Abel.

'Well ya can keep that,' said Milly, 'for being such a good boy.'

119

'Gaw, fanks Milly,' I said. Georgi's eyes nearly came out of his head when he heard Milly say that.

'Giss a tanner, Al,' he said.

'How can I give ya a tanner when I've got to give Fred 'arf of it?' I said to him.

'Ya nuffing but a tight barsted,' Georgi said to me.

'Why don't ya all have a tanner each?' said Milly from the bed, 'and that way there will be no fighting.'

'I don't want no bleeding fighting around her,' bawled Ma Taylor, 'so give him his sodding tanner.'

I gave him a tanner and he said, 'Gee fanks, Al, you're a good old mate.' I fawt, *that ain't wot he said a few seconds ago.*

Arfter a few days in bed, Milly was up and about again and she was nearly back to her old self. Me and Fred went to see her all the time she was in bed.

'Ya sure gave us a fright, Milly, when ya was ill wiv all that blood on ya bed,' I said to her one night.

'Ya, I must have done, me ducks, but ya old Milly ain't going frew that again for no barsted. I'll make the sod wear a french letter the next time.' Me and Fred looked at each uvver.

'Wot do ya mean, Milly?' Fred asked.

Milly smiled and said, 'Ya'll know wot I mean when ya get a big boy.'

Chapter Seven
Hanging at Stink House Bridge

One summer's arfternoon arfter dinner the whole gang of us were playing down by the canal. We were amusing ourselves by jumping from barge to barge when Gobber picked up a lump of wood and, pretending it was a gun, pointed it at Bomber and shouted, 'Bang, you're fucking dead, Bomber.'

'Piss awf,' Bomber shouted back. Poor old Bomber was a born loser. He didn't have a muvver to look arfter him – she ran away and left him wiv his sister, and went on the game in Limehouse. We used to call him Bomber on account of the pilot's helmet he always wore 'cos he never had a hair on his head. They kept shaving it all awf at the school clinic as he had some kind of skin disease. Laugh . . . he would sit at the back of the class wiv this bleeding helmet stuck on his nut and he always had a snotty nose.

'Hey, Bomber,' I used to say to him, 'ya brains are coming down ya nose,' and he would wipe his jersey sleeve across his nose. 'Ya can write ya name on his jersey sleeve where it was so stiff,' old Fred used to say.

The smells that came from him were nobody's business though it wasn't his fault. He had nobody to give him a barf. Anyway, back to our game of cowboys and Indians. Bomber continued to complain.

'Why do I always have to be the one dead?' he moaned. 'Why can't Tommy or Al be dead for a bleeding change?'

'Because I said "ya bleeding dead and so you're dead",' said Gobber.

Before we knew it, it turned into a full-scale game of cowboys and Indians. Bomber, Gobber and Tommy were Indians, while me, Fred and Georgi were the cowboys. Fred was self-appointed sheriff.

A fight broke out between the cowboys and Indians and Sheriff Fred said firmly, 'All those Indians we capture are going to hang.'

'You're not going to fucking hang me,' shouted Gobber as he leapt from barge to barge.

'Bang, ya barsted. You're copped one in the leg,' said Georgi to Bomber.

Bomber collapsed on a barge, still defiantly shouting his Indian call. Chief Indian Gobber tried to pull his brave to safety, but it was too late. Fred, the sheriff, was on them like a ton of bricks. Chief Gobber ran for his life, leaving the injured Bomber to the mercy of the brutal sheriff.

'Right, let's hang the Indian barsted,' shouted Georgi.

'Get that rope,' shouted Fred, the sheriff, pointing to a rope on one of the beautifully painted barges. I got the rope dutifully and handed it to the sheriff.

'Don't give it to me. Hang it on that tree over there,' he ordered.

'Wot fucking tree?' I asked.

'The Stink House Bridge, ya silly sod. Make out it's a tree.'

I slung the rope over one of the girders.

'Put a slip knot in it,' shouted Georgi who by now had a blood lust. So I done as I was told.

'Right, pull it up,' he told me. I pulled the rope up to bring it level wiv a terrified Bomber's neck.

'OK, ya dirty redskin. Have ya got anyfing to say before ya die?' asked the sheriff.

'I'm a terrified brave but I ain't talking,' said Bomber, his knees knocking.

'Right, let's hang him and hang him high,' said Georgi.

And wiv that, Georgi put the rope round Bomber's scraggy neck. And before you could say Albert Pierpoint, Georgi and Fred started to yank at the rope. The next fing I saw was Bomber being pulled in the air. he was about a foot off the ground when all of a sudden he started to make a funny sound and began desperately to tear at the rope round his neck.

Gobber, realising what had happened, yelled, 'Let him down, ya silly basters. He's choking.' Georgi let go of the rope and Bomber came down wiv an almighty bump onto the towparf.

We quickly released the noose. His face was as red as a beetroot. He tried to say somefing not too complimentary but he couldn't get the words out. As he gasped for breath, a red weal around his neck, I said, 'There he goes again. Bleeding shamming.'

'I ain't bleeding shamming,' Bomber finally said. 'Ya nearly strangled me, ya stupid barsteds.'

Just then, Tommy shouted out, 'Look, there's two water rats

having a fight,' and we all ran to where he was pointing, leaving
Bomber still on the floor, contemplating his scrape with eternity.

Meanwhile we were on the towpath cheering as two water rats
as big as cats were knocking fuck out of one anuvver. Still
holding his froat, Bomber staggered onward and said, 'Smash
that big barsted with that lump of wood on the floor, Gobber.'
Gobber stepped forward and brought the piece of wood down as
hard as he could. But before he could do it, the rats made their
escape and ran for their lives.

'Oh shit, ya missed,' I shouted.

'Look,' said Fred, 'they've gawn back in the drink.'

'Let's get them,' shouted Georgi. He immediately began
stripping off his togs but he was too late. By the time he got
completely undressed the rats had gawn.

For the rest of that arfternoon we went swimming in the canal.
Those lazy summer afternoons down at that canal was out of this
world to us kids. When I look back to it now, it was like the Souf
of France for most of us – except for poor old Bomber who used
to get it in the neck from us.

I shall never forget the day Bomber attempted to run away
from home. He wanted to get away from his old man. He started
arfter his dad had been out on one of his marathon drinking
sessions. He was as drunk as a brewer's horse when I saw him
staggering down the street.

'Look out,' I said to Bomber, 'here's ya old man and he's as
drunk as a barsted.'

'I'll have to go in now that barsted's home,' said Bomber. His
old man was reeling all over the road as he tried to walk. Then
he went into his usual routine. He started shouting at the top of
his voice to his neighbours: 'Come on out, ya barsteds. I ain't
fucking scared of any of ya.'

Gobber summoned up courage and shouted at him, 'Shut ya
mouf, ya old piss cart.'

'Leave awf, Gobber,' said Bomber, ' 'e'll go bleeding mad in
a minute.'

'Piss on the lot of ya,' shouted Bomber's old man.

'Ya, and piss on you too,' replied Gobber.

Just then, Bomber's old man fell arse over head in the gutter.
As he lay there we all ran to pick him up amid the fag ends. As
we got him back on his feet, he spotted the cowering Bomber.

'Ya little barsted. Ya pushed me over,' he shouted at him. Wiv that he viciously punched poor old Bomber on the conk, making Bomber's snub nose bleed.

'I never pushed ya,' shouted Bomber who by now looked as if he'd done fifteen rounds wiv Joe Louis. 'Ya fell.'

'Don't ya fucking lie to me, ya little barsted,' shouted Bomber's old man. And as he said it, he brought his boot up as hard as ne could and kicked Bomber in the belly. Bomber screamed wiv pain.

By this time, my mum came out, and so did some of the uvver women down the street.

'Leave him alone, ya pissy arsed barsted,' shouted my mum.

Gobber's muvver then came running across the street, and as she got to Bomber's old man, she flew at him like a mad woman. She clawed all his face down wiv her fingernails, and then she pulled him down on the ground by his hair. My muvver urged her on.

'He wants a bloody good hiding, that barsted, the way he treats those two kids of his.'

Bomber's old man was bawling and shouting on the ground and somehow he managed to get onto his unsteady feet. he was in a right old state, and as he staggered down the street, all the women, most of them wearing curlers, jeered at him. He seemed oblivious of the abuse as he staggered along the street, effin' and blindin'.

'Ya want to poison that old barsted,' Gobber's muvver said to Bomber. 'Ya would be better awf wivout him.'

'It's all right for you, Mrs White,' said Bomber, 'but he'll bleeding kill me when I get in.

That night we were all hanging around in the street when Bomber came towards us wiv a battered cardboard box under his arm. Fred saw him first. We all ran up to him.

'Where ya going,' Bomber?' Georgi asked.

'I'm leaving home.'

'Wot's in the box, Bomber?' asked Fred.

'It's me gear, ain't it?' replied Bomber.

'Wot fucking gear?' asked Georgi.

'Well I've got a bit of bread.'

'Wot, wiv butter on?' asked Gobber.

'Leave awf, Gobber. Since when did I have butter on my bread? It's bleeding dry! But it's better than nuffing, ain't it.'

'Wot else ya got in the box? Let's have a look,' said Tommy.

Bomber put the box down under the light of the lamp post and

124

took awf the lid as we gathered round. In it was all Bomber's worldly possessions. Tommy put his hand in the box and pulled out a dirty old rag.

'Wot the bleeding 'ell's this?' asked Tommy.

'It's me towel,' said Bomber.

'Ya towel?' said Tommy. 'It's got all fucking holes in it.'

'Well that's all right then,' said Bomber. 'I won't have to wash so often, will I?'

'Where do you fink you're going, Bomber?' I asked him.

'Well, I was finking of going down Soufend and nicking a boat and going to America to make a lot of money, and when I get back I fought I'd buy a nice house for me and my kid sister to live in.'

'Wot about ya old man, Bomber?' asked Gobber.

'Fuck that old barsted. I hope he's dead by the time I come back.'

'Ya never going to get there, Bomber,' I said.

'Why ain't I?' asked Bomber.

'Well, for one fing, you can't row ya bit all the way to America, and for anuvver fing, here comes ya old man.'

And sure enough, Bomber's old man was roaring down the street arfter Bomber. As he drew near, so he shouted out to Bomber, 'Get ya fucking self back in that bleeding house and put ya bleeding sister to bed, ya little barsted.' Bomber picked up his luggage and went home like a little pig wiv its tail between its legs. Bomber's old man went up the street to have anuvver bellyful of beer. As for Bomber, he never did leave home until eventually he got sent away to a kids' home as his old man wouldn't look arfter him and his two sisters.

He never cried the day they came for him to take him to the home. There was no tears left in him.

'Ya know wot, Al,' said Fred. 'That Bomber will be better awf in a home, won't he?'

'I suppose so,' I replied.

It was six monfs before we saw Bomber again. I shall never forget that day. it was on a Sunday and arfter we came out of church where we had been singing in the choir we decided to go down the canal and have a game of cards wiv the rest of the gang. Well, one of the kids was posted as look-out as we was playing for money. Ya 'ad to 'ave a look-out in case Old Bill came along. We was having a nice game when the kid that was standing look out said, 'Blimey, it's old Bomber.'

There was Bomber coming down the canal as large as life. None of us could believe our eyes. He was coming towards us grinning all over his boat race.

'Hi Bomber,' shouted a couple of the kids and the next fing we knew we was all crowding around him. No more was there the old pilot's helmet. In its place was a lovely head of well-kept hair and the old dirty jersey was gawn for good.

'How ya going, Bomber?' asked Fred.

'You look smart,' I told him.

And then he started to tell us all about the home he was in and how he had a barf twice a week. All the kids was asking him questions.

'I'd love to be barfed by one of those nurses,' sex-mad Gobber said.

'Wot's the mungy (food) like?' I asked him, and he told us all about the lovely food and how they had meat on a Sunday and baked spuds and jelly for arfters.

'Wot about the birds?' asked Gobber. 'Do they sleep in the same rooms as the geezers?'

'Of course they don't,' said Bomber.

'Fuck that then. I ain't going to no bleeding home if I can't sleep in the same room as the birds,' Gobber said.

'They wouldn't have ya if ya swear like that,' Bomber told him.

None of us could believe our ears that Bomber didn't swear any more. We all knew that the old Bomber had gawn forever. I learned years later that Bomber had gawn into the navy and became a warrant officer (Good luck, Bomber, wherever you are).

There was hundreds of kids like Bomber in the East End and most of them never had a break like him.

One morning I got up early to try and get a day's work in the market as I wanted to go to the pictures that Thursday night wiv Fred. I ended up getting a job helping out on a vegetable stall but, as usual, my muvver fawt I was at school. I'd been working for about an hour when I saw Gobber and Bomber on the uvver side of the street. They were playing hookey as well. As I was about to call them, the geezer who I was working for asked me to go and get a sack of spuds awf of his barrow that was parked round the corner, a few streets away.

126

'Righto, guv,' I said, 'one sack of spuds coming up,' and awf I went to the barrow. I shouted arfter Bomber and Gobber. ' 'Ey, Gobber, wot ya doing away from school?'

Gobber turned around and said, 'The same as you, ya ponce.'

'Where are ya going, Al?' asked Bomber.

'I'm going to get a sack of spuds awf a barrow round the corner,' I told him. 'Why? Are ya going to give ma a 'and, then?'

'Ya, we'll give 'im a 'and, won't we, Gobber?' said bomber.

'Yea, but I want a bung (payment) for it,' replied Gobber.

'I can't bung ya yet,' I said. 'I don't get paid awf of the geezer until tonight.'

'Fuck that then. I ain't lifting no sacks of spuds if I ain't going to get bunged for it,' said Gobber.

'You'll give me a 'and, won't ya, Bomber?' I asked.

Bomber looked at Gobber and said, 'Come on, Gobber. Let's give 'im a 'and. Arfter all, he is our mate.'

'OK then,' said Gobber, 'but I ain't lifting more than one bleeding sack.'

Kidding Gobber on I said, 'You're a good mate, Gobber. When I get paid we will all go in Jones's coffee shop and I'll buy ya a dripping teacake each.' By this time we had reached the barrow wiv its load of spuds and uvver veg on it.

'OK Gobber,' I said, 'get hold of that sack of spuds on top.'

'Piss awf, you ain't my bleeding guvner,' said Gobber, frowing 'is 'ands in the air.

'Now don't be like that, Gobber. Ya eiver want to help me or ya don't,' I told him. By this time, Bomber had got hold of one end of the sack.

'Come on, Gobber. Stop fucking about and get hold of that bleeding end,' said Bomber. Gobber did as he was told and they lifted the sack of spuds awf of the barrow and put it on the ground.

'Anyone would fink they were bleeding 'eavy,' said Gobber as he let the sack fall to the ground.

'Well, if you fink you're so fucking strong, you bleeding well carry them,' said Bomber.

I fawt, *'Ere we bleeding go again. By the time I get these bleeding spuds round to the stall it will be time to pack up.* Then I fawt to myself, *Harryboy, you have got to use a bit of the old grey matter wiv this ponce Gobber.*

'Gobber,' I shouted, 'do me a favour and piss awf. Ya as weak as a virgin in a bleeding convent.'

'Who's bleeding weak?' asked Gobber, flaring up.

'Well the way you're bleeding performing, it's enough to make the angels cry, ain't it, Al?' said Bomber.

Just then, the geezer who I was working for on the stall came round the corner.

'Where's them fucking spuds I sent ya for over 'arf an hour ago?' he yelled.

'I am getting them, guv,' I replied. Wiv that, Gobber started to put on a bit of a show.

'Don't worry, guvnor,' he said, 'I'll have them on ya stall in a jiffy.'

'Where's he come from?' the geezer asked me. 'Who the bleeding hell does he work for?'

'He's wiv me, Guv,' I said. 'He's going to give me a 'and wiv the spuds.'

The geezer looked at Bomber and said, 'Wot about him?'

'He's wiv me, guv,' Gobber chipped in.

'Now let's get fings straight. Who's working on me stall and who ain't?' asked the geezer.

'Well, I've done all the work all morning guv, ain't I?' I said.

'Well I ain't paying fucking free of ya and that's that,' he replied. And wiv that he went to pick up the sack of spuds, but before he could pick them up Gobber had the sack of spuds in his arms.

'It's OK, guv. I've got them. Ya get back to ya stall and I'll bring them around to ya,' said Gobber.

'OK then,' said the geezer, and awf he went back to his stall wiv the free of us following behind.

Arfter we had gone about twenty yards, Gobber was going all colours of the rainbow wiv the weight of the spuds.

'Ya want a 'and, Gobber?' said Bomber.

'Naah, leave awf. I can carry a dozen more like this,' said Gobber frew urgent pants of breff. I fawt, *the way you're going on, me old son, you'll end up shitting yerself by the bleeding time ya get to the stall.*

Well, he made it wiv a lot of puffing and blowing, and I could see it was a big relief when he put the sack of spuds down. Between puffs and blows he said ' 'ere you are, guv. One sack of spuds.'

'It's about bleeding time. Ya can tip them over into that barrel,' said the geezer to Gobber.

'Righto giv, I'll do that,' I said, and I went to tip the spuds over into the barrel.

'No ya fucking don't. That's my fucking job,' said Gobber. I fawt, *if ya want to do it mate, you bleeding carry on and fucking do it.*

'We don't want no bleeding bovver, Al,' said the geezer. 'Let him tip the spuds and you can go and serve that lady.'

'Righto, guv,' I said and awf I went to serve some old dear wiv a cabbage and some tomatoes. All this time, Bomber had been standing by the side of the stall.

'Wot shall I do guv?' asked Bomber.

Pushing a shilling into Bomber's hand the geezer said, 'Take that jug and go and get a jug of tea.'

'OK, guv,' replied Bomber. And as he walked away to the coffee shop, the geezer called arfter him. 'And don't forget me bleeding change.'

We had a day's work on the stall, and when it was time to pack up, we all had our jobs to do.

Bomber had to go and get the barrow and Gobber and I had to help sack up what veg was left over on the stall.

'Wot ya going to buy wiv ya wages, Al?' said Gobber. 'I ain't going to buy nuffing,' I said. 'I am going to save it for the pictures on Thursday night. Me and Fred is going to the fleapit to see a jungle film.'

Bomber arrived back wiv the barrow and we started loading the stuff onto it while the geezer rolled the tarpaulin and pulled down the struts from awf the top of the stall.

'We're all loaded up, guv,' said Bomber.

'Right, take it round to the "lock up" in Willie Street. Unload it and come back 'ere for the stall.'

'OK guv,' I said and, wiv Gobber in the sharfts, we began to push the heavy barrow round to the 'lock-up'. That was about five minutes away from the market.

'Go on me old son,' Gobber shouted to Bomber. 'Show them how to go, me old son.'

Gobber was going like a good'un when we approached the hill in Willis Street. Now that hill was a barsted by the end of the day, wot wiv all the muck that had dropped awf all the barrows belonging to the stall-holders in the market. There was all kinds of rubbish, such as cabbage leaves and mud from the wheels of the barrows. Wiv all the pushing and shoving we had now reached the top of the hill.

' 'old it,' said Gobber. 'I've to 'ave a blow (rest),' and wiv that we stopped on top of the hill.

'Come on, Gobber. Stop pissing about. It's getting late and I've got to get home,' I told him.

'Wait a bleeding minute, can't ya. This bleeding fing is bleeding heavy.'

'Heavy my bollocks. Ya as weak as old Nick,' shouted Bomber. I fawt, *Bomber, that's the last fing ya should have said to him*.

'Who's fucking weak? I'll show ya. Give us a push,' shouted out Gobber.

Well we just did wot he asked and awf he went down the bleeding hill pulling the barrow careering behind him. What wiv the weight of the barrow and the stuff piled on top of it, it was impossible to hold it. The next fing I noticed was his legs started to go as they was going ninety to the dozen. Then it happened. Gobber went arse over bollocks. The barrow was now out of control and going under its own steam. The next fing that happened, the barrow ended up going frew the door of a boozer.

'Fuck me, Bomber,' I said, 'look at that,' and we both stood there wiv our moufs open. The bar of the boozer was covered in shit. There was brussel sprouts and cabbages and spuds all in the bar. The guvnor of the boozer went potty. And the two old girls who had been drinking by the door screamed for their lives and ended up behind the counter. The door of the boozer was hanging awf its hinges.

'I am fucking awf,' said Bomber. 'It ain't my fault,' and he scarpered a bit lively.

Poor old Gobber was recovering from his mishap and he was back on his feet and running for all he was worf up Railway Street out of the arms of the guvnor of the boozer. I fawt, *Harryboy, it's time ya had it on ya toes too.*

I ran back into the market wiv the boss of the boozer shouting, 'Come back here, you little barsted.' As I went into the market, I went slap bang right into the arms of the geezer who owned the barrow.

'Come on. I've been waiting for you to bring the barrow back,' he shouted.

'I ain't got ya barrow,' I said. 'Gobber's got it round the corner.'

'You bleeding kids are more trouble than ya worf,' he said and he went awf in search of his barrow.

We stayed out of the market for a while, but if I had to go up

130

there for my old muvver I would always run past the stall on the uvver side of the street. We never got paid for the job and Gobber and Bomber never got their dripping teacakes from Jones's coffee shop.

If ya nevver had a swimming costume at our school ya couldn't go swimming. So you was left behind and told to read your books. Arfter the teacher went awf wiv the uvver kids to the swimming barfs, we ended up playing truth and dare. Well, it was my turn to take a dare. The kid arsked me wot I wanted to do.

'Tell the truff or take a dare?' he said.

'Dare,' I said.

'I dare ya to piss in that flower vase.' I done just that and I put the vase back on top of the cupboard.

Well, that bleeding vase was there for weeks and no one could guess where the smell was coming from. When the sun came in frew the window it shone right on this bloody vase. I mean, wot wiv the glass, it made the sun stronger, and boy wot a bloody stink.

All the teacher could say was, 'Have you pissed yourself, Ellis?' Poor old Bomber got the blame for any smell in the classroom.

'No sir, I ain't,' Bomber replied. All the kids laughed and finally the caretaker located the smell.

Well, the next day when we went to school, old Gibbo, our teacher, was going mad. Arfter we all got in the class and settled down, Gibbo said, 'Right, it was one of you. I don't know who but I am going to find out.' And wiv that he was getting the cane out of the desk drawer.

'One of you has urinated in this flower vase,' and he pointed to the vase on the desk.

'Wot's the silly old barsted talking about?' I whispered to Georgi who sat next to me.

'He means someone 'as pissed in the vase.'

'Oh,' I said. 'I wonder who done that?'

Georgi wasn't there the day the Phantom Slasher struck. Gibbo was going red in the face trying to find out who done this terrible deed. Arfter searching every face in the class for an answer he made a beeline for poor old Bomber.

'Wot about you, Ellis?'

'It wasn't me, sir,' said Bomber.

'Sit up straight, you scum,' he said and he gave poor old Bomber one on the nut wiv the cane.

'Oh, that hurt,' said Bomber.

'It's not harf as hard as it's going to be for the one who did it when I find him,' bellowed Gibbo.

By this time Gibbo's blood pressure was way up and he was nearly pulling his hair out wiv rage. Arfter picking on a few more kids he got round to me.

'Wot you got to say for yourself?' he said, looking me straight in the eye.

'Who? Me, sir?' I asked.

'Who do you think I am talking to, that moron sitting next to you?' and he pointed to Georgi.

'I don't know who pissed in ya old flower pot,' I said to him. 'Besides, if I did I wouldn't tell ya.' Well, he nearly went frew the roof and before I knew it, he was pulling me out of my seat.

'Get out here,' he was shouting as he pulled me along by my ear.

'He ain't done nuffink,' Georgi shouted. 'Wot ya picking on him for, ya old ponce?'

'You get out here as well, you scum,' he yelled at Georgi, who left his seat and joined me in front of the class.

'Do you know wot I fink?' said Gibbo. 'I think that you, Hunter, are the ringleader of this lot and I think that you are the one that urinated in that vase. And I am going to make sure that I punish you. Hold out your hand.'

'I ain't done nuffink, ya got the wrong one,' said Georgi. And wiv that old Gibbo started to whack Georgi wiv the cane across the back. I fawt, *that old barsted's going too far.*

'Leave him alone ya old barsted,' I shouted. 'It was me who pissed in ya old flowers, and I'm glad I done it too.' Well, Gibbo went white.

'So it was you, was it?' he shouted at me and all the time he was waving the cane in the air. 'Right, hold out your hand,' and wiv that he began to whack me across the hands wiv the cane.

Arfter he had whacked me about six times on each hand I couldn't feel a fing, so I just stood there and laughed at him.

He flung the cane across the room and he yelled at me, 'Get out of my sight, you scum,' and I knew then that I had broken his spirit.

Me and Georgi retured to our seats and old Gibbo just sat

down at the desk wiv his head in his hands and when he finally looked up I could see he had tears on his cheeks.

Arfter a while in the midst of the silence of the class I stood up. He looked at me and said in a voice that seemed too weak to speak, 'Yes, Hollis.'

'I am sorry, sir.'

He wiped his face wiv a white handkerchief and said, 'Thanks, Hollis, sit down.'

Poor old Gibbo. Wot he had to put up wiv from us lot was enough to turn anyone's hair grey.

Opposite our school was a small fruit-and-veg shop and sometimes on our way to school Georgi, Fred, Tommy and me used to put a farving each and buy a pennyworf of carrots for dinner.

One day, Tommy said, 'If we keep on eating these bleeding carrots we will turn into bleeding rabbits.'

Sometimes we would get a pennyworf of speckty apples if they had any and we would put the apple between bread and have an apple sandwich.

One day Tommy found a maggot in one of his apples.

'Look,' he said, 'I've got a bleeding maggot.'

'Ya bleeding lucky,' said Georgi. 'Now ya can have a meat-and-apple sandwich.' Laughter was the only fing that we got free in those days.

On the corner of our street there was a sweet and tobacco shop run by a little fat Yid and his wife. Bernie Joseph was about five foot free, wiv a red rosy face and black curly hair. He was as round as a barrel. He was hen-pecked by his wife, and wot old muvver Joseph said was law. She was as fat as her old man, dark-haired, and about five foot two. She always looked as though she wanted a good wash and all the kids called her 'Soapy Joseph'. If any of us kids went into the shop for somefing, the two of them would widdle out just in case we nicked somefing. But we had as much chance of having a feeve up in that shop as we would trying to nick the Crown Jewels. As a matter of fact, to nick the Crown Jewels would have been easier.

One day, my old lady sent me over to the shop to get somefing and Fred and Georgi was wiv me. On the way we were discussing wevver or not we could feeve somefing from the fat pair.

'I bet I could nick a lucky-dip bag from the barrel,' said Georgi.

'Leave awf,' said Fred. 'That barrel is right under their bleeding noses and you've got no bleeding chance.'

'I know,' I said, 'why don't we knock the empty lemonade bottles over and while old Bernie is doing his nut, Georgi can have a feeve up.'

Well, that was our plan, and true to pattern, as we entered the shop so old man Joseph came from out of the back room. As always, close on his 'eels was Soapy.

'Vot's all der noise for?' he asked. Just then, there was a fucking great crash and empty lemonade bottles spilled all over the gaff.

'Wot's happening?' asked a startled Soapy. And before we knew it, she was round from behind the counter wiv Bernie close behind.

Out of the corner of my eye I could see Georgi diving his grubby hand into the lucky-dip barrel and he was stuffing his plunder up 'is jersey. He was grinning all over his boat race. Soapy sank to her knees and began picking up the fallen lemonade bottles. At the same time as she bent over so she was revealing all the good Lord had given her and believe me, it wasn't a pretty sight. By this time Georgi had slipped out of the shop, leaving me and Fred picking up the empty bottles.

'Dat's a bloody fine mess ya make,' Bernie was repeating.

'Sorry about that, Mr Joseph,' I said.

'Vell, vot's done is done. Vot does ya vonts?' he asked. I gave him my order of one gobstopper and Fred and me couldn't get out of the shop farst enough to see wot Georgi 'ad nicked.

Georgi was waiting for us around the corner. As we got up to him Fred said, 'Wot ya get, Georgi?'

'I got free lucky bags, didn't I?' replied Georgi, and wiv that he handed Fred and me a lucky bag each.

Wiv trembling fingers we opened our booty. Inside there were a few little sweets and a cheap lucky charm.

'There ya are. I told ya I could get somefing,' Georgi was saying as he stuffed the few sweets from his dip into his norf and souf.

'You're a right fucking lad, you are, Georgi,' Fred said. And we all had a good laugh about our escapade. They were the best sweets I had ever tasted.

A few days arfter we had nicked the lucky-dip bags, Fred and

134

I was walking past the shop and old man Joseph was sitting on a chair outside. As we approached him, so he jumped awf the chair and said, 'You're just the boys I wont.'

'Aye aye, Fred,' I said, 'he's tumbled about the lucky-dip bags.'

'No, he couldn't have or he would have copped me yesterday when I was in his shop getting somefing for me old lady.' *That's true*, I fawt.

'Wot ya want, Bernie?' asked Fred.

'Vell, ya know I've got a cat dat is having some badies soon. Vell I vont ya to do a little job for Bernie and I will give ya a penny. That's a lot of money for such a little job,' said Bernie.

Fred and I fawt the matter of for a while then Fred said, 'OK, Bernie. It's a deal.'

We followed Bernir into the back of the shop where he picked up this big tabby cat that was sitting on some boxes. Putting it into Fred's arms he said, 'Dere she is.'

'We can't take her like that, Bernie,' I said. 'We will have to put her in a sack or somefing.'

'I ain't got no bloody sack,' Bernie replied.

'Well give us an old cardboard box, then,' said Fred.

'OK. A cardboard box I have, but no sacks.' He produced a cardboard box from out of an old cupboard and Fred put the cat in it.

'There ya are, Bernie,' said Fred, and at the same time he put out his hand for the penny.

'Ven ya gets back I vill pay ya,' said Bernie.

'Nope, money first or we don't do the job.' Ya see, we had dealings wiv Yids before.

'All right, all right,' said Bernie, frowing his hands in the air, and then pushing the penny into Fred's grubby hand.

So we left the shop wiv the poor old cat in the cardboard box. As we got a little way up the street, we saw Gobber and Bomber.

'Wot's in the box, Fred?' asked Bomber.

'It's a bleeding cat.'

'Where ya taking it?' asked Gobber.

'Down to have it put to sleep,' I told them.

'Who's bleeding cat is it?' asked Gobber.

'It's old Joseph's and we've got to get rid of it for him,' said Fred.

'He gave us a penny to do the job,' I told them.

Just then a fire engine came rushing round the corner. One of the factories down by the canal was on fire.

'There's a bleeding fire,' shouted Gobber.

'Let's follow them,' shouted Bomber. And we all took off like greased lightning in chase of the fire engine, Fred trying to keep up wiv the cat still tucked under his arm.

By the time we got to the factory it was well alight. There were flames coming out of all the windows and the firemen were drawing water out of the canal and spraying it all over the inferno. By this time a big crowd had gathered outside the burning place.

'Let's go over the wall,' said Gobber. 'We can see better by the towparf.' So we all began climbing over the wall to the canal.

As I was halfway over the wall, Fred said to me, 'Get 'old of this bleeding cat, Al.' He handed me the cardboard box so he could also get over the wall.

As I was halfway over the wall, Fred said to me, 'Get 'old of this bleeding cat, Al.' He handed me the cardboard box so he could also get over the wall.

When he got down from the wall I said, 'Wot ya going to di wiv this bleeding cat?'

'I don't know. I want to see the fire,' replied Fred.

'Frow the fucking fing in the bleeding drink,' said Bomber.

'That way it will save ya a job of going all the way to the High Street wiv it,' Gobber said Wiv devastating logic. 'Give us the ponce 'ere. I'll show ya wot to do wiv it.'

Before we knew wot was happening Gobber frew the carboard box in the drink wiv the cat inside. It sank to the bottom as the bubbles came up and as far as we were concerned, that was that. Awf we went to watch the fire.

A few days later, Fred and me were in old Bernie's shop buying some more sweets with the money we had earned selling firewood. Bernie and his wife were behind the counter.

'Come on then. Vot ya vont wiv ya money?' he asked.

Fred was looking at all the sweets in the jars and was about to make up his mind when Bernie looked up and went as white as a sheet. And wiv his hands up to his cheeks, he shouted, 'Yor, yor, it's a bloody ghost, mummer.'

I looked around and there was the bleeding cat as large as life, sitting on some boxes. I pulled at Fred's jersey and said, 'Aye up, Fred, his fucking cat's back.'

136

When Fred saw the cat he said, 'Fuck me. I fawt he was bleeding dead, the barsted.'

'Vot's she doing here?' asked Bernie.

'How the bleeding hell do I know? We slung the bleeding fing in the drink,' said Fred.

'I told you to take the fing and have it put to sleep,' shouted Bernie. 'And anuvver fing, Where is the money I gave you?'

'Fucking spent. Where do ya fink it is, ya old ponce?' said Fred.

'Fuck awf out of my shop and don't ever come back,' Bernie shouted, and wiv that we ran out as farst as our legs could go.

When we were well out of sight of Bernie's shop I said to Fred, 'How the bleeding 'ell did that little barsted get out of that bleeding box?'

'I don't bleeding know,' said Fred, 'but I can tell ya one fing, the poor little barsted is still alive.'

By my firteenf birfday I was earning sixpence a week and wiv that I was able to take my lovely Diane out from time to time. It would cost me all my week's wages for one night out wiv her but it was worf every penny. Georgi and the rest of the gang didn't like me going about wiv her and one night Georgi let me know it in no uncertain terms.

'I don't know why ya want to hang around that bird,' he said. 'She's nuffing but bovver.'

'If ya don't like it ya know wot to do,' I said.

'I'll punch ya bleeding head in,' he said.

'Leave awf. Ya couldn't punch a hole in a bleeding doughnut,' I said and wiv that he slung me a right hander which caught me right at the side of the ear'ole. The next fing I knew, we was on the ground punching fuck out of one anuvver. Georgi ended up wiv a bloody nose and a torn shirt and I lost two front teef. Poor little Diane also witnessed this savagery. She was bawling her eyes out, but like all the birds, she loved it, knowing two geezers were fighting over her. Arfter it was all over we ended up the best of pals again.

On our way home I said to Diane, 'I showed that barsted Hunter, didn't I.' And she looked at me wiv those heart-melting dark eyes and said, 'Yea, you was the winner, Al.' I was so proud when I heard her say that.

It was around this time that there was some talk about a geezer called Hitler. Of course we didn't take much notice of it as we was only kids and we didn't understand. Little did we know that

137

he was going to change all our lives and as you know, that barsted turned out to be Lord High Executioner of all times.

On my firteenf birfday, I had my first pair of long trousers. To me they was real, long strides. Usually I went out busking in a pair of my bruvvers' cut-down strides. The old lady bought them in a stall in the market for twopence. By the time she had taken them up and given them a good wash and pressed them they was 'ansom. They was also lovely and warm. I said to me old mum, 'They're just wot I wanted for the winter. It won't be so cold when I take the old man out now, will it, Mum?'

'I'll try and get ya a nice big jumper next week. Old Solly had a nice one on the stall but he wanted a tanner for it,' she said. Old Solly was a fat greasy Yid who had a second-hand stall in Chris Street Market, the same market that I used to work in.

'If he's got that jumper next week I'll get it for ya and then ya old chest will be lovely and warm.' I fawt, *that will be 'ansom as it did get cold in the winter wot with the fog and the rain. It was enough to kill a donkey awf.*

Apart from old Solly selling second-hand clothes in the market, there were also free old women who sold the same sort of fings. They never had a stall and they would lay a bit of old black cloff down on the ground and frow all the old clothes down on it. Then women bargain hunters would all gather round and pick up the old clothes and ask how much they were. There would be old coats, old socks, jackets, ties, trousers – in fact, all sorts of old clothes. Ya could buy a good pair of trousers for sixpence.

These women were known locally as the old girls. If my mum ever got me anyfing from them and if I should ask where it came from she would say, 'From the old girls.' We would always look round at the old girls if I was out shopping wiv the old lady.

Sometimes one of these gnarled old girls would pinch up a bunch of socks and say, ' 'Ere, who wants this lot? Only a penny.' There could have been about four or six pairs of old socks in one bundle. All they needed was a good wash.

I said to my mum one dar arfter we had watched the hard-selling trio in action, 'Where do they get all those old clothes from, mum?' She told me that they came from the rich people who had a lot of money.

'Would you like to be rich, mum?' I said.

'Not as rich as that, that I could afford to frow away clothes like that,' she said.

'I'd like to be rich,' I said.

'Yes, and wot would ya do wiv all the money?' she asked.

'I'd buy you a nice new coat and a nice pair of shoes, and ya wouldn't have to wear those old lace-up boots any more,' I told her. But we were only dreaming . . .

I shall never forget the night me and my old man got lost in the fog. We had been working a few boozers over the river (souf London) when the fog started to come down.

'The fog's coming down, Dad,' I said, 'and I don't like to look of it. If it gets too fick they will stop the trams and we may have to walk all the way home.'

'I tell ya wot we will do, son. We will work The Crown and finish awf at the Star and Garter,' said the old man. *Thank heavens for that*, I fawt, as I didn't fancy that long walk home.

We got to the Rose and Crown in Lewisham all right and we managed the Star and Garter but when we got out of the Star and Garter ya couldn't see a hand before ya.

'Blimey, dad,' I said, 'I can't see a fing.'

'Don't worry, son. Get me near the pavement and I can feel my way to the tram stop,' said the old man.

Well, we started to walk to the tram stop and we had been going for about ten minutes when a figure loomed out of the fog.

'Is that you, Bill?' a voice said. It was old Tom, one of the regular customers from the Rose and Crown. 'It's me, Tom,' he said.

'Oh, it's you, Tom,' said the old man.

'Wot ya doing going this way?' asked Tom.

'We're looking for the tram stop.'

'It's a few yards up the road, son. If ya keep on this side ya will be all right,' he said as he bid us goodnight.

We started to walk towards the tramp stop as Tom had directed us. Arfter a while I started to get worried as I could not see the tram stop.

'Blimey Dad,' I said. 'I can't see nuffink.' Just then I saw a faint blue light.

'We are near the coppers' station, dad,' I said.

'How the hell did we get up this way?' said the old man. 'I fink we'd better go in the nick and see if they can help us.' And wiv that we mounted the station steps. It was the first time I was pleased to be in the nick. It was so nice and warm inside. I looked up at the big clock above the counter and it said five to eleven. I fawt to myself, *Blimey, we have missed the last tram home*.

There was a young scarp behind the counter. When he saw the old man was blind he said, 'Can I help you, sir?' *Blimey*, I fawt, *he's posh calling the old man sir*.

Well, we seem to be lost,' the old man said to the copper.

'I should think so. A bat would get lost in that lot out there,' said the copper. 'Where was you making for?'

'We want to get the last tram over the river,' the old man told him.

Just then the door opened and in walked anuvver copper. He was a lot older than the one behind the counter and as luck had it, he knew the old man.

'Hello, Bill. Wot ya doing here?' he asked. Well the old man told him about how we got lost and how we came to be there.

'Well, I tell you one fing, Bill. You won't get no tram home tonight as they stopped them running over an hour ago.'

'Wot are we going to do, Dad?' I said.

'Don't worry, son. We'll soon get you and ya Dad fixed up. But first let's have a nice cup of tea.' And he said to the young copper, 'Put the kettle on, son. How far have ya got to go, Bill?'

'Poplar,' said the old man.

'Blimey, that's a walk,' said the young copper, pouring milk into the empty mugs he had put on the counter.

Just then the kettle started to boil. The young scarp made the tea and arfter he had poured it out he gave us a mug each.

'Here ya are, old man,' he said, handing a mug of tea to me dad.

'Drink ya tea, Bill, and I'll see wot I can do for ya,' said the old copper. And wiv that he went frew a door behind the counter.

'Old Joe will get you fixed up,' said the young copper. 'He's been in this nick so long he nearly owns it.'

Me and the old man sat down on a bench by the counter and drank our tea. Arfter a while the door opened and back came Joe followed by an inspector.

'This is the gentlemen I told ya about, sir,' said Joe.

'I hear you are having some trouble in getting home, old man. We can't have that, can we,' said the inspector.

'Yus guv. Me and the boy here seem to be lost and now your

140

man here tells me that they have stopped all the trams frew the fog and we have to get over the river.'

'Well now, don't you worry. We will fix you and the boy up for the night. That's if you don't mind bedding down in a cell.'

'I'd like to get home if I could, sir, as the wife will be worried about the boy,' said the old man.

'You'll never make it, Bill,' said Joe.

'You leave this to us,' said the inspector and wiv that he picked up the phone. 'You say you live in Poplar?' he asked the old man.

'Yes, that's right sir,' and the old man gave him our address. Arfter a few seconds the inspector broke the silence.

'Hello. Is that Poplar? This is Lewisham here. Inspector Dent speaking. Can you send one of your chaps round to a Mrs Hollis?' and he began to explain the situation. Arfter a while he put the phone down and said, 'There you are, Mr Hollis. All fixed up. Poplar police are going to send a man round to let your wife know wot 'as happened.' The old man fanked him for all he had done for us.

'By the way, wot was you and your boy doing over by the river in the first place?' he asked. The old man told him wot had brought us over the river and the inspector became very interested and asked the old man to show him his concertina as he was in the police band and he was interested in music. The old man took the concertina out of the bag and started to play a few tunes.

While he was playing the doors burst open and a couple of young coppers marched in a drunk, and the next fing we know, this drunk started to dance all round the nick. Well, the coppers weren't going to stand for that.

'Come on Frankie,' said one of the coppers, 'let's go. It's bedtime,' and they marched him awf to the cells to sleep it awf.

'He's a regular customer here,' said old Joe. 'We have him in about three times a week at least. It beats me where he gets his money from.'

The inspector looked at his watch and said, 'It's about time we got you and the boy bedded down, Bill.' He was calling me Dad by his first name now and I could see the old man liked it.

'Show Mr Hollis and his son to their room, constable,' he said, and added, 'as a matter of fact Bill, it's a cell but it sounds better if we call it a room.'

The old man fanked him once more and we followed old Joe

down the corridor. We could 'ear old Franky snoring his drunkness away a few cells down the corridor.

'Here were are, Bill. This is it,' said Joe as he led us into the peter (cell).

It was the first time I had ever been in a police cell and it wasn't to be the last as I was to find out later on in life. The cell was a small brick room wiv painted walls and a small window wiv fick bars up it. There was two wooden benches down each side of the wall and in the corner there was a carsey pan wiv a wooden seat.

'Don't take any notice of the poetry on the walls, son. None of it will ever be published,' said Joe wiv a laugh. 'There's a couple of blankets there just in case you get cold,' he added and bid us goodnight. He looked over his shoulder as he was going out of the door and said, 'I'll wake ya wiv a nice cup of tea in the morning, Bill,' and he went out leaving the door ajar.

I put the blankets on the wooden benches that already had mattresses on. We began to settle down for the night.

'You all right, son?' asked the old man.

'Yus Dad, I am OK. Wait until I tell the gang about this in the morning. None of them will believe me,' I said.

'Yea, but we know it's true, don't we, son?' he replied.

Old Joe was as good as his word. There he was in the morning, standing beside the benches wiv two big mugs of steaming tea.

'Here we are, Bill. Did you sleep all right?' he asked.

'Lovely, fanks Joe,' replied the old man.

'Well, I shall be going awf duty soon, but I'll see ya on the tram when you are ready,' said Joe.

When we left, we shook hands wiv all the coppers that had helped us the night before. Inspector Dent said he would look out for us the next time we worked over Lewisham. We said goodbye to him and the old man fanked him once more. When we got home the old lady said she was worried out of her mind when the copper from Poplar nick came to the door and told her wot had happened to us. I told her all about it and how old Joe had brought us a nice cup of tea.

'That was nice of him,' she said.

The old man and me saw a lot of old Joe and the inspector whenever we was working Lewisham and we got to know the inspector very well. I sometimes looked up and he would be standing there listening to the old man playing as we stood in the doorway of one of the boozers we may have been working. of course I told Georgi and Fred about me and the old man spending the night in the nick but as usual they didn't believe me until my old man told them it was true.

By the early 1930s, fings had begun to change. Welsh miners made a march to London. There was hundreds of them. I saw them. Their faces were lined wiv years of hard work in the mines, trying to earn a crust of bread for their loved ones. They was all singing, 'Land of Hope and Glory'. I told the old man about it, and he said, 'It will give the poor devils a break from being underground in the dark and damp.' A few years later old King George died. I remember my old dad saying, 'Gawd rest his soul. He had everyfing in life but he took nuffing wiv him.'

We all went to the school church the day they buried him and we all wore a black arm-band and arfter the service we had the rest of the day awf.

'We never had the day awf when old Kate snuffed it did we,' said Fred.

'She was only an old piss artist. Besides, ya always get a holiday when the King dies,' said Georgi.

As a matter of fact that old King did us a favour. A few weeks later his son was crowned King and we all went to a party and they called it a Coronation party. We ended up having a free feed up and arfter the party they gave us all a mug each wiv the King and Queen's head on it. My bruvver ended up using mine as a shaving mug. Fred's mum wasn't impressed, however.

'It ain't bloody mugs we want,' she said. 'It's bleeding food.'

Around this time there was a geezer going round the East End wiv a gang that called themselves the Black Shirts. They was always punching up wiv the Yids around Whitechapel. My Dad said they were a bad lot and he told me to stay away from them as there was always trouble wherever they held their meetings. But when you are fifteen you are like the cat, curious. So one night, when they was holding a meeting up in Whitechapel Road, about four of us went to have a look at wot was going on.

When we got there there was a big crowd and there were coppers everywhere. Up on a platform, there was a geezer giving a speech and he was yelling his head awf and saying all sorts about the front wheel skids and wot we should do wiv them.

'Them old Yids ain't that bad,' I said to Gobber. 'Wivout them we wouldn't be able to earn on a Saturday morning.'

143

'Ya, that's true, Al,' Georgi said.

'I know some dodgy Englishmen,' Fred said.

'Who do you know that's dodgy?' asked Gobber.

'Well you're a dodgy barsted to start wiv,' Fred said to Gobber.

'He ain't English,' said Georgi, 'he's bleeding Chinese.'

'Piss awf,' said Gobber. 'I am a Cockney,' and he spat on the ground. The geezer up on the platform was still shouting and bawling. All of a sudden someone at the back of the crowd slung a brick and it hit him right in the kisser knocking him out cold. Before we knew wot was happening everyone started fighting and there was blood everywhere.

'Let's piss awf,' I said to the lads, and we had it away on our toes a bit lively. That was the first and last time we ever went to see the Black Shirts.

I never liked violence, even though I was quick-tempered. I would flare up and be sorry afterwards. Violence is a terrible fing. When I fink of all the violence I have seen, I sometimes wonder how we survived. It's a funny fing. It seems that poverty and violence always go togevver. Where there's poverty there's violence. Sometimes the violence is unnecessary but it seems that there will always be poverty. Gang warfare creates violence and greed creates poverty. There was always one gang or anuvver in the East End and I have seen how violent they could be.

Like the time they ran a lorry over poor old Happy's legs and put him in a wheelchair for the rest of his life. Everyone knew Happy. He was about forty years old wiv scars on his face and a broken nose. He was about five foot eleven and he always wore a flat cap and an old overcoat. Someone had named him Happy as he never smiled. It was common knowledge that he was also a grass. One day Happy started singing to the Law and he ended up getting two geezers bird. One got free years and the uvver got five. The word was out to get Happy at all costs and get him they did. When Happy knew the gang was arfter him he went into hiding.

One day one of the gang saw him getting awf of a tram and he followed him to where he was living and he went and informed the firm that was arfter him. That same night they went and dragged him out of his digs and bundled him in a lorry. They drove him out to Epping Forest. Arfter working him over they laid him down and the loory ran over his winnypegs. Happy had paid for his singing.

Happy wasn't the only one to fall foul of a violent gang. There

144

was Johnny the Greek. The gang he upset ended up nailing him to the billiard-hall floor. I used to run errand for the boys in the billiard hall in West India Dock Road. Like if anyone wanted a bet put on, I would take it to the local bookie. Johnny the Greek was about five foot six tall wiv black hair and dark eyes. he had a light-brown skin. His family came from Greece but he was born in London.

Johnny the Greek had been messing around wiv a bird whose bruvver was a member of one of the local gangs. And Johnny had put this bird in the family way and he said the baby wasn't his and he said he wasn't going to marry 'that cow'. Well, the girl's youngest bruvver heard about this so he came in the billiard hall to sort Johnny out. However, this kid came awf worse as Johnny gave him a good hiding. When this kid's bruvver found out he had been done over by Johnny all hell broke loose.

Johnny was telling all the boys in the billard hall about how he didn't care about this young kid's bruvver. I'd just come back from running an errand and I saw these four big geezers coming up the stairs of the billiard hall behind me, but I took no notice as I didn't know who they were. Well, they followed me in the billiard hall and made straight for Johnny the Greek. When he saw them, the look on his boat race was one of fear. They didn't say much. The only one that said anyfing was the girl's bruvver. He grabbed Johnny by his jacket and said 'Bubble and squeak (Greek) I'll teach ya to keep your hands awf of my sister, ya barsted.'

No one moved. We all just stood there, transfixed. Two of the gang got hold of Johnny and force him to the floor of the billiard hall. The bruvver of the girl produced a hammer and some big nails out of his overcoat pocket. I couldn't quite see what was going on. The next fing I knew wat that all four of them had Johnny on the floor and he was screaming like a baby. I fink I will 'ear those screams till my dying day and I shall never forget it.

Arfter a while all four began to leave. As they made towards the door one big fller put his finger to his lips and said, 'Yous lot, shut it,' and they all left. All the geezers who had been playing billards rushed to help Johnny. He was lying on the floor on his back wiv his arms outstretched. The barsteds had driven a nail frew the palms of his hands. When I saw wot they had done I felt sick. The boss of the billiard hall, Alfie Brown, was trying to get the nails out of Johnny's hands. All the time Johnny was crying.

'Don't move,' said one of the geezers, 'we'll soon have ya up Johnny.'

Arfter a while they managed to free Johnny from the floor. He got up holding his hands across his chest and he kept repeating, 'Oh my God! Me hands, me hands!' No one suggested calling Old Bill. That would have been like committing suicide. Two of the geezers took Johnny home. The next time I saw him he had both of his hands bandaged.

Johnny went to his grave wiv those scars on his hands. There was no retaliation from him. How could there be? Johnny was just one against a brutal gang. It's the same old story. The strong always survive and they go on inflicting pain and misery among the weak.

When I was young I used to dream of going away to a place where everyfing was nice and clean and no one used violence to gain wot they wanted. My dream did come true later on in life but it took God to make it come true. They say God works in mysterious ways and to me that is true as I will tell you later on in my story.

All along West India Dock Road you could see rows of shops that catered for seamen. The docks were at the end of the road. The shops sold such fings as uniforms, seaboots, and pullovers. Ya could go in any one of these shops and buy a shark knife or for 'arf a crown you could buy a brass knuckle-duster. it was so easy to buy fings connected wiv violence.

Those knuckle-dusters were a terrible weapon. I saw two seamen having a fight one night and one of them had a knuckle-duster and he punched the uvver geezer right in the face wiv it. It was as though someone had opened up his face wiv a meat cleaver. They was fighting over some old brass. It's a funny fing wot men will fight over. I hope she was worf it.

The lady coppers in those days used to wear navy-blue uniforms wiv black high-legged boots laced up to the knees and a navy-blue top. They would frighten the life out of ya if ya was to meet one of them in the dark. The nickname for them was Liz. If we was swimming in the canal and one of them was coming along the towparf and one of the kids spotted her, they would shout, 'Look out, old Liz is coming,' and we would scarper, because if one of them caught ya they would whack ya on the bare arse wiv their gloves. So we made sure we didn't get caught by them. Those lady coppers had a lot to put up wiv in Limehouse wot wiv the drunks and the prostitutes, but they could look arfter themselves those old birds.

I saw one of them having a do wiv two brasses one night. 'Liz' had been trying to take one of them to the nick and the uvver one had jumped in to help the uvver brass from being nicked. They both had her on the ground and they were like a couple of mad women. In the fight this old lady copper had lost her helmet so one of the brasses seized the opportunity and grabbed a handful of the lady copper's hair. As she did so, this lady copper swung round and hit this brass right in the gut. She let go of the lady copper's hair and sunk to the ground wiv a moan.

Arfter that it was just plain sailing for the lady copper. She just got hold of the uvver brass and sent her flying along the pavement. Before those two brasses knew where they was they was put on a wheelcart and carted awf to the nick. They were a regular sight those wheelcarts in Limehouse. They were like a long board wiv two wheels and they had a hood which went right over the top and they had big levver straps at the sides so when they got a drunk who was a bit hard to handle they would get him down and cart him awf to the nick. they were handcards and they were kept in the yard at Limehouse nick.

Limehouse nick was a dirty old brick building wiv stone steps going up the front. And over a door hung a blue lamp advertising their trade and inside it stunk of disinfectant. The walls was painted cream and green. It was a tough nick. It had to be wiv all the villains they had to tame. It was no good one using kid gloves. Violence had to be met wiv violence. Even so, wiv all the violence around me, my childhood was a happy one. We was always finking up ways of earning a copper of two or getting up to some kind of mischief. A favourite stroke of ours was to sling stink bombs in the nick doorway and run for all we was worf. Lord help ya if ya got caught. Ya was in for a good hiding awf of old Bill. We would run round the corner and walk back a few minutes later to see some young constable cleaning out the doorway and cursing to himself. We would go by and say, 'Paw guvner, wot a stink,' or I would look at Fred or Georgi and say, 'Paw, have ya shit yaself?' and we would run awf laughing, and shouting, 'Limehouse nick is a shithouse nick and it stinks and so do all the coppers.'

The way we used to make our stink bombs was we would go round the back of the picture house and get the old cuttings out

147

of the dustbin. these were film cuttings. We would roll them up in paper as tight as we could, leaving a little bit of film sticking out at the end. We would then light it wiv a fag end and when it started to flare up we would blow it out and it would smoulder and send off clouds of smoke and the stink was horrible. the films in those days were made of celluloid.

It was certainly a tough area but no matter where you went ya couldn't find a better crowd of people. If ya was in bovver there was always someone to help ya out. Even though I was in the choir at the school church I never had much time for religion. It was just one big giggle and somewhere to go out of the cold on a winter's night when it was choir practice. It's a funny fing, the warmf ya can find in a church. If was just life to us and the only fing we knew. To me life is just a book. Every day is a page and the more you do the more pages there is.

Chapter Eight
I baptise you . . . wiv black ink

I suppose we was lucky compared to some kids. We always managed to keep our heads above water. The fing was ya had to fight to live and my old Dad always managed to bring home the bread. No matter wot kind of wevver it was, the old man always went to work to get a crust of bread for us kids.

Poor old Fred's Dad was taken very ill one day. Fred's Dad worked driving a water cart. He was a tall man wiv brown greying hair. He loved his horses. When he got home from work one night around nine o'clock, I often heard him say, 'Oh well, I've bedded my darlings down for the night.' He meant his horses.

Fred came to our house just as we was having our tea. We never had much. It was only bread and dripping.

'Ya had ya tea yet, Fred?' I said and he said, 'Ya, Al,' but I could see he was looking longingly at the bread on the table.

'Wot ya have for ya tea then?' I asked him.

'Oh, not much,' he replied, but I could see he was lying. I fawt, *there's somefing wrong here.*

Well, we finished our tea and there was a few crusts of bread that one of my sisters had left on the table. My two sisters went out to play and the ole lady was at the sink washing up the tea mugs. All of a sudden Fred nicked the crust awf of the table, and put them in his pocket. He fawt I didn't see him take them. I fawt, *Well I'll be a monkey's uncle, the geezer is hungry.*

'Let's go, Fred,' I said and we went out in the street.

When we got outside I said to him, 'Ya sure ya had ya tea, Fred?'

'Of course I have,' he said looking at the ground.

'You're a bleeding liar. Wot ya nick that crust awf of our table for if ya had ya tea?' Poor old Fred went as red as a baby's bum.

'Well I'm hungry,' he said and wiv that I took him back to the old lady.

When we got back indoors the old lady was washing the table top. She stopped wot she was doing and looked up and said, 'Wot the bloody hell do you want? I fawt you went out to play.'

'Muvver,' I said, 'Fred ain't had no tea.'

'Wot ya mean he ain't had no tea?' she asked.

'Are ya potty or somefing muvver? He's had no tea on account that his dad is ill and his muvver ain't got no mungy in the house and she ain't got no money to send for the doctor to see his dad.'

'Ah, you poor little sod. Sit yaself down there and I'll give ya some bread and dripping,' she said, pointing to the table and wiv the next breff she said, 'Wot's wrong wiv ya farver, son?'

'I don't know but he can't breeve and he can't get his breff.' All the while the old man was earwigging (listening).

' 'as the doctor been to see him?' he asked.

'No, me muvver said she ain't got the money to send for him.'

A doctor in those days cost 2s 6d, that's if you wasn't in the Sick Club where you worked. As Fred's dad was out of work and living on the Board of Guardians he had to find the money for the doctor.

The old lady had given Fred somefing to eat and she said, 'Arfter ya get that down ya we will go and see wot we can do for ya dad.' At the same time she was pulling her old shawl round her shoulders.

When we got to Fred's house his Ma opened the door and called out 'Ya there, Rose?' and wiv that Fred's mum came to the door.

'Oh hello, Lil. Come in, girl. Don't stand there,' and we followed her to the kitchen. As I said before, the old lady was only five foot nuffink and she didn't care about no one. If she had anyfing to say she would come right out wiv it.

'Wot's this young Fred tells me about Jim being ill?'

'I don't know wot's the matter wiv him, Lil. He's been in bed for free days now and he can hardly breeve,' replied Fred's muvver.

'Let's have a look at him,' said the old lady, and we all marched into the bedroom.

Fred's old man was as white as a ghost and he was breeving very farst. Well, we all stood there looking at him, but it was the old lady that broke the silence.

'Blimey, Rose. I don't like the look of him. Ya better go and get old Doc Lowder in to see him.'

'Leave awf, Lil. I ain't got no bleeding money for bread, let alone doctors,' said Fred's mum.

'Ya get him here,' said the old lady as she was opening her purse and taking out half a crown.' And you two can go and get a bit of shopping while we wait for the doctor,' she said to me and Fred.

Old Doc Lowder was a good old geezer. Everyone liked him. He'd made a living in the East End since he was a young man but how he did it I shall never know. He'd brought many a cockney urchin into this world including yours truly. He was five foot six tall wiv greying hair. He wore gold-rimmed glasses and carried a little brown Gladstone bag. If you couldn't pay him he would say, 'Ho well, we will leave it till the next time.' He never did get his money. Mind you if ya never had the money for the prescription at the chemist ya went wivout.

Arfter we returned from the shop old Doc Lowder finally arrived on his old bicycle. When he arrived we was all in the kitchen. As soon as he got in he went to the bedroom wiv Fred's mum.

'Wot ya fink's wrong wiv me dad, Al?' said Fred.

'I don't know, but my old lady said she didn't like the look of him.' Even though Fred's farver was a barsted to him, I could see he was worried.

'Oh he's all right. He's only god a cold,' I said.

Arfter a few minutes the doctor and Fred's muvver came into the kitchen.

'Well, that's it my old dear,' the doctor was saying as they came into the room. 'You see, his lungs are so congested we must get him in as soon as we can.'

Well, we all knew wot that meant. Fred's dad was going into hospital. Fred's mum fanked the old doc and gave him his harf crown and wiv that he left, saying he would send for the meat wagon.

It wasn't long before the ambulance arrived and all the neighbours came out to see wot was going on. They carted Fred's old man awf to St Andrew's Hospital, Bow. The old lady stayed to help out while Fred's mum went to the hospital wiv Fred's old man. Me and Fred went back to my house to see if my dad was okay.

As we got in my house the old man said, 'Is that you, Harryboy?'

'Yus dad,' I replied.

'Wot's wrong wiv old Jim?' he asked.

'Well, we don't know yet but old Doc Lowder 'as sent 'im to the hospital as he 'as got congestion in the lung,' I told him.

'Blimey, as bad as that is it?' said the old man, not knowing Fred was in the same room. I saw the look on Fred's face.

'Don't worry, Fred, he'll be all right,' I told him.

'Yus, he will be all right in a few days,' chimed the old man.

'Besides, my mum's down there so it will be OK, won't it dad,' I said.

To me, my mum was the end of all fings bad. But it wasn't all right. Fred's old man only lasted a few days and he died of congestion of the lungs. My old lady said there wasn't much they could do for him as he was too far gawn. Maybe if Fred's mum could have got the doctor sooner it would have been OK. It didn't take Fred long to get over it. He was back to his old self arfter a few weeks.

When I listen to the way people go on about the way fings have changed, wot they don't know is that a lot of so-called innovations like Chinese restaurants we had in the East End years ago. We had one in Limehouse when I was a saveloy. The most noted place for Chinks was Pennyfields, a street awf of West India Dock Road which is till there to this day. Ya could see all sorts going on in Pennyfields. Ya could see the old cufflinks in the poppy kitchens (opium dens) having a right old time. They were in a world of their own.

The Chinese used to run a game called puck ar poo and you could win a lot of money on this game. All ya do is to put marks down on a bit of paper. How it worked I don't know. I remember my old dad won firty pounds once on puck ar poo. We all went potty. There was new coats and shoes for the girls, and a new pair of boots and long trousers for me. Poor old mum bought a lovely new rug to go in front of the fireplace, and it looked lovely. It was the first rug we ever had. She said she was going to take it up during the day and put it down at night to save the wear.

'Leave awf, muvver. No one will see it,' I said. But she was like that my old mum. She loved to keep fings nice. She would scrub my sisters' pinafores until they was white and then she would starch them. She would spend hours scrubbing and washing just to keep us clean and tidy. There was one kid at our school, he never seemed to have a clean jersey and I used to fink to myself, he could do wiv a muvver like mine.

Life went on as usual in the East End and the old man was still busking in all kinds of wevver. My bruvver Albert teamed up wiv a team of dancers, and they started working in the West End. Albert told me that the medzers was a lot better there.

I said to the old man one day, 'Why don't we try the West End one of these nights, Dad?'

'No, son, I'd sooner stay round the old East End.'

'Why?' I asked him.

'Well wot would all our old punters say if they never saw us around anymore?'

'I suppose you're right, Dad.'

But I always had a yearning to work amongst the bright lights. I had never been up there but Albert had told me all about the fine ladies and gentlemen he saw there and how they were all dressed up in their finery. He would tell me of all the lovely ladies in their long dresses and I would lie in bed listening to his tales until I fell asleep, dead tired.

I would tell Georgi and Fred of all the stories that Albert told me about the glittering West End and I would say, 'I'm going up West one of these days.' Georgi and Fred would laugh and say, 'Leave awf, Al. It's a million miles away.'

Somehow I suppose they were right. The people who could afford to live in the West End had no idea of the way we lived in the East End. I never wanted a lot of money so I never dreamed of riches. But no man should have so much while the uvver man has so little. God sends us into this world naked and we leave it the same way.

Live was wot ya made it in the East End. It was hard for almost everybody. It was the conditions we all lived under. The houses was infested wiv rats, more so in the houses by the docks. I remember an old nightwatchman once told me that he saw an army of rats on the move. He was on duty one night outside the docks as the local council had the road up. he was sitting alone in his hut by the coke fire when he heard this sound. He thought it was the wind at first, and it was getting louder, so he got up to have a look. He nearly died of fright at what he saw.

'Wot was it?' I asked.

'Son, there was millions of the barsteds all running across the road to the uvver side of the docks. I just froze wiv fright. There was one big one leading the rest and they all fanned out like a pyramid. It's a sight I never want to see again.'

Old Pop, the nightwatchman, was a little old man, about five foot free, wiv white hair and grey eyes. He wore an old grey overcoat and a flat cap. He worked for the local council so when

153

they dug up the road he would be there to light up the red lamps and look arfter the tolls. We would sit for hours listening to him round his old coke fire. He would tell us tales of the First World War. He told us how he got gassed in the trenches of France and how he saw his pals get blown to bits and how some of them ended up wiv no arms and no legs. At that time they were just stories to me. Little did I know that I would see war for myself later on in life.

It was nice sitting in his hut wiv the glow of the fire casting shadows on the canvas of the hut. We sometimes shared his supper wiv him or we would go up the market and nick a few spuds awf of the stalls and take them back to him and he would bake them for us on a shovel over the fire. Some of the kids never had a fire at home so it was a treat for them to be nice and warm and listen to the old nightwatchman's stories. He used to laugh and say that all his mates died to make this a land 'fit for heroes to live in.'

'You got any medals, Pop?' Tommy said to him one night.

'Yus, I've got some medals son. They're in a drawer at home.'

'Why don't ya wear them them?' said Fred.

'I'd sooner leave them where they are, son. They bring back too many bad memories,' he said as he gazed into the fire for a moment as though he was dreaming of a place far away. But then he added, 'I'll show ya me medals tomorrow night.'

'Gee,' said Tommy. 'I will be here to see them, Pop.'

As we all left him and bade him good night, Tommy said, 'Ya won't forget to bring ya medals tomorrow night, will ya, Pop?'

'I'll bring them, son,' he replied and awf we all went.

The next night we all went expectantly to the hut and there he was, sitting, looking into the fire, smoking his pipe.

'Hiya Pop,' Georgi said to him and we all piled into the hut.

'It's bleeding cold tonight, ain't it Pop?' said Gobber.

'Ya but ya get used to it on this job,' he said.

'Have ya brought ya medals to show us, Pop?' asked Tommy. Wiv that Pop got up and went to a ragged old overcoat that was lying on the bench, and he pulled from the pocket a dirty old bit of rag and started to unwrap it. He then held up a long row of medals wiv their faded ribbons of all colours. We all looked at them wide-eyed as he told us wot they were for.

'They're lovely ain't they, Al?' said Tommy.

'Ya,' I replied, 'but they want cleaning, don't they Pop?'

'Why don't ya clean them, Pop?' asked Tommy.

'Wot's the use?' he said. 'Ya can't clean the blood that was spilt for them. Do ya see that one?' He pointed to a medal in the shape of a star. 'Well, that's the Mons star. You know, I lost four mates in that battle.'

'Did we win, Pop?' I asked.

'Win, son? It was one big balls up and it should never have happened.' And he went on to tell us all about it.

I told my Dad about old Pop having all those medals and that he never wore them.

'Ya can't eat medals, son,' said my Dad.

They say that laughter is the spice of life. The biggest reward for me was to 'ear people laughing. The more laughs we got, the better the show, even when I was at school (when I was there, that is). I loved to dress up to make the uvver kids laugh, and being a daredevil was anuvver of my weak points. I would do anyfink if someone dared me to do it, and I would do anyfink for a giggle. Like the time I put black ink in the font at church. Ya should have seen the uproar the following Sunday.

It all began one night at choir practice. The choirmaster had been having a go at me all frew the practice so I said to Fred, 'I ain't coming no more.'

'Why ain't ya, Al?' Fred asked.

'Well, he keeps blaming me for everyfing.'

'Well, ya do piss about wiv the girls,' said Fred.

On our way out frew the vestry I saw a bottle of black ink.

'Give us that bottle of ink,' I said to Fred. 'Wot ya want it for?' he asked.

'I'm going to hide it and that old ponce won't be able to find it and he will be doing his nut when he 'as to fill in his books.'

But on our way out, one of the uvver kids said, 'I dare ya to pour it in the font, Al.' So wivout any more ado, I did just that and we all ran awf laughing.

The following Sunday we went to the morning service at St Gabriel's and as usual at the end of the service the vicar read out the notices for that day. I heard 'is voice in the distance saying, 'And the christening of Mr and Mrs Butler's son will take place in the font.'

'Blimey, wot about the bleeding ink?' I whispered to Fred.

'Wot bleeding ink?' he asked. And then, like me, he remembered.

155

'Wot we going to do?' he asked.

'We can't do nuffing, can we. We'll just have to leave it, won't we,' I said.

Arfter the service was over we was in the vestry and Fred said, 'Wot happens when they christen that saucepan lid this afternoon?'

'I don't know,' I said, 'but I am coming back to find out for a giggle.'

In the arfternoon we went back to church, and as we got to the church door, old man Butler and his old woman was coming along wiv the christening party. We all piled into the church and stood round the font.

The old vicar started the christening service, and he was holding the kid over the font and he plunged the little christening cup into the font and he was saying, 'I name thee Robert George in the name of the . . .' and by this time he had poured all of the bleeding holy water over the saucepan lid's winnypeg. And then it happened. The bleeding kid started screaming his head oawf and his little bald head was covered in black ink. 'Blimey,' the shocked father of the child said, 'that water ain't been bleeding changed for bleeding years.'

The old vicar just couldn't understand it and he didn't know wot to say. Me and old Fred nearly pissed ourselves laughing. The poor little saucepan lid had black ink all over his little head, and old Ma Butler was saying, wiv tears rolling down her cheeks, 'Oh me poor little babby, he's all black. And look at his lovely shawl. It's bleeding rotten.'

The red-faced vicar was saying how sorry he was and that there would be a full inquiry into the matter. The choirmaster was running about like a blue-arse-fly putting clean water into the font. Old Grandfarver Butler was doing his nut and he fretened to burn the church down. The old vicar finished the job and was apologising all over the place and he was blaming the old choirmaster for not seeing that everyfing was OK for the christening.

'Wait till the vicar gets hold of him on his own,' I said to Fred, 'he'll bleeding kill him.'

The poor old choirmaster was doing his nut when we went to choir practice the following week He was asking all the uvver kids if they knew anyfing about the ink in the font, but it was more than their life was worf to come copper so we was never found out.

Arfter that episode the old choirmaster was at the church checking the font before every christening.

The name of the vicar was Farver Brown. He was tall and skinny wiv brown hair, brown eyes and long bony fingers. When I mentioned his fingers to Fred once, Fred said, 'Ya, I've notice that. That is frew having his fingers in the collecting box.'

At that time I had only one more year to do at school and out of that year I only went for the last two monfs.

'You'd better finish awf the last two monfs at school or ya won't get a character reference when ya leave,' said Fred.

'I don't need one for busking,' I told him.

'Are ya going to do busking when ya leave school then, Al?'

'Of course I am. I've got to take the old man out, ain't I? Wot's good for my Dad is good for me. Besides, my Dad's dad was a busker and so was his dad, so wot else is there for me?' I said.

By the time I left school I was taking the old man out full-time and my bruvver Albert was still working in the West End on his own. I left school around 1933. There was no celebration on the last day. I fink they were pleased to get rid of us. I wasn't sorry to leave. I hated the place. Fred, Georgi and Tommy all left school at the same time as I did. Fred started work wiv his farver in the dog-biscuit factory, Georgi worked in a timber yard, and Tommy started work wiv his farver in the council yard. We were always the best of mates and spent as much time togevver as possible. Even though they was earning more money than me, they would share when we all went out togevver.

'Why don't ya take a job in a factory, Al?' Tommy said to me one day.

'That's OK but you can all get the sack and I can't,' I replied.

Tommy's sister Diane was growing up nicely and all the boys were beginning to chase her wivout success. She was going to a better school as she was a bit brainy and her farver stopped her from going around wiv the gang.

Gobber White had been nicked and put into a home. My mum said, 'He'll end up on the end of a rope, that boy.' And he did.

The old choirmaster left the church and there was also a new vicar. When we all left school we had no time for choir practice. We started hanging around Tony's café in West India Dock Road. It was a small place wiv about eight tables. We could all get in there, swopping tales and eating a plate of chips which cost

157

ya fourpence in them days. We couldn't go and hang around Bob's coffee-stall any more as he died the same year we all left school.

One night we was all sitting in Tony's dafé having a cup of tea and we were discussing where to go.

'I know,' said Fred. 'Let's all go up the West End.' Well, we was all in agreement and awf we all went.

We finally found our way to Leicester Square and discovered it was a different world to wot we had been used to. It was every bit as glittering as Albert had said. There was bright lights everywhere, and I knew that night that I was destined to work there. By the time we had finished looking around open-mouthed we had missed the last bus home, so we had to walk all the way back to the East End. But to me it was worf every minute of it.

It was very late by the time I got home and when I got indoors the old lady had waited up for me.

'Where the bloody hell have ya been?' she bawled at me as I walked frew the door. 'And wot have ya been up to?'

'I ain't been up to nuffing Ma. We missed the last bus home,' I told her, 'so we had to walk all the way home.'

Well, she rattled on a bit more and arfter a while she began to listen. I told her all about the sights and all about the bright lights as ya see she had never been up the West End like me.

'I fawt I might have seen Albert up there working,' I said. Mum said that Albert had been in bed ages ago, and she added, 'That is where you should be.'

Before we said goodnight she said, 'Don't worry ya mum like that again, boy, let me know where you're going.'

'OK muvver,' I said. 'God bless,' and when she kissed me on the cheek I knew I was safely home.

The next day I told my bruvver Albert about my adventure the night before.

'Ya want to stay away from there,' he warned me. 'Besides, the ladies and gentlemen's a lot of villains up there.'

'You go up there,' I said.

'Only because I work up there,' he replied.

'Why don't you take me up there to work wiv ya?' I asked.

'And who's going to take the old man out if I take you wiv me?' he said.

'I tried my utmost to get the old man to work the West End but he wouldn't have it, so I was condemned to the East End for a few more years.

By 1937 there was a lot of talk about that guy called Hitler and how he was beginning to push some of the small countries around. One night I was out busking wiv the old man when one of the punters in the bevvy we was working said to him, 'Ya fink there's going to be a war, Bill?'

'I hope not, mate. I had enough of the last one,' replied the old man.

Everywhere we went there was talk of war.

'It will be awf one of these days wiv those barsted Germans,' said Georgi's old man.

'Do ya fink so, Mr Hunter?' I said.

'Well, it stands to reason,' he replied. 'Wot ya fink they're sending Chamberlain over there for?' And he went on to say how the world was getting overpopulated and the only way to stop it was to have anuvver war.

When I told my Dad this he said, 'Take no notice of him, son. He talks a lot of rubbish.'

Fings seem to be improving at home. We even had a few mats on the floor instead of the old lino. My eldest sister was at work and the few bob she brought home seemed to help out a bit more. My mum bought me my first suit. Even though it was two sizes too big, I fawt it was smashing. I shall never forget when she gave it to me.

She had bought it awf a secondhand stall in the market. I had been out wiv the old man all day and when we got home she said, 'I've got somefing for you son, but first ya can eat ya supper.'

Well, arfter the supper of bread and dripping she gave me this parcel and said, 'Here ya are, try that on.' Well, when I opened this parcel there was this suit.

'Blimey, muvver,' I said, 'where did ya get that?'

'Try it on and let's see how it fits ya,' she said, ignoring my question.

I hurriedly started stripping awf my uvver clothes, and finally put this suit on. Hodling my arms out I said, 'How does it look, Mum?'

'It's a bit big but I'll soon fix that,' she said.

The old man wanted to feel the cloth and he said, 'That's a good bit of stuff, that.'

'Wait till the boys see me in that,' I said. 'They'll all go potty.'

'Ya mean Diane when she sees ya,' said my sister.

'Why don't ya keep ya big mouf shut,' I screamed at her.

Well, Mum was as good as her word. By the time she cut a bit awf of the strides it didn't look so big. My bruvver Albert said he would lend me his stook (scarf) to wear round my bushel and peck and he showed me how to press the strides. Well, the next night I couldn't get into that suit farst enough so I could show it awf to the boys.

When I finally got dressed, I went up to Tony's Café and I peeped in the door to see if all the boys were in there before I made my grand entrance. Well, there they are, all sitting at our usual table. As I walked frew the door, Tommy was the first to get a load of me.

'Blimey,' he said, 'look at Al,' and the rest of them turned round to have a butchers' hook.

'Where did ya get that suit?' asked Georgi.

'How much did it cost?' asked Fred.

They were all asking questions at the same time and I just stood there wiv my hair all greased down wiv about 'arf a pound of margarine that I had nicked out of the cupboard and Albert's borrowed stook tied in a knot wiv a brass ring around it that my sister had lent me. Arfter I had told them all about the suit, I had a cup of tea. But I was still standing up by the table.

'Why don't ya sit down, Al?' asked Tommy.

'He's bleeding frightened to in case he creases his trousers,' said Fred.

'Yea, it will cost us a tanner a minute to talk to him, won't it Al?' said Georgi and we all ended up having a good laugh. I took care of that suit as if it was the only suit in the 'ole world and I pressed the trousers every time I went out in it.

In those days the music hall was a great fing and we all started to go to one each Monday night. It was the only time I could go out and enjoy myself as I was out busking wiv the old man the rest of the week. We would all save fourpence out of our money and we would give it to old Tony to mind for us and each Monday night he would hand it back to us in the café. We would go up in the gods at the Queens Theatre, Poplar. However, it was at the Hackney Empire where I saw the first comedian I ever saw on stage. It was dear old Max Miller. I said to Fred one night in the interval, 'I'll be up there one of these days,' and he laughed and sayd 'Yus, sweeping up.'

160

Going to the music hall became a regular fing for us and I never knew then that I was destined to work wiv some of the biggest stars in showbusiness. One night I asked Diane if she would like to go wiv me to the music hall and she said she would. I took her to the Queens and there was an act on the bill and this guy was playing the spoons.

'Ain't he good?' she said,

'Ya, but he ain't as good as me,' I said.

'Well, why ain't you up there, then?'

'I will be one of these days,' I replied.

One day my bruvver Albert said he would teach me to tap-dance. It took me free monfs of hard practising before I could do it properly.

'It would be good, Al,' said Albert, 'if we were to do a routine togevver,' and he was finking about getting a show togevver and taking it out on the road.

'Wot about working the West End wiv it?' I said.

'I said I was only finking about it,' he replied.

'You're all bleeding shit. Ya don't mean wot ya say,' I said.

'How can we work the West End?' said Albert. 'You know I am wiv the Lunar Boys, and I can't let them down.'

The Lunar Boys were well-known in the East End and the West End. They would put on a fifteen-minute show right in the middle of the street and they would draw big crowds. Another famous street group used to put on a drag show. It consisted of about seven ome palones (nancy boys) all dressed up in women's clothes. They would form a line in front of a barrel-organ and start danging. Some would do high kicks while others would do the splits and all the time they would be screaming at the top of their voices, in a very high pitch. They would put on a very good show. The street urchins would sit on the kerb and laugh and clap till their little 'earts were content. All the old girls would come out in the street and watch the show. While the excitement was going on, one of them would bottle.

One day they came down our street and we was all sitting on the kerb watching them.

' 'Ey mate,' said Fred to one of them, 'ya want to see him dance,' and he pointed to me.

'Can ya dance, love?' he asked me.

'Yea, me bruvver learned me,' I told him.

And the next fing I knew he was pulling me out in front of the barrel organ and I started dancing like a good'un. One of the old girls who had been watching the show went and told my Mum to come and have a look at me dancing. Well, all the kids was shouting and clapping.

Arfter the show, one of the ome palomes came over and said how they liked the way I worked and would I like to join them for the rest of the day?

'How much will I get for a day's work?' I said, and he was just about to tell me what I was worf when the old lady came up and said, 'Piss awf. He'll end up as bent as you are,' and that was the end of that. And that was the first time I walloped (tap danced) in public, but it wasn't to be my last.

My bruvver started courting a nice girl called Edie and there was some talk about them getting married and all the family was in agreement, as Edie was one of us, a real cockney. Edie was about five foot one wiv black hair and grey eyes. She became the best bottler in the West End.

Well, they ended up getting married and they had a real cockney wedding. They got married in my old school church, St Gabriels and as I stood there it brought back a lot of memories. Arfter the wedding we all had a beer up.

'I wouldn't mind but I can't even get pissed on my own wedding day,' Albert said to me.

'Why is that?' I asked.

'Well I've to go to out to work tonight. I can't mess around now. I've now got an old woman to keep,' he said.

The old lady let Albert and Edie have the back bedroom to live in and they gave the old lady harf-a-crown a week for the latty (room) and that went towards the Duke of Kent (rent). The whole house was only ten shillings a week. We was a happy family even though the house was infested wiv rats. It was a god-forsaken hole. As a matter of fact, I don't fink God ever fawt about it, but we knew nuffing else.

I have not yet mentioned Bill, my eldest bruvver. There is not a lot to say about Bill. We loved him as bruvvers should do. He was completely different to Albert and me. He went out busking wiv the old man before I was born and when he started work, Albert had to take the old man out. Bill was a good'un. He started work at the local biscuit factory at the age of fourteen and he was there until he died. He used to bake the biscuits. He died on the operating table at the London Hospital in Whitechapel Road. My eldest sister Lily also took my Dad out busking,

162

she took him out a long time before I did so you see we have all had our turn of busking. My youngest sister was still at school.

By 1948 I reached my sixteenf birfday. That geezer, Hitler, was by now stirring up a lot of trouble. In 1938 I had done my first-ever stage show. It was a concert for a load of old people at the local town hall. There was an advertisement in the local rage asking for talent to appear in an old people's show.

'I am going round the town hall to see about it,' I said to Fred and Georgi.

'We'll come wiv you and we can have a giggle,' said Georgi. So awf we went.

Well, when we got to the town hall and went inside, there was a big geezer on the door. He looked at us and said, 'Well, wot do ya want?'

'We've come about this,' I said and showed him the advert that I had cut out from the paper.

'Oh I see,' he said. 'Ya want to be in the ballroom,' and he told us where to go.

When we got to the Poplar Town Hall ballroom there was some more people there and there was an old bird up on the stage playing a piano.

'Blimey Al,' said Fred, 'listen to her knocking fuck out of those ivories,' but I was too engrossed wiv the stage.

'Never mind about her,' I said, 'look at that greengage (stage).' It was a lovely stage wiv beautiful curtains and red and green spotlights. There was a few people up on the stage rehearsing their own act.

Arfter we had been standing there for about four minutes a grey-headed man came up to us and asked us wot we wanted.

'He wants to be in your concert, guvner,' said Georgi pointing to me.

Well, the geezer looked at me over his glasses and said, 'Wot do you do?'

'He can tap dance, can't ya, Al?' said Fred before I could answer.

'Is that so? I would like to see that. Follow me,' he said. We followed him down to the stage.

'Wot do you call yourself?' he asked.

'Harry,' I replied.

'Is that your stage name?' he said wiv a laugh.

'I ain't got a stage name. I go out busking,' I said.

'You do wot?'

163

'He goes out busking wiv his farver,' said Georgi.

'Do you mean you go round the pubs busking?'

'That's right,' I said.

'How old are you?' he asked.

'Sixteen, guv,' I answered.

'You're not very big, are you,' he said.

By this time we had reached the stage and the old geezer shouted out, 'Just a moment everybody,' and they all stopped wot they were doing and looked in our direction. there was a moment of silence.

'This is Harry, and he tap dances and he wants to join our little show,' said the man. There were a few smiles from those up on the stage and then he said, 'You go up there and show us wot you can do.'

As I climbed the stairs at the side of the stage my heart was pounding like an African drum and I felt full of joy.

'Just a moment, son. Would you like Mrs Tate to play for you?'

'Can ya play "Bye Bye Blues"?' I asked.

'Certainly,' she said and awf she went.

Well, I had to stop her as it was too slow. We finally got togevver and it went like a bomb.

When we had finished everyone was clapping and Fred and Georgi were shouting, 'More! More!' The old geezer came running up on the stage and he put his arm around my shoulder.

'That was fine, son. You'll do. What do you think, Mrs Tate?' he asked the pianist.

'That was lovely, Mr West,' she replied, and that was how I got to know old Mr West who had been running shows for charity for years. he was about five foot eight, wiv grey hair and green eyes. He wore a dark blue suit wiv a silver watch-chain across his derby kelly. There was no name to the show. It was just a get-togevver for the old folks. I did my first audition there at the Poplar Town Hall and I did my last-ever show there many years later.

Well, all frew that week all the spare time I had I spent rehearsing. I had to go back four times to the Town Hall before the show, and each time I couldn't get up on that stage farst enough. On the night of the show I was the first one there at the hall. Eventually the uvvers arrived and there was a lot of hussle and bussle going on backstage. Mr West was running around and giving orders and Mrs Tate was getting her music sheets togevver.

164

Old Mrs Tate was a nice old lady. I fink she also played the organ in a church somewhere. She was a small woman wiv her hair in a bun at the back of her neck. She wore glasses and had red rosy cheeks and blue eyes.

Well, the show got under way and the punters seemed to be enjoying it. Then it came to my turn and old Mr West told me to stand by. As I was standing in the wings I could 'ear Mr West saying at the top of his voice, 'And now ladies and gentlemen, we have somefing different.' He seemed to be going on forever about how old I was and how small I was and all at once Mrs Tate started to play my music and before I knew it I was out on stage doing my stuff.

At first I fawt everyone had gawn home as I couldn't see nuffing but blackness as the lights were so bright. But I still went on walloping. Arfter I had finished everyone clapped and I heard shouts of, 'More! More!' and I knew it was the gang. They had all loyally come to see me on what was my first stage appearance.

Chapter Nine
A family at war

In September 1938 old Neville Chamberlain went to Germany to see Adolf Hitler. He returned wiv that famous piece of paper which he claimed would bring 'peace in our time'. But despite that, fings still looked desperate.

One night while we was out busking my old man said to me, 'I don't like the look of it, son.'

'Do ya fink there will be a war, Dad?' I said.

'Lord only knows, son. I don't dare fink of it.' I told him that Pop the nightwatchman said that the Germans drop gas on ya and it burns all ya face and eyes and he said ya can die wiv it.

'I know, son. I saw it in the First World War.'

'Do wars come in numbers then, Dad?' I said.

'War can come any time, son,' he replied.

I told him that Georgi's dad said wars were a racket and they were only started to make money for the rich.

'I told ya before not to take any notice of wot Sam Hunter said. One of these days he is going to get into trouble wiv the fings he says,' said the old man.

Everywhere we went there was talk of war.

'If there is a war I am going to join the army,' Georgi said one night in Tony's café.

'Leave awf,' said Fred. 'They wouldn't have ya as you't got flat feet.'

'Who's got bleeding flat feet?' retorted georgi. And wiv that he pulled awf his boots to reveal 'ols the size of spuds in his socks.

We all laughed and one of the uvver boys said, ' 'ey Georgi, the Germans will run for their lives when they see your boat race.'

'I am going to join the Navy,' said Fred. 'It's the best.'

'How can ya make that out, Fred?' asked one of the boys.

'Well, my dad was in the Navy in the First World War, so if it was good enuff for him it will be good enuff for me.'

'My old man said that if there's a war it won't last long,' said

Tommy. 'He reckons it will only last about six monfs.' Little did we know that night wot terrible times lay ahead of us.

About this time Gobber came out of Borstal after being put away for two years. He went there for nicking some cakes out of a shop. The old baker got hold of him and sent for Old Bill. But it never seemed to have done Gobber much good. He told us one night that he learned more in the two years he was in Borstal than he had learned all the time he was at school.

'Why?' I asked him. 'Did ya do sums and reading, Gobber?'

'We had some lessons, but I now know how to take the back awf of a Peter (safe).'

He reckoned he learned more about feeving than anyfing else. He described it as a house of learning, not of correction as the magistrate had told him when he sent him away.

About free monfs arfter Gobber got out of Borstal he started going around wiv a bird called Rosie. I can remember one of the boys saying to him one night, 'Gobber, you'll end up wiv a dose of Albert Docks (pox) awf of that bird. She's had so many geezers she's lost count.' But it made no difference to old Gobber.

'It won't last long as she's always going wiv different geezers,' said Georgi.

'Old Gobber will end up doing her in,' I said.

Lovely Diane went into hospital the day Chamberlain came back from Germany. She was in St Andrews Hospital.

'Do ya fink she will be all right, Tommy?' I asked him, as I was worried about her.

All that night in the café when I met the boys I wasn't my usual self and they knew it.

'Wot's the matter wiv ya, Al?' asked Georgi.

'Don't ya know?' said Fred. 'He's worried over his bird being in hospital.'

'Don't worry, Al,' said Gobber. 'She will be OK.'

'Why don't we all go and see her on Sunday and cheer her up?' said Georgi.

'Yus, we can nick a bunch of flowers out of the park for her,' said Fred. 'And we can have a whip round and buy her a nice box of chocolates.'

'Ya, I can hold the money,' said Gobber.

'Leave awf. I wouldn't let ya hold my cock, let alone hold the money we are going to buy the chocolates wiv.'

It was all arranged that we would go and see her on Sunday.

'You will have to nick the flowers on Saturday night,' I told Tommy, 'and keep them in water in your house until we are ready to go to the hospital on Sunday.' We all agreed to put fourpence each towards a box of chocolates.

On Sunday we all got dressed up ready to see Diane in the hospital. We met at Tommy's house and when I saw the flowers they had nicked from the park the night before I said, 'Blimey, wot did ya do, nick all the bleeding weeds in the bloody park?' It was the biggest bunch of flowers I had ever seen.

'If ya going to nick anyfing make sure ya nick it big,' said Gobber.

'You can say that again,' I said.

On our way to the hospital, Tommy told me all about the flower raid on the park as I could not be there. I had to go out working wiv the old man. Before we set awf for the hospital there was nearly a punch-up over who was going to carry the flowers.

'I ain't going to carry them,' said Tommy. 'I had enough carrying them in the dark last night wivout carrying them in the daylight as well.'

'Well, I am bleeding sure I ain't going to carry them,' said Fred.

'I don't want to be seen wiv a bunch of bleeding flowers,' said Gobber.

'Well, it looks like it's down to you, Al,' said Georgi.

'Ya, it's your bleeding girl,' said Tommy.

'Leave awf. I'll look a right berk carrying them, won't I,' I replied.

Well, ya wasn't wiv us last night when we nicked 'em, so you should be the one to carry them,' said Fred.

'OK then, I'll carry them,' I said reluctantly, and we all set awf for the hospital.

When we got there, Tommy's muvver and farver was waiting outside in the corridor leading to the ward. When Tommy's old man saw us all, he said, 'Wot the bloody hell do you lot want?'

'We've come to see Diane,' Tommy said.

'Where di ya get those flowers from?' Tommy's farver asked me.

'We bought them between us,' said Gobber.

168

'They're lovely ain't they, Tom?' Tommy's muvver Rose was saying.

'Yus, they are nice, ain't they,' Tommy's old man replied and wiv the next breff he said, 'I don't want no pissing about when we get inside.'

Just then a young nurse came along and said, 'They only allow two visitors around a bed at a time.'

'Oh, all right,' said Tommy, 'we will have to take turns to go and see her then,' and we all agreed to wait outside in the corridor.

Just inside the corridor there was a trolley wiv a pile of clean sheets on it.

'My old lady would love a pile of those sheets,' said Gobber.

'Keep ya bleeding mince pies awf of them. Do ya want to get us all nicked?' said Georgi.

'I'm only kidding,' said Gobber.

Arfter a while Tommy's dad came out of the ward and said, 'It's all right. There's about four visitors around one bed.'

'Wot's good for them is good for us,' said Tommy and we all pined in the ward.

When we got to the bed, there lay Diane, and she looked as lovely as ever. The ward she was in was a long one wiv beds each side. She was sitting up in bed dressed in a blue nightdress wiv little roses embroidered on it. her black hair was tied at the back of her head wiv a white silk ribbon.

She gave us all a smile and said, 'Wot do you lot want?'

'We come to see ya, sis,' said Tommy, 'and we brought ya some chocolates and look at the lovely flowers we got for ya.' I handed her the flowers and as she put them to her face to smell them she looked like an angel.

'Ya don't look too bad, do she, Al?' said Tommy.

'No, ya look OK,' I told her. Then I noticed that Gobber was missing.

'Wot happened to Gobber?' I said.

'I suppose he is outside wiv my old man,' said Tommy.

It was time for us to go and as we was saying our goodbyes to Diane, Tommy kissed her on the cheeks and said, 'I'll see ya later, sis,' and then he said, 'Go on, Al, give her a kiss.'

'Leave awf,' I said.

'Go on,' said Tommy's muvver. 'Don't be shy.'

As I bent over to kiss her I felt the warmf of her face. I kissed her on the cheek and said, 'See ya then, Di.'

169

'Some geezers get all the luck,' said Georgi, and we all laughed.

We all waved goodbye to her from the doorway as we went out of the hospital.

'Wot happened to Gobber?' I said.

'I bet he went for a piss,' said Georgie.

'I fawt he was wiv Tommy's farver,' I said.

As we got to the hospital gates I turned round and saw Gobber coming up behind us. By this time Tommy's muvver and farver had left us and gone ahead. Gobber caught up wiv us as we got outside the gates.

'Ya took ya bleeding time, wot ya been poncing about at?' asked Fred. And wiv that, Gobber started to laugh. We all wanted to know wot the joke was.

'Wait until we get down the road and I will tell ya,' said Gobber, and he started to run. Well we all knew he had been up to somefing so we all ran arfter him.

Fred jumped on his back and said, 'Come on Gobber, wot's the joke?' and we all ended up jumping on him.

'All right, fuck ya. I'll show ya it ya let me,' and we all let him go. Just then he opened his shirt and from the front of his trousers he pulled out a bed sheet. He then did the same from the back of his trousers.

'Wot ya want to go and nick them for, ya barsted?' said Tommy. 'If ya had got caught we would all have been nicked.'

'Well, I nicked them for my old lady,' said Gobber.

'When did ya nick 'em?' said Fred. 'I never saw ya.'

'Course ya never. I nicked them when ya were in the ward and I shot in the piss house and put them down my strides.'

'You're a dirty fucker, Gobber, nicking fings from a hospital,' I said.

'Leave awf. They've got plenty and we ain't got none so I helped meself, didn't I,' he said.

Well, we all told Gobber wot we fawt of him but it made no difference. It was like water on a duck's back.

'Don't say a word to Diane about it or she will go mad,' I said to Tommy.

'She didn't look bad, did she Al,' he said.

'No, she looked all right,' I replied.

'Ya should have seen her the day she had her operation,' said Tommy, She looked terrible then. Fank God she is OK now.'

It's a funny thing how people turn to God in a crisis. I have heard some right villains call out, 'Oh my God,' when they have been hurt in some way. Like the time poor old Billy Day got his lot. He never did an honest day's work in his life and he was known locally as a right villain.

He was a fick-set guy wiv blond hair and blue eyes. He was up to all sorts of villainy. he used to break into warehouses and nick anyfing he could lay his hands on. He worked in the docks unloading the ships.

I saw him have a fight one night in the bevvy wiv a Dutch seaman, and this big Dutchman was getting the better of Billy. So Billy done no more. He took the marble top awf a table and he smashed it right in the Dutchman's face. The dazed Dutchman sunk to the floor of the boozer and his face was streaming wiv blood. Someone said that it was only the weight that stopped the geezer from being killed as it was too heavy for Billy to give it a good swing.

Arfter a few years Billy started to go straight as he got married and he told me he was going to settle down. His old man got him a job in the docks and the story goes that one day Billy was working in a ship's hold unloading the cargo, when out of the blue, the iron ball that was swinging from the crane swung round and hit him right in the back of his head.

One of the boys who had been working alongside of him, said, 'He went down like a wet sack and his last words were "Oh my God!" ' and he rolled over and died. At his funeral six of his mates carried him to the grave. Even villains cry.

In 1938 Gobber got nicked again. This time for breaking into a wine shop and nicking some bottles of gin and whisky. However, he was lucky as they put him on probation for two years.

'You'll never learn, will ya, Gobber?' I said to him, but he just spat on the ground and laughed.

'Wot did ya bird, Rosie, say?' said Fred.

'I am the boss out of us two,' said Gobber defiantly.

'Leave awf. She knocks fuck out of ya. She's the boss and no mistake about it,' said Fred. Rosie was taller than Gobber so she would fight wiv him like a man.

The years was slipping by and it was coming up to Christmas. The old man and I were still trudging the streets of the East End trying to get a living. It was a hard life but we was happy and I was glad I had the experience of coming up the hard way. That is why I never wanted to be rich. If you're rich it is so easy to get

171

wot ya want. My old Dad used to say, 'To want fings is life. Ya never see a happy millionaire. This is because they have everyfing they want.'

A few weeks before Christmas I was rehearsing for the Christmas show wiv old Mr West and old Ma Tate at the local church hall and I made it quite clear to Mr West that I wasn't to let the rehearsals interfere wiv my busking, as it was near Christmas, and me and the old man had to get all we could. Mr West said he understood and we came to an arrangement about the rehearsals.

I told the old man about the concert and he said, 'That's all right, boy. We can start early on the day of the concert and we can finish in time for ya to get home, have ya tea and then you can do your stuff at the concert.'

The shows were always on a Satuday night so I would start work about ten in the morning and finish about six. That would give me time to get home wiv the old man and get ready to go to the Town Hall by eight o'clock. The old man was a stickler for work. To him busking was as though he worked in a factory. He would start at a certain time and finish at a certain time.

The old lady was running around getting a few fings for Christmas. My two sisters made some paper chains to decorate the living room. Even though Gobber was on probation he was still nicking fings left and right. He said to me one day, 'We ain't going wivout nuffing for Christmas. Even if I have to 'arf inch the bleeding crown jewels.'

Christmas came and went and the Christmas show went down well and everyone like it. We all had a laugh and enjoyed ourselves. But it was as though everybody knew there was a shadow hanging over them.

On New Year's Eve 1938 Fred slipped on some ice on his way to work and ended up in hospital. He then worked round the council yard locating vans. When we all went to see him at Poplar Hospital he was lying flat on his back on a wooden board on the bed. He had somefing wrong wiv his back.

'That's the sort of beds ya get in the nick,' Gobber said.

'How do you know, Gobber? You've never been in the nick. You've only been in Borstal,' said Georgi.

'Well, that's wot the beds are like in Limehouse nick cos I've been there the last time they nicked me,' he said.

'Leave awf, they wouldn't make ya sleep on a board, would they Al?' said Fred.

'Well, I know they have got boards in Lewisham nick cos me and my dad slept there the night we got lost in the fog.'

'There ya are,' said Gobber wiv a grin.

There was about four of us round Fred's bed when a young nurse came up and said sternly, 'Only two visitors at a time allowed round each bed.' Of course, Gobber was in like a shot.

'Don't worry, darling. We ain't going to nick ya old bed. Now if you was in it I wouldn't mind.'

'Leave awf, Gobber. You're making her blush,' said Georgi.

'Nurses don't blush,' said Tommy.

'I bet it would take a lot to make you blush, wouldn't it darling,' said Gobber. By this time this little bird was getting hot under the collar. Gobber said it was because she was bending over tucking in the bed sheets.

As she bent over Gobber said, 'Blimey, black stocking tops and white flesh.' And he flung out his arms and said, 'Take me darling, I'm all yours.'

'Take no notice of this team, nurse. They don't mean anyfing,' I said, and she gave me a little smile.

'Come on you lot,' I said. 'Fred's mum is waiting outside to come in.'

We all said goodbye to Fred and as we began to walk away he said, 'Look out for my old lady for me Al, will ya?'

'Don't you worry, my old son,' I said. 'My old lady will see she don't go wivout anyfing.' My word was as good as my bond. Fred's muvver came and had her dinner wiv us all the time he was in hospital.

Arfter Fred came out of hospital he couldn't go back to work for at least free weeks so one day I said to him, 'I'll take ya out busking wiv me if ya like Fred.'

'Wot do I have to do?' he asked.

'Ya don't have to do nuffing much. All ya have to do is bottle.'

'OK I'll have a go,' said Fred.

Well, laugh . . . I took him wiv me and the old man around Lewisham. We had it all arranged. I was to play the spoons, the old man was to play the concertina, and Fred was to do the bottling.

I told him wot to do and he said, 'If ya show me first I'll know wot to do.'

'OK,' I said.

Well, at the first boozer I left the old man in the doorway

173

playing and I said, 'Come on, Fred, I'll show ya how to bottle,' and round I went wiv Fred following me up behind.

'Wot's all this, Harryboy?' said one of the punters. 'The game must be good if ya got to get help.'

'Ya must be joking, guvner,' I said. Poor old Fred went as red as a beetroot.

When we had finished I said, 'There ya are. There's nuffing to it.'

Well, we got to the next boozer and I opened the door and said to the guvner behind the bar, 'Is it all right to have a go, guvner?' Ya see, a good busker always asks the guvner of the boozer before he starts to perform. In fact, there wasn't one pub guvner who refused us permission to play. You must remember in them days there was no TV in the pubs there is now and none of them took a backhander from us. We only made enough to live on.

Well, as we was on our usual round the guvner knew us.

'It's OK, Harryboy,' he shouted back from the bar and the old man started to play a couple of numbers and I said to Fred, 'OK Fred. Go on and bottle,' and I pushed him frew the door.

When we had finished Fred came out of the bar and I said, 'Wot's the mezzers jaggs? (How much is there?)' and when I looked in the bottlin' bag he had a penny.

'Wot the fucking hell ya been doing.' I said. 'Ya should have at least a tray saltie (freepence) awf of that bevvy.'

'Wot's the mezzers ya jaggs?' asked the old man.

'A saltie,' I replied.

'Well, they wouldn't give me nuffing,' said Fred.

I saw a little smile across the old man's face and I knew wot he was finking. Ya see, there is a right way and a wrong way to bottle. Ya don't just hold the bottling bag and walk by. You'll end up getting nuffing like that. So you have to go right up to the punter wiv a nice smile and at the same time ya gives him a salute by touching ya cap wiv ya forefinger and ya say, 'Jolly good luck, sir.' And ya don't move till he bungs ya (gives ya somefing). And then ya move on to the next punter. Ya didn't cop awf of everyone as in them days they were nearly all skint.

Well, when I told Fred this, he said, 'It's harder than working. I'd sooner stick to my own job.'

The old man said to me arfter we got home, 'I am afraid, son, young Fred won't make a busker.'

'Ya know wot, Dad,' I said. 'I fink you're right.'

Old Fred finally returned to work and I used to pull his leg and say to him, 'Ya want to come out busking wiv us Fred?'

'Not likely. It's hard work,' he would reply.

When me and the old man was out togevver we had many a laugh about poor old Fred's lesson in busking.

My old Dad used to say, 'Ya got to be born to it, son,' and born to it I was. As I told you before, it was a hard life, but I don't fink I would have had it any uvver way. it's wot was handed to me the day I was born. If I had to do it all over again I would do so because that's wot God wanted me to do and I have done it the best I know how. Maybe I should have done more, I don't know. But God stopped me from doing more as you will find out as my story goes along. Ya see the book of life is brief and once you have read the pages you can't go back to them.

People were getting worried in 1939 as the shadow of war was getting closer and closer and on September 1939 just one year after Chamberlain had been to Germany to see Hitler, we was at war.

I shall never forget my poor old Dad's face when we heard it on the radio. He just listened and he went white. I watched him reach out and take my muvver's hand in his and he said, 'We will be all right old girl, wiv God's help.'

I can see those two pairs of work worn hands stretched across the old wooden kitchen table and my muvver's voice was saying, 'Wot about me boys? They will have to go.'

That night we all met in Tony's café.

'Wot ya fink about the war, Al?' asked Fred.

'It won't last long,' said Georgi. 'My old man said so. He reckons it will only last a few weeks.'

'Wot does your old man know?' said Tommy.

'All he knows about is going away to sea and coming home and putting ya muvver in the family way,' Gobber said.

'Your old man's a randy old barsted, Georgi.' All Georgi done was to laugh about it all.

The next fing the government done was to issue everyone wiv gas masks. We all had to go to the old school to get fitted wiv them. Gobber came out wiv two – one he was issued wiv and one he nicked.

'Wot ya want two for, Gobber?' I said.

'In case one don't work,' he said.

175

'If it don't work ya won't have bleeding time to put the uvver one on,' said Tommy wiv a laugh.

To us it was a big giggle in those first days of the blackout when everyone had to cover their windows so the Germans on an air-raid couldn't be helped.

Gobber nicked more gear than bleeding Ali Baba. If ya wanted anyfing in the food line Gobber had it. He said, 'I ain't going to bleeding starve when I can nick it.'

Tommy's dad had to go in the army as he was in the Army Reserve and Georgi's old man went back to sea. People were busy filling up sandbags and taping their windows. It was supposed to be a protection from blast.

A lot of the men we knew were already in the Forces and there seemed to be more birds in the bevvies than men. However, people seemed to be more friendly towards one anuvver. I suppose it was because they didn't know wot was going to happen next. Everywhere me and the old man went they was good to us and we seemed to be doing all right as all they wanted was music and a singsong. It was as though they had no tomorrow.

One night Gobber came into the café and told us Rosie was in the family way.

'Wot ya going to do about it, Gobber?' I asked.

'I'm getting married, ain't I?' he replied.

'Ya could get old Ma Taylor to get rid of it for ya,' said Fred. 'She takes care of all the brasses that get in the family way round here.'

'Leave awf. I'm getting tied up and that's that,' said Gobber.

'Ya can't look arfter ya bleeding self let alone get tied up to a bird for the rest of ya life,' said Tommy.

Well Gobber married his Rosie at Poplar Registry Office but just before he got married he got nicked again. he was arrested for nicking a load of sacks from the sack factory. There was about free fousand sacks on the lorry. he planned to charge two shillings a sack once he found a buyer.

When the coppers nicked him, all the boys shouted, 'Let him go ya dirty barsteds.' But it was no use. Gobber was nicked and that was that. Well, they let him out on bail but he didn't turn up for the court hearing so the magistrates at Thames Police Court issued a warrant for his arrest.

On the day he got married Old Bill was waiting outside the

registry office for him. Laugh . . . There was Rosie wiv a lump on her belly as big as a football and Gobber done up in his old man's suit that was two sizes too big for him. The collar of the shirt he was wearing was like a horse's collar. All the boys went down to the registry office to wish him and Rosie luck. No sooner had he come out arfter the ceremony than Old Bill jumped on him and took him to the nick.

'That's the end of his bleeding honeymoon,' said Fred.

No sooner was Gobber in the nick than Rosie was having it awf wiv anuvver geezer at the wedding knees-up. It was a Saturday that Gobber got nicked so the police held him in the police cells all over the weekend and he had to go to court on Monday morning. As soon as the magistrate saw Rosie wiv her lump on her belly and heard how they only got married on Saturday they was a bit each on him. Arfter the Old Beak had given Gobber a bollocking he told him he had to go into the Army or he would go to jail. Gobber picked the Army and boy did that Rosie have a good time while he was away.

The night before he went away, all the gang went round to his muvver's house for a piss up. It was a farewell party for Gobber. There was all kinds of drink there. There was no need to ask where it came from. All Gobber kept on saying was, 'Drink up. It's all down to the peanut man,' meaning it had all been nicked.

Everyone had a good time at Gobber's party and he was telling us wot he was going to do wiv the Germans when he got over the uvver side.

'Leave awf, Gobber,' said Tommy. 'You'll run for ya bleeding life,' and all the boys agreed.

'I don't know wot I am going to do wiv that little slut, Rosie, while he's away, Harryboy,' said old Ma White. 'She'll be out wiv Tom, Dick and Harry.'

'This is one Tom she won't be out wiv,' said Tommy. We all had a giggle.

'I wouldn't touch her wiv a barge pole,' said Georgi.

Tommy was laughing to himself and I asked wot the joke was.

'I was just finking, Al. That's just about wot she can take – a barge pole.'

'You're a dirty barsted sometimes, Tommy,' I said. 'She may be all right once the baby's born, Ma.'

'I don't fink so, son,' she said. 'That kind don't change their stripes. Ya know, the dirty cow don't even change her bleeding drawers.'

Gobber's baby was born in March 1940 and I was eighteen when his baby was born. I didn't know that by October of that year I would be in the Navy. My bruvver Albert had already been in the Army for some monfs. The people from the National Society for the Blind had been to see my dad about being evacuated out of London but the old man wouldn't hear of it.

He said to the geezer that came to see him, 'Guvner, that swine ain't going to move me out of London, so you can go back to your office and tell them so.' The geezer went on to say how silly the old man was not to go and how the Germans might start to bomb London.

'It can't be worse than the last lot and I went 'arfway frew that until I copped this lot.' He meant he was blinded by an explosion on board his ship.

Well, the geezer went away but before he left he said, 'I will be back to see you again just in case you change your mind.'

'They ain't shifting me out of old London,' said my Dad when he'd gone.

In August London had its first air-raid. I took the old man and the old lady to the air-raid shelter and the next morning arfter it was all over I had a go at my Dad about being evacuated.

'They won't bomb us no more. They only done that last night to frighten us,' was all he said.

'Leave awf, Dad,' I said. 'They've blown 'arf the bleeding street away. And besides, wot is going to happen when I have to go away?'

'It will be a long time before you have to go,' he said.

'Don't you believe it. Georgi 'as gone in the army and he is only fre monfs older than me. And Fred goes in the Navy nest monf, so how long do ya fink it will be before they send for me?'

My old man had tears in his eyes when he said, 'Wot would I do in a strange place, son? I would be lost. And besides, how would me and ya muvver live away from old London? And anyway, I'm not taking charity from no one.'

'It's not charity, Dad. Everyone 'as to go.'

Poor old Mum looked up and said, 'Don't worry how we are going to live. I'll soon get a bluddy job scrubbing for someone.'

Well, the bombers came back next night wiv their deadly cargo and that was it.

'I am going to see that geezer from the Blind Society and get you and Mum and the girls out of all this,' I told the old man.

It took me a few days to get it all fixed up. The old man didn't like it but in the end he went wiv my Mum and two sisters. They were sent to a lovely seaside town called Scarborough.

When the geezer from the Blind Society told us where they were going, I said, 'Blimey, I've never heard of it.' But he assured me it was a smashing place as I was to find out later. Anyway, he said Scarborough was the only place to go to at that time.

It was a few days arfter I got the old man and the old lady fixed up that I got a letter telling me that I had to go for a medical.

'It's the first time anyone 'as even written to me,' I told the old man. And it was true. I'd never received a letter from anyone before.

I had to go on the Friday for the medical and as I went frew the door the old man said, 'Don't forget, son. Ya want to go in the Navy and don't let them palm ya awf wiv anyfing else.'

Well, when I got to the medical centre at Whipps Cross there was a hundred geezers there all stripped to the waist.

'Where do I go to join the Navy, guvner?' I said to the geezer on the door.

He looked at me and said, 'I don't fink you're big enuff,' and he laughed. Then he said, 'Go to room four.'

When I got to the room there was a big geezer sitting at a desk and he looked up abruptly and said, 'Name?' I told him my name and he took the letter from me and told me to sit down until I was called.

I sat down next to a geezer and he said, 'Ya come for a medical, mate?' I told him I had.

Arfter a while a geezer came out of a small room and shouted out, 'Henry Hollis?'

'That's me, guvner,' I said.

'Come alone, lad,' he said and I went into the room.

When I got inside there was a doctor at a table and he asked me a few questions and then he told me to strip to the waist. I done as I was told and before he started to examine me I said, 'I want to go in the Navy, guvner.'

He looked at me and said, 'You're a bit short,' and he started to examine me. Arfter he had finished he said, 'Hollis, you're as sound as a bell.'

'Well, am I in the Navy now?' I asked.

He smiled and said, 'There's more to it than that I'm afraid,' and he told me to go to anuvver geezer across the room.

I picked up my clothes wiv one hand and I walked across the

179

room to the uvver geezer. He told me to sit down and he started to look into my eyes wiv a light.

Arfter a while he said, 'That's fine, young man.'

'I want to go into the Navy, guvner,' I said.

He smiled and said, 'All right son. Go in the next room.' I fawt, *this is a right old lark going from one geezer to anuvver*.

Well, when I got in the next room there was an old bird in there wiv a white coat on. I was still holding up my trousers wiv one hand and my clothes in the uvver.

'Drop your trousers and bend over,' she said.

'Do wot?' I said, finking I was hearing fings.

'Drop your trousers,' she said, sternly this time.

Holding onto them I said, 'I ain't doing that in front of you, missus.'

She looked at me and said, 'Don't be silly. I am a doctor.'

'I don't care if ya old muvver Riley,' I said. 'I ain't doing that.'

She went to the door and I heard her say, 'We have got one of those in here,' and in walked anuvver doctor.

'Now then young man. Wot's all this about?'

'She wants me to take my trousers down and I ain't having none of that.'

He laughed and said, 'But this lady is a very good doctor.'

Well, arfter him telling me how she saw to men in the altogevver each day, I meekly let my strides down to my ankles.

She looked at my manhood wiv a big light and I fawt, *this bird sure likes an eyeful*. Then out of the blue she got hold of my cobblers and said 'Cough.' Boy, did I go red and, to put a cap on it, she said, 'Bend over,' and she looked right up my bottle wiv the light. I couldn't pull my trousers up farst enuff.

'That didn't hurt, did it?' she said, and wiv the next breff she added, 'You have passed A1.'

'Does that mean I am in the Navy?'

'That's not up to me,' she said. 'That is up to the man outside.'

Well, when I got outside, I said to the geezer, 'I want to go in the Navy or I ain't going at all.'

He laughed and said, 'Well, I'll say this for you my lad. You've got guts. Why do you want to go into the Navy?' and I told him that all my uncles had been sailors and that my Dad was a sailor.

'All right son,' he said, 'let's have a look at your card.' And I handed him the card that the lady doctor had given me.

He looked at it and said, 'You're just five foot two.'

'I know that, but wot about the Navy?' I said.

Well, he could see I had made up my mind about being in the Navy and he said, 'OK son, you will be hearing from the selection board.' And wiv that I left and walked out into the brilliant sunshine.

When I got hom I told the old man and the old lady that I had passed for the Navy. The old lady burst out crying and said, 'That's the last of me boys now.'

'Don't cry, Mum,' I said. 'I'll be OK. I can swim.'

The day came when I had to take them all to Kings Cross Station to be evacuated to Scarborough. We travelled to Kings Cross Station by underground and bus, loaded down wiv all the stuff they were allowed to take. I can remember Dad clutching his old concertina all the way to the train. We never had much to say to each uvver and I knew wot he was finking. I always knew.

I kept saying to my old mum, 'Don't worry, Mum. We will soon be togevver again,' and wiv tears running down her cheeks, she replied, 'I hope so son, I hope so.'

We said our goodbyes wiv tears and hugs and as I stood and watched the old steam train chug out of the station and out of sight I felt so alone.

When I got home, the old house was empty. The old wooden table where we had so many discussions, was scrubbed clean and the teacups were just where the old lady had left them, all neatly put away on the sideboard. I lived in the old house till my call-papers came, which was only a matter of a few days.

That night Tommy came round to ask me if I would like to go and have tea at his house, and I was only too pleased to accept. When I got there his sister Diane was there and she helped me forget the sad events of that day. I don't know if she pitied me or not but that evening, I ended up going to the dolly mixtures wiv her. I held her hand all the time but my mind wasn't on the film. I was finking of my Mum and Dad and wondering where they were at that time.

When we came out of the pictures we walked home. We stopped in the doorway of a shop and Diane said, 'Wot's wrong, Al?'

'Nuffing,' I replied. 'I am just finking of me Mum and Dad.'

'Don't worry,' she said and as she said it she took me in her arms. I just broke down and cried like a baby but I felt safe in her arms, just like a child. She was so warm and so real.

Arfter a while I said, 'Ya must fink I am a right berk acting like this.'

'You're not a berk,' she said. 'Youre one of the best.' Before I knew wot was happening I found I was kissing her, and that was the first time I ever kissed her properly.

She was so lovely that girl. I ended up taking her out a few times arfter that until I went in the Navy. As a matter of fact, Diane was my first real love.

Then it came, that letter telling me to report to the Navy at Portsmouf on 1 October 1939. Tommy was waiting to go in the Army, so on 1 October I started working for the King. Tommy and Diane saw me awf at Waterloo Station.

As I shook Tommy's hand he said, 'I'll be seeing ya, me old son.' I wanted to take Diane in my arms and hold on to her. I was longing for someone to comfort me, but wiv Tommy there I held back. As I kissed on the cheek, she said, 'Don't worry, Al. We'll soon all be togevver again.'

I got on the train wiv my old battered case and looked out of the window. There was a soldier saying goodbye to his wife. I heard her say to him, 'Come back soon, darling,' and just then the train lurched forward. I managed to wave to Tommy and Diane and she moufed somefing to me frew the winder, but I couldn't make out wot she was saying and I never found out.

In the packed train there was a lot more geezers going to the same place as I was and we soon all got talking to one anuvver. When we arrived at Portsmouf station, there was a couple of geezers waiting to meet us. We was all told to get into a big truck and then they took us to a barracks. To me it looked like a prison, wiv its big gates and its guards wiv rifles. I fawt, *wot the bleeding hell have I let meself in for?* The smallest geezer of the two who had met us from the tain was bawling his head awf.

'All right you lot, get out and fall in over there, and be quick about it. The quicker I get you in the sooner I can have my tea,' he was saying.

All the uvver geezers were out of the truth and I was the last. As I could not find my case I was looking for it.

'Oi you, ginger,' I heard him shout.

I looked up and said, 'I've lost me case.'

'Never mind ya bloody case. Get yastelf out of that truck before I put ya on a charge,' he was yelling. I fawt, *I ain't even got a fucking uniform yet and this geezer wants to put me on a bleeding charge.*

Just in the nick of time, one of the boys from the truck came up and said, 'I fink this is your case,' and he was holding up the old case that I had borrowed from Tommy. I got out of the truck and by this time the geezer was red in the face.

'Wot's your name?' he yelled at the top of his voice.

'Hollis, guvner,' I said. I fawt he was going to have a fit.

'Guvner!' he yelled. 'I am Chief Petty Officer Swain and you call me Sir or Chief.' I fawt, *I don't care if ya old King Cole. Ya ain't going to make me look a berk in front of all this mob.*

'I won't be calling ya anyfing the way you're carrying on,' I said. 'You'll 'ave a bleeding 'eart attack if ya ain't careful.' By this time all the uvver lads were grinning.

'OK. That's it. Come out here you,' he yelled, pointing at me.

I don't know wot he had in mind, but just then a tall greyhaired man came to the top of the steps leading to an office and he said, 'Come on, Chief, we haven't got all day. Let's get these men through.'

'Yes sir,' said Swain and wiv that he looked at me and said, 'I'll see you later, me lad.'

We was all called into the office one at a time as our names were called. The lad that found my old case was Scots and we became great buddies. He said to me, 'He sounds a bit of a villain don't he,' and he looked towards old Swain.

'Yus,' I said, 'but we tame villains where I come from,' and he laughed.

It was my turn to go in the office and Swain sure let me know it. He yelled at the top of his voice, 'Hollis, Henry.'

'That's me,' I said.

'Come on then and be smart about it,' he yelled, and before I knew it I was in the office.

The tall man who came out to the top of the steps was sitting at a desk wiv anuvver geezer and I noticed he had free gold rings on his sleeve.

'Wot is your name, lad?' he asked me as he looked up from some papers he had been reading.

'Hollis, guv,' I answered.

'Say sir when you address an officer, lad.' It was that geezer Swain poking his nose in again.

Before I could say 'Sir' the geezer wiv the free gold rings said, 'Thank you Chief Petty Officer. Wot was your job in civvy street?' he asked me.

'I never had a job. I worked wiv me Dad.'

'And wot did you do with your father?' he asked me.

'We went out busking togevver.'

'Busking!' he said, and wiv that the grey-headed man leant across to him and he said somefing to him.

'Oh I see,' he said, looking surprised.

'And what was your part in all this? Did you sing or something?'

'No sir,' I said, and I went on to tell him all about how the old man was blind and how we was the fird generation of buskers.

All of a sudden he became very interested and arfter I'd finished telling him he said, 'You sound a useful lad. Maybe we can use you in our concert party.'

I fanked him and as I was going out of the door he said, 'Look arfter him, Chief. He will be very useful around Christmas.' I fawt, *that's a giggle asking Swain to look arfter me. The old barsted don't even like me and I've only been on the job for two hours.* Old Swain (the old barsted) was five foot eight wiv greying brown hair, brown eyes and a red face – frew too much shouting no doubt.

The next day we all got given a uniform and the next fing tha happened was we were all to be inoculated. There ws one geezer in front of me and he was about six foot tall and we ended up calling him Lofty. Well, as soon as he saw the needle he took a flat dive on his old boat race.

I said to the Scots boy, who by this time I was calling Jock, 'Wot's the good of him? He'll shit his bleeding self if a Jerry chases him wiv a bayonet.' Mind you, come to think of it, so would I.

I came to know that Scots boy very well and soon we was inseparable. Where you saw Jock you would see me. Like me, he wasn't a big'un. he was five foot free tall with blond hair and blue eyes.

On the fird day I was given the job of sweeping the barrack room. I'd done 'arf of it and I was sitting down 'aving a bit of a blow and I faw to myself, *I know wot I'll do. I'll write a letter to the old lady and let her know where I am.* I got me writing paper out of my case and I settled down to write. I'd just finished and was just about to seal down the envelope and all hell broke loose.

'Wot the bloody hell do you fink you're doing, Hollis?' came this booming voice. There was no need to look up as I knew it was my old friend, Chief Petty Officer Swain.

Before he could say anyfing I said, 'I am writing a letter. Wot ya fink I am doing? Waiting for a bus?'

Well, he just about went mad. He started to lay the law down and he was yelling at the top of his voice.

'All right,' I said, 'don't do ya nut. Are ya potty or somefing?' Well, that done it. He exploded.

'You get this room cleaned up and you be outside the Master of Arms office at two o'clock. You're on a charge me lad.' And wiv that he steamed out of the room saying somefing under his breff. I fawt, *Cobblers to ya*.

When Jock came in for lunch I told him all about it.

'Wot can they do to you?' he said.

'I don't know,' I replied. 'They seem to have a lot of funny ideas. They fink this barracks is a ship. When they let ya go outside the gates they call it going ashore. If ya ask me, Jock, I fink they're all potty.'

At two o'clock I was outside the Master of Arms office and there was two uvver geezers there waiting to be called.

'Are you on a charge mate?' I said to one of them. He nodded so I said, 'So am I.'

He looked at me and said, 'Ya better not go in there wiv those overalls on. They'll go mad and you'll be on anuvver charge.'

'Wot ya supposed to wear then.' I asked him.

'Full rig,' said the uvver geezer who was standing there, 'and if I was you I would go back to your barrack room and get changed like us.'

Before I could make up my mind wot to do there he was, the mouf himself, Chief Petty Officer Swain. He had more mouf than a cow 'as udders.

'Wot the bloody 'ell are you doing in those overalls?' he yelled at me.

'Ya never told me I had to wear me sailor's suit. All ya told me was to be here at two o'clock.'

'Suit? Wot the bloody hell at ya talking about, lad? You mean the King's uniform.' I fawt, *how the fuck can it be the King's when it belongs to me?*

'I'll tell you wot you're going to do, my lad. You're going back to your mess and you are going to change into your uniform and you are going to be back here in fifteen minutes,' he said.

I fawt, *you've got some hopes. It's five minutes there and back and I've got five minutes to get ponced up*.

Arfter one big rush I finally got back to the office. Old big mouf was still inside wiv one of the uvver lads that was outside

185

when I first arrived. I waited for a few minutes and out came this lad.

'Watch it,' he said, 'he's in a right old mood that old barsted in there. I've just got seven days confined to Barracks.' I fawt, *If he got seven days CB for just walking across the parade ground, I'll get bleeding life for writing a letter.*

'Right, lad. When you get inside come smartly to attention, off cap and give your name and number to the officer of the watch,' said old Swain.

Well, I went as smartly as I knew how and came to attention dropping my cap in the process. There was anuvver petty officer and an officer wiv two gold rings on his sleeve.

'Name and number lad,' said the uvver petty officer.

'Holls PJX3 . . . er . . .' All of a sudden I couldn't remember my number.

'Come on lad, wot's your number?' said the petty officer.

'I know it's free somefing,' I said.

'How long have you been in the Navy, Hollis?' asked the officer.

'Free days, sir.'

'Three days and you are in trouble already. What is the charge, petty officer?'

'I caught this man writing a letter in working hours, sir,' said old Swain.

'Don't you know you are not to write letters in the working period?'

'I didn't know I couldn't write a letter, sir,' I replied.

'Who was this letter to?' he asked.

'To my muvver sir,' I said.

'Was it important?'

'Well, sir, she doesn't know where I am, so I fawt I would write and let her know and I'd just finished when he came into the room shouting his head awf at me.'

'You mean Chief Petty Officer Swain.'

'That's right, sir,'

'You don't address a Chief Petty Officer as "him". You address him as Chief Petty Officer, do you understand?' he said.

'Yus sir,' I replied.

There was a few moments silence while the officer looked at the paper on his desk. Then he looked up and said, 'As you have only been wiv us for a few days and you are not used to our ways

186

yet, I am going to overlook the matter and hope I never see you in front of me again, do you understand?'

'Yes sir,' I said.

'All right. You can go, and if I was you, young man, I would learn your number off by heart or when it comes to pay day you'll get no pay, will you?' he said.

'No sir,' I said. And wiv that I was marched out of the office by Chief Petty Officer Swain.

When we got outside old Swain said, 'You should think yourself lucky, lad. If you had been in the Navy for a couple of monfs you would have been in for it.'

'Yus chief,' I said.

'Now go about your work and don't let me catch you out of line again,' he said, and that was my first test of the Navy. Six weeks later I was a full-blown sailor, or at least they said I was.

We had all finished our training and we was all given fourteen days leave. I spent my leave wiv the old folk and my two sisters in Scarborough and it took me a full day to get there. When I finally found the place where they was living I was just about all in wiv all the travelling.

My old Mum shed a few tears when she saw me standing at the door. Arfter a while when we all settled down, Mum was telling Dad how nice I looked in my uniform. Arfter we all had supper, me and the old man sat down and had a long chat. I could tell he wasn't happy about being away from London and not being able to earn his own living. I told him not to worry as it would soon be all over and we could all return to dear old London and we could go out to work and meet all our old punters. But I knew by the look on his face that he knew uvverwise.

I had a nice time wiv the family and then it was time for me to go back. They all saw me awf at the station. The old lady cried a little and when I shook the old man's hand I felt him grip my arm wiv the uvver hand.

'I'll keep my old strill (musical instrument) in trim,' he said and I could 'ear by the quivering tone of his voice that his old heart was breaking inside.

'I'll see ya, Dad,' I said and I got on the train. As it pulled out of the station and I was at the window waving goodbye I felt like saying, 'Fuck the Navy,' and I wanted to get awf of that train and say to the old man, 'Come on, Dad. Let's go Joegering.' But like millions of uvvers I had to do my bit for King and Country.

187

When I got back to Portsmouf I saw Jock getting awf of the same train as I did from London.

'You must have been on the same train as I was,' he said.

'How come?' I asked.

'Well the train from Edinburgh stops at York and you must have got the same train and you had to change at York for the London train.'

He told me wot a good time he had wiv his family and how he didn't want to come back and when I told him I felt the same way, we had a good laugh and before we knew it we was back in the barracks.

'Can you imagine old Swain's face if we didn't turn up from leave?' I said. 'He would just about go potty wiv happiness. He is just waiting to get me in front of the guvner, the old barsted. I know he don't like me. If he starts having a go at me now I am back I will end up giving him one.'

'You can't do that,' said Jock, 'you'll end up getting life in the glasshouse.'

Arfter that first leave, fings seemed to settle down and I began getting used to the ways of the Navy. I said to Jock one morning when we was on parade, 'If ya stand next to me we will get detailed awf for the same working party,' and it worked out just as I said. We were both detailed for the same job togevver.

As the PO came along the line he said, 'You two – chapel cleaning.' I gave a little smile to myself as chapel cleaning was one of the best jobs in the barracks.

When we got in the chapel I said, 'There you are, me old son. I told ya, if ya stick wiv me we'll end up owning this bloody Navy.' There wasn't much to do in the chapel, only a spot of dusting as it was only used on Sundays, so once we had finished we sat down and had a laugh and a joke (smoke).

'Ya know wot, me old son,' I said. 'We could get this job regular.'

'How come's that?' asked Jock.

'Well all we have to do when the PO comes down the line to pick out the working parties is for me to say "chapel cleaners, sir".'

'He won't stand for that,' said Jock.

'He will if we have buckets and brooms wiv us.'

'Where the bloody hell are we going to get buckets and brooms from?' asked Jock in his broad Scottish accent.

'Easy, just leave that part of it to me.' I knew where there was buckets and brooms kept, just behind the door outside the PO's office, so arfter we finished our work I told Jock of my plan.

Well, I got two brooms and two buckets. The only fing was that the buckets had painted on them in red paint 'PO's Office'.

'We can't use those wiv that mark on them,' Jock said.

'Wot's stopping us from taking the marks awf and painting on them "chapel"?' I said.

'You'll never do it,' was his reply.

'You watch me.' I told him to go and get our teas while I got the buckets and brooms organised and that I would see him in the mess later on.

'We will be in a right old mess if this scheme of yours don't work,' he said.

'Don't worry me, old son. I've never let ya down yet, have I?' I said to him.

Awf I went to the carpenters shop. I said to one of the boys who was working there, 'Hey mate. Have ya got any sandpaper I can have?'

I couldn't have asked a better geezer. He turned out to be one of me own, a cockney. he was called Frank Swaby.

'Whereabouts do you come from up the smoke me old son?' Frank asked me. And when I told him he put out his hand and said, 'Put it there. I come out of Bowen Street,' (awf of Chris Street in the market).

'Fuck me,' I said. 'I know a few geezers who live in Bowen Street,' and I mentioned a few names of some of the lads he also knew.

'Wot job did ya do on civvy street?' he asked. And when I told him he said 'Ya ain't the geezer who used to go round the bevvies wiv the old blind man, are ya?' And when I told him that I was he said, 'That's funny, my old man knows your old man. They call your dad Blind Bill, don't they?'

'Yes,' I said.

'Fuck me, it's a small world ain't it me son,' he said picking his nose. 'Now wot is it ya want? Ya can have anyfing in the bleeding shop.'

Well, I told him all about my scheme and we ended up having a laugh about it.

'You leave it to me, me old son, and I will make a proper job of it for ya,' he said. 'Ya see, I've got the proper stencils. If ya going to pull a stroke like that ya want it to look right, don't ya.'

'Good on ya, me old son,' I said. Arfter about an hour he had finished the job and ya couldn't tell the difference.

The next day me and old Jock was on parade wiv our buckets and brooms and as the Petty Officer walked along the line, picking out the working parties, he came to me, and before he could say a word I said, 'Chapel cleaners, sir,' and at the same time I made sure he saw the buckets and brooms, and wivout batting an eyelid he said, 'OK, off you go.'

Me and old Jock laughed all the way to the chapel and our little scheme worked like a charm. We had the job for the next nine monfs. Our routine was to do a bit of cleaning and dusting in the morning and in the afternoon arfter lunch we would have a sleep behind the altar. We even bought an alarm clock between us so as we could wake up when it was time to knock awf.

I remember the time when Jock picked an argument wiv a big Frenchman. I couldn't tell ya wot it was about or the way it started: all I know was the Frenchman ended up minus his Hamstead Heaf (teef).

Ya see, all the gunners in the Navy carry their gas masks slung low on their shoulder so Jock and me were no exception. I had my gas mask hanging from my shoulder when the argument started.

'Forget it,' I said to Jock. 'We will end up getting nicked and put in the chokey.' But this big Frenchman wasn't having any.

'You fucking Englishmen are no fucking good,' he said and wiv that he spat right in Jock's boat race.'

Well, I done no more. I pushed Jock to one side and as I did so I let the strap of my gas mask slip from my shoulder and I caught it wiv my hand and I gave it one almighty swing and 'it this Froggy full in the norf and souf and there was blood and Hamsteads everywhere. The Froggy screamed like a pregnant elephant. The next fing I saw was two coppers coming across the road to see wot it was all about.

'Johnalderly, ya Jaggs doie bald omes,' I said to Jock, forgetting Jock didn't know the busker's language. So before he knew it I was away up the toby (road) wiv Jock behind me. We dived in the nearest bevvy until it was closing time. The fights that Jock got me into was nobody's business. The funny fing about it was we were both only five foot two nuffing. It's a wonder we both didn't get killed by some of the big'uns he picked on.

Chapter Ten
Adolf gives me that sinking feeling (and a wife)

One day we got the buzz that there was a big draft to be made up for one of the aircraft carriers and that it was going to the Middle East.

'I don't want none of that Middle East lark,' I said to Jock. 'I want to stay in England so I can be near my old Mum and Dad if anyfing happens.

One day I was in the carpenters' shop talking to my old mate Frank from Bowen Street and I told him about the draft.

'If ya don't fancy it, Harryboy, ya want to volunteer for somefing else,' he said.

When I told Jock wot he had said, Jock said, 'I know, mine sweepers.'

'Bleeding mine sweepers?' I said.

'Why not?' he replied. 'Ya only go out to sea a few days at a time and the rest of the time you're in harbour.'

Well it sounded OK and when I told Frank he said, 'It ain't a bad idea. There's one good fing about it. Ya won't get sent overseas, will ya? But on the uvver hand, if them Jerries catch ya sweeping the Norf Sea, Gawd help ya. They'll knock ten buckets of shit out of ya.'

'Well, it's better than going overseas for a couple of bleeding years, ain't it?' I replied.

So we ended up volunteering for training for mine sweepers.

Arfter a few weeks training we was transferred to Lowestoft on the East Coast to make up the crew of a mine sweeper. Before we left Portsmouth I ended up having anuvver run in wiv old Swain and getting seven days CB. But I still had the last laugh on the old barsted, for as we was leaving in the back of the lorry on our way to the station for Lowestoft, he jammed his hand in the tailboard of the lorry. He was on guard at the main gate and it was his job to inspect all vehicles entering and leaving the barracks.

191

When he saw me in the back of the lorry wiv the rest of the lads he said, 'Seeing that you're aboard Hollis, I'd better have a good look in here. You might have next week's wages in there.'

All the lads laughed and I said, 'Ya got to say somefing ain't ya, big mouf.'

He replied that it was a good job I was being transferred or he would put me on a fizzer for being cheeky and wiv that he slammed the tailboard catching his hand in it. He went as red as the Soviet flag and called me all the barsteds under the sun. The lorry drove out of the gates wiv yours truly laughing his head awf and old Swain shaking his fist at me and yelling at the top of his voice how he would get me the next time he saw me.

I put two fingers up and shouted, 'Up ya, ya old barsted.'

'I wouldn't like to be in your shoes if he catches up with you, you cockney barsted,' said Jock.

Before we left Portsmouf I ended up selling the buckets and brooms to two of our mates for two pounds and I told them how to go about the job. Me and old Jack went out on the beer wiv the two nicker the night before we left.

I shall never forget the first time I set eyes on that old minesweeper. 'It looks like somefing out of the bleeding ark,' I said to Jock.

'It is the bloody Ark,' he replied.

'It must be fifty years old if it's a bleeding day,' I said.

As a matter of fact we ended up nicknaming her The Ark.

The skipper was a toff and he knew how to treat the boys. He had been a trawler skipper before the war and he knew the Norf Sea like the back of his hand. He was always concerned about the crew. The crew consisted of Chief Petty Officer Webber, four stokers, two leading seamen, six ordinary seamen, and an overworked cook. Sometimes one of the boys would take a turn of cooking.

Chief Petty Officer Webber came from the West Country. He was as round as a barrel wiv a rosy red face, and he loved the Cockneys, so you can guess I got on wiv him like a house on fire. He had been in the Navy since he was a boy, and he knew all the tricks of the trade.

One day I said to Jock, 'Ya know wot Jock, it's the best idea I've had yet, getting us transferred to this old tub.'

'Piss awf, it was my idea,' said Jock looking me straight in the eyes.

'I don't care who's blessing idea it was but it was a good move getting away from that old barsted Swain,' I replied.

Well, we settled down in that old tub and we looked upon her as home. The rest of the crew turned out to be a great bunch of boys, and when we wasn't at sea we had some grand times togevver. Apart from Jock I became great pals with Geordie, a tall Newcastle lad wiv brown eyes. We all drank in the same boozer when we went ashore and there was one of the locals who used to play an old piano that stood in the corner of the bar. We had some right old sing-songs. All the lads would sing a song in turn. Jock's favourite was, 'I belong to Glasgow'. I used to shout out to him, 'Get down ya old ponce, you came from Edinburgh.'

One night it was Chief Petty Officer Webber's birfday and we got him as drunk as a brewer's cart horse and he ended up doing a strip in the middle of the bar. He was right down to his underpants when the landlord stepped in and stopped him. All the boys booed and shouted, but no way was the landlord going to let him go any furver. We got him dressed the best we could and took him back to the ship.

When we told him the next day wot he had done, he said, 'I will never be able to hold my head up in Lowestoft again.'

The next time we went into the boozer the landlord said, 'Here chief, here's something for you,' and he handed the old chief his vest. Poor old Chief Webber went as red as a beetroot and all the boys gave him a big cheer. Arfter a few rums he had forgotten all about the strip tease the night before and he was singing like a good'un.

Lowestoft was such a different place to the red tape of Portsmouf. One cold December arfternoon we left harbour at about four o'clock and the wind was blowing and it was ice-cold. It seemed to go right frew ya clothing. We were about four hours out at sea and I had just come awf of the bridge arfter doing my watch. I went down to the mess and as I passed the galley I got a mug of steaming tea awf of the cook.

When I got into the mess Jock said to me, 'More bleeding tea?'

'Ya bleeding need it arfter coming awf that bridge. It's like a fucking ice box up there,' I replied.

Arfter I drank my tea, I said to Jock, 'Oh well, I fink I'll take a shower and get a good scrub down.' That was the only fing good about that old tub, the Navy had fitted it out wiv a nice shower.

I had finished my shower and I was stripped to the waist arfter putting on my trousers and seaboots and I was in the process of drying my hair when it happened. At around eight o'clock there was an almighty explosion and the old tub shook from stem to stern. I fawt to myself *God, wot 'as 'appened*?

I made my way to the stairway leading to the upper deck. The first bloke I saw coming towards me was Chief Petty Officer Webber.

'For God's sake son, get on top,' he shouted at me, and before I could ask wot was wrong, the skipper was shouting frew a megaphone at the crew to abandon ship. I had no time to return to the mess for my tin helmet and oil skin. By the time I got on deck I had pulled my jumper over my head. I could see the skipper out of the corner of my eye shouting at the top of his voice frew the megaphone. Then a voice behind me shouted, 'For God's sake lad, get those seaboots off. You won't stand a chance in that swell.'

I must have broken all records in taking them heavy seaboots awf. I looked up once more at the bridge and I could see the skipper counting the boys as they went over the side, and all at once I had joined them. As I struck the ice-cold water it seemed as though my guts had been tied in a knot. As I came to the surface I could see a dinghy bobbing up and down in the swell about twelve yards away from me.

The next fing I knew I was swimming towards the dinghy. The freezing water had brought me back to my senses. I could make out there was about five blokes in the dinghy waving their arms at me. As I reached the dinghy, I could see two hands stretched out to me and someone shouted, 'It's Cockney.'

I gripped the outstretched hand and found myself being pulled from the cruel sea. The first face I saw that greeted me was Jock's. I was so cold I couldn't speak. We just cuddled up to each uvver. He put his arms around me and I wanted to crack a joke and say somefing like, 'Shall we go steady, darling?' but it just couldn't come out of my chattering mouth.

I looked back at the old tub and I could see smoke bellowing out of the paint locker, then the hatch of the paint locker blew awf and there was flames about forty foot high and they seemed to light up the whole of the Norf Sea.

We all lay in shocked silence there and watched the old tub go down to her resting place at the bottom of the sea. One minute the whole area was lit up and the next there was complete darkness. I shall never forget the way that old tub went down. It was as though I was losing a part of me.

There was no heroes that night. There was no one singing 'Land of Hope and Glory.' We were all shit-scared. The cold was now biting right frew to my bones and everywhere was as black as coal. One lad began to vomit all over the inside of the dinghy. I don't know if it was nerves or the amount of water he had swallowed when he went over the side of the old tub.

In the darkness a voice said, 'Are you all right, mate?' and the lad who had been vomiting replied, 'Yea, mate. I think I have swallowed harf the bloody North Sea,' and it was just those few words that started us all talking. Someone else said, 'I wonder what 'as happened to the uvver lads. Do you fink they got off all right?' and someone else was asking wot happened. But no one seemed to know.

'I fink we hit one,' said the lad who had been vomiting.

'No, I don't fink so,' said Jock. 'If we had we wouldn't be here now. It's more like that we've been tin fished (torpedoed). What do you fink, Al?'

'All I know is I am breaking my neck for a piss and I am so bleeding cold I fink it would be impossible to find my bleeding cock,' I said, and that seemed to cheer them up a bit.

Then one of the lads said, 'Does anyone know the time?' I fawt, *Wot the bleeding hell does the geezer want to know the time for? 'as he got a bleeding train to catch?* We was tossed about for hours and it seemed like years. All frew the night the wind blew and the biting cold was unbearable. Sleep was out of the question so we just lay there staring into the darkness. I fink that was the longest night I have ever known.

As I lay in the dinghy being tossed about like a cork, my mind wandered to the old folk and my two sisters in Scarborough. I prayed to myself and fanked God that they were safe and tucked up in their warm beds. A lump came to my froat as I lay there and fawt of my old Dad and how a year or so back he was happy going on his rounds busking. I fawt of all the boozers we used to work and of all the old customers he knew in them. I fawt of Georgi and Fred and wondered where they were at that moment and I prayed to God that they weren't going frew wot I was going frew at that time. Then I fawt of my lovely Diane. I fawt how lovely it would be to feel her arms around me and to feel the warmf of her body so close to mine to keep out this stinking cold, and then I fawt, *'Suppose I don't ever see her again?* I loved her

195

so very much at that moment and my chest felt heavy where my 'art was longing for her. I wanted to shout, 'Please Di, please help me, please help me,' and then I felt warm tears running down my cheeks and I was so afraid of wot lay ahead for us. I wondered if the old house in London was still standing. I don't know if I dozed awf at that moment or not but I seemed to lose myself. And then I found myself saying, 'Oh God, when will it all end?'

'Did you say somefing, Al?' Jock said.

'No mate,' I replied, 'I am too fucking cold to speak.'

We watched the dawn come up and I licked my lips, but all I got was the taste of salt. I would at that moment had given anyfing for a hot drink of some sorts. Fings seemed to be a bit better in daylight and the wind had died down but there was still a swell on. As I lay there and looked round at the uvver lads in the dinghy I fawt, *Wot a sorry looking lot we are*.

Arfter about an hour the sea seemed to be a lot calmer. Then, all of a sudden, someone screamed: 'There's a ship. It's a bloody ship, I tell you.' It was Geordie the stoker and he was yelling at the top of his voice.

We all looked in the direction he was pointing and saw it for the first time. It seemed a million miles away and I wanted to go down on my knees and give fanks to God.

'Let's all wave,' someone said. 'They are bound to see us.' The next fing I knew I was grasping Jock's hand and as we looked at each uvver, I could see the tears rolling down his cheeks.

I took him in my arms like a child and said, 'It'll be all right now, me old son. They'll see us,' and he was crying like a baby.

'Here we are, you barsteds,' Geordie was shouting. 'Come and get us.' All the lads was waving and shouting for dear life. And then I heard it.

'Listen,' I shouted, and we all seemed to look up into the sky, and there it was coming towards us.

'It's a bleeding Jerry,' said one of the boys.

I fawt, *Oh God no*, and one of the uvver lads said, 'No it ain't. It'a flying boat.' I knew then we was safe.

I looked at Jock and said, 'There ya are, me old son. I told ya we would be OK.' As for the rest of the lads, some was crying and some was laughing and screaming.

The plane few over us a few times and each time he got lower until we could see the man inside. He seemed to be flapping his wings each time he flew over us. A few minutes later he was heading towards the ship and we watched the plane getting smaller and then he came back and flew above us for wot seemed like ages. All the time the ship was coming nearer, and before we knew it we was all climbing up the rope nets that had been lowered over the side.

It was a Corvette that picked us up after our twelve hours of fear in the sea.

As I got to the top of the rope net, a voice said, 'Give us ya hand, son.' I gripped that hand for dear life and was pulled onto the deck. As I reached the deck someone slung a big fick blanket around my shoulders and then I found myself being lifted up into someone's arms. I can never describe the feeling I got when I felt those arms around me if I live to be an 'undred.

An hour later we was in the ship's sick bay and provided wiv dry clothes and a big mug of hot rum and we were told to drink as much hot tea as we wanted. Later we found out that the Corvette had been searching for us all night long. It seemed that our old skipper had got a mayday call out over the wireless before the old tub went down.

As I lay in my bunk that night, I had made up my mind that the Navy had had it wiv me. No way was I going to go frew anyfing like that again.

The captain of the Corvette came to see us and had statements taken from all of us as the Admiralty would want to know what happened. We all told him wot we knew and he told us to relax and get rested up.

It was around midday when he came back into the sick bay.

'Don't get up lads,' he said. 'I have some good news and some bad news to tell you.' We all listened to wot he had to say.

'First of all,' he went on, 'your captain and some more of your lads have been picked up, but there is still two of your crew unaccounted for, but we are still searching for them.

We all seemed to shoot questions at him at once. Someone asked who was missing and someone else wanted to know wot had happened. All he could say was, 'I can't tell you yet.'

As he left to go out he turned round and said, 'By the way, I will be putting you ashore at Great Yarmouf. I fawt, *I couldn't give two monkeys' bollocks where ya drop us as long as we are safe*. It was around free o'clock that arfernoon we reached Great Yarmouf on the English East Coast.

As we pulled in the quay at Great Yarmouf the door of the sick bay opened and one of the attendants said, 'Come on lads, you're home.' As we all walked unsteadily from the sick bay, the Captain was watching us from the bridge. I wanted to go up to him and shake him by the hand and say, 'Fanks, mate,' but ya don't do fings like that in the Navy.

As we all walked down the gangway to the naval ambulance that had been waiting for us, we were cheered by the onlookers. A few fishermen came forward to help us into the ambulance. People was shouting, 'Good luck boys,' and someone patted me on the back and said, 'All the best, chum.' As we got into the ambulance and drove away, people were waving.

'There ya are, me old son,' I said to Jock. 'You're a fucking hero.'

They sent us to a civvy hospital in the town and by the time we reached it we were all back to our old selves.

'We could get a bit of leave out of this lot,' one of the lads said.

'Piss awf,' said old Geordie, the stoker, 'you've got some bluddy hopes.'

'Wot do we have to do to get leave in this man's bluddy navy?' I said. 'Get fucking drowned every time ya want bleeding leave?' They all laughed.

'I don't know,' said one of the uvver lads. 'My hoppo (mate) got sunk and arfter he came out of sick bay he got fourteen days' leave.' 'Aye that's right,' said Jock. 'I've heard of that meself.'

'Leave awf,' I said. 'Wiv our bleeding luck we will all end up in chokey for not bringing the old tub back. I'll tell ya one fing me old son,' I added to Jock. 'If I get any blooming leave it will be the last the bleeding navy is going to see of me.'

'Wot do ya mean, Al?' he asked.

'Wot ya fink I bleeding mean? I am going to piss awf and I am not coming back.' Jock looked at me as if I had two heads.

'They'll bleeding shoot ya if they get hold of ya,' Geordie butted in.

'They will have to get me first,' I said. 'Besides I'd sooner be shot than go frew that fucking lot again.' There was silence. Then Geordie said to the lad who first brought up the subject of leave. 'How long was your hoppo in hospital for?'

'I don't think he was in for more than a week. All I know was he got fourteen days' leave when he was discharged from hospital.' he said.

'Well let's hope they keep us in for a week. I could do with a bit of leave. My old woman must be getting a bit fruity. I haven't seen her for five months,' said Geordie.

That night, arfter a day of tests and doctors examining us, we was all tucked up in nice clean beds. i lay there in the dark and my mind drifted to the two boys that was missing and I prayed to God to let them be safe and sound.

The next morning we all saw the doctor again, and he asked me if there was anyfing I wanted.

'There is only one fing I want, Doc,' I said, 'and that's a few days leave.'

Wiv that he smiled and said, 'That is not up to me, that is up to the Admiralty, but I'll see wot I can do.'

As I left the room where I had just seen the doctor, I saw Jock waiting outside and he pushed a newspaper into my hand and said, 'Look Al, we're bloody heroes.' I read the front page and screaming from the paper was the headlines. "CREW OF MINE-SWEEPER PLUCKED FROM THE CRUEL SEA'.

'That's a bloody lot of good,' I said. As I read on I learned that the rest of the crew had been picked up – all but two. The story went on to say that they were still searching for them but there was little hope.

'Who do ya fink is missing, Jock?' I asked.

'I don't know but maybe we will get some news later on today.'

When we got back to the ward, all the rest of the boys were sitting round a big fire at the end of the ward and Jock and I went to join them.

Geordie looked up from the paper he was reading and said, 'I wonder where the rest of the boys are?' and wiv that a little old geezer who was sitting in an armchair, that looked as though it was about to swallow him up, said, 'They may have taken them to anuvver hospital.' I fawt, *Ya silly old sod. That's brilliant, that is. Course they've gawn to anuvver hospital or they would be here wiv the rest of us.*

'I am glad they have brought us here instead of taking us to a military hospital,' one of the lads said.

It was free days before we learned the full story of wot happened. It seemed there was an explosion in the engine room and that the two boys that went down wiv the ship were a leading stoker and an ordinary stoker. Wot led to the explosion we never knew, but I always said to Jock, 'One of these days this old barsted is going to split herself wide open.'

The rest of the crew were picked up and taken to Lowestoft. We spent a week in that civvy hospital and all the time we were there we were treated like royalty. After the week was up we were sent back to Lowestoft where we met the rest of the crew and we all swapped stories of wot happened. The following Sunday we all went to church for a memorial service for the two boys that went down. As I stood in the church I vowed to myself that I would never end my days at the bottom of the sea.

Five days later we were all sent back to our home base which was Portsmouf, for redrafting. As we went frew the gates of Portsmouf barracks, I said to Jock, 'Ain't it fucking marvellous, of all the sodding places to go to it 'ad to be here where that barsted Swain is.'

'Cheer up, Cockney,' said Geordie, 'perhaps they have sent the old barsted on draft.'

'Leave awf, Geordie,' I said, 'wiv my luck I'll probably end up in the same duty watch as the old barsted.'

We had no sooner got to the main office and got the lorry unloaded when he appeared. One of the lads said, 'Hold tight, Cockney, here comes your mate.' And wiv that I looked up and there he was, the mouf himself. When he saw me he just didn't know wot to say.

'Oh no, not you,' he said pushing his cap to the back of his head. Before he could say anuvver word I stepped forward and stuck out my folk (hand) and said, 'How ya going, Chief?'

He could do no more but shake my hand. Ya see I caught him awf guard. He dropped my hand like hot shit.

'I don't want no bovver from you,' he yelled. 'I've got enuff to put up wiv around here,' and wiv that he stormed awf into the office.

'If I was you, Cockney, I'd stay clear of him,' Geordie was saying.

'Ya know wot, Geordie, I fink ya got somefing there, me old son,' I said.

We all got settled into the mess that we were allocated to and then we did the usual routine of having our paybooks stamped and seeing the MO. The next day we were all given fourteen days' survivors' leave. Jock travelled wiv me on the same train and I left him at York. As I shook him by the hand, I said, 'Well, mate, I don't expect I will see you again.' The look on his face was one of surprise.

'What the bluddy hell do ya mean, man?' he was asking.

'Just that. I ain't coming back and that's that.' He was saying somefing like: 'Don't be a bluddy fool man, they will shoot ya when they get hold of ya.'

'They will have to get me first,' I said. Just then his train began to move out. I didn't know wot the future held for me then as I watched him waving to me until he was out of sight.

My two sisters were waiting for me at Scarborough station when I got awf of the train as I had sent my old mum a telegram saying I would be home that day. Arfter the greetings were over on the station, my eldest sister, Lily, told me that they were now living in a nice flat over the top of a shop. My youngest sister Rene asked how long I was home for. I didn't answer her question.

When I got home the old lady and the old man was indoors. Arfter mum had dried her eyes and fings settled down, Mum told me how she came to rent the flat. I did not tell them of the past events as I did not want to worry them. Besides, that sort of fing is best forgotten. Dad seemed to be settled down and I fink he knew in his heart that he would never again walk the streets of London playing his old concertina.

At tea that night, Dad looked up and said, 'How long are you home for son?' I didn't know wot to say. I just said the first fing that came into my head.

'Oh, they are going to send me a telegram if they want me,' I replied. I knew then I wasn't fooling the old man. He didn't say anyfing. He just went on eating his tea. Arfter my fourteen days' leave was over I was still at home. On the fifteenf day I knew I was in trouble

One night about four weeks later while I was having a drink wiv the old man in a pub, he said, 'Why don't ya want to go back?' I didn't know wot to say to him.

'Ya know you're in bad trouble don't ya, son?' he said. 'They will be coming to look for ya.'

All of a sudden I blurted out, 'No, they won't. They don't know where I live.'

'Don't talk silly, son,' said my Dad, 'they will have your address from the book you allow your muvver to draw money on.'

'Well I ain't going back on my own,' I said. 'If they want me they will have to come and get me.'

And get me they did. It must have been about two monfs arfter we spoke about it in the boozer that I was in the bedroom laying on the bed playing wiv my sister Lily's baby, when there was a bang on the door. Dad went down to open the door to find

201

out who it was, and just as he opened the door there was a big scuffle and I heard the old man saying, 'Wot's going on?'

There must have been eight of the barsteds. They had crowbars and all sorts. One of them had pushed the old man over and, as I reached the top of the stairs, I could see my Dad trying to get up. I saw red and went for them. 'Ya fucking barsteds,' I shouted, 'Can't ya see he is blind?' I kicked out for all I was worf but I had no chance. I was captured.

There was an inspector and four coppers. The inspector turned out to be a good guy. They took, me back upstairs to the living room and the inspector was saying how sorry he was as he did not know the old man was blind. Poor old mum was crying her eyes out.

'Don't worry, mum, they can't shoot me,' I said and before I knew where I was, I was outside and in a car on my way to the local nick to await an escort to come and take me back to Portsmouf.

That night Mum and the old man came to see me in the police station. Mum kept saying wot a silly boy I was and how I was in bad trouble. The inspector came in and said that I would be going back to Portsmouf the following day as there was an escort on the way up to take me back.

I said goodbye to the old folk and the next morning, at around ten o'clock, I heard someone say, 'Where is the little barsted?' I fawt, *I know that voice*. It was Geordie. he had been picked to be one of the escorts. A copper opened the cell door and in walked Geordie.

'Cockney, you are a no-good barsted,' he said wiv a big smile.

The leading seaman in charge of the escort produced a pair of handcuffs from his pocket.

'There's no need for them,' said Geordie, 'he ain't no criminal. He is only a few days over leave.'

'OK Geordie,' said the leading seaman, 'if you trust him it's OK by me.'

'Fanks mate, I don't want to be seen wearing those bleeding fings,' I said.

By the time I got back to Portsmouf I was feeling lousy. I fawt I was getting a right old cold. We got back into barracks late that night, and just before we got to the gates, the leading seaman put the handcuffs on me and he said, 'If anyone asks if you have been sackled (handcuffed) all the way, say yes.'

'OK mate, fanks,' I said.

As luck had it, old Swain wasn't there to see me arrive, but when I got into the office, the Master at Arms was a right old barsted. He started to lay down the law and he was shouting at the top of his voice.

I fawt, *You're fucking mad you, ya silly old barsted*. He ended up by saying 'We have places for blokes like you.' I was put in a big room wiv about five uvver geezers and I found out that they had all done the same as me. I fawt, *I am not the only one then, am I*?

By the morning I could hardly breeve and the sweat was pouring awf of me and it felt as though I had a hammer banging inside my head. Around ten o'clock, we were all marched over to go in front of the captain in charge of the barracks. They made us double march all the way across the parade ground and I could hardly keep up wiv the rest.

One by one we were each called in to see the Captain and as each of the lads came out they were telling the uvvers wot sentence they had got.

'What did you get, mate?' I said to one lad next to me who had just come out.

'Twenty-eight days in Kingston,' he replied. 'Where the bleeding hell is Kingston?' I asked. He was just about to tell me that Kingston was a naval detention centre when the petty officer in charge shouted 'Keep quiet, that man,' pointing to the young lad.

As I waited my turn to go into the office, I fawt I was going to die. I was leaning against the wall and I could 'ear someone saying, 'Wot's the matter with you man, are you drunk?' I tried to tell him I was ill, but before I could get it out it was my turn to go in.

Someone was shouting out my name and number, and someone else was shouting 'Double march.' But all the time it seemed as though they were calling from miles away.

I stood in the captain's office, the sweat running awf of me. He asked me if I had anyfing to say, and I replied, 'No.'

The next fing I heard him say was, 'Ninety days' detention.'

I left the office wivout a word as I could not be bovvered. When we all got back to the Master-at-Arms' office, we were told to get our kit, and each of us was sent to our mess under escort to get the rest of our stuff. I was just about all in, but I was determined not to let them see I was ill.

Arfter lunch we were all waiting to be taken to Kingson. While

I was waiting by the door, old Swain came in. He took one look at me and said, 'I told you you wouldn't amount to nothing, didn't I, Hollis?' I fawt, *Piss awf, ya old barsted*.

He was saying somefing else but I could not 'ear him. he seemed to be a million miles away. I then heard a voice shouting, 'Pick up ya kit and get fell in here.' I followed the rest of the lads and then I found myself climbing up into a truck, handcuffed to anuvver lad. They closed the tailboard of the truck and it drove out of the gates.

We arrived at Kingston Detention barracks around free that arfternoon. I couldn't see wot it looked like as the truck was frew the gates and the gates were slammed arfter us. Then it started – all hell broke loose. There was a chief petty officer in naval uniform wiv white gaiters and white belt carrying a truncheon and from his side there was a chain wiv a big bunch of keys on it.

He locked the gates arfter us and shouted, 'Right, all in, sir.' At that moment anuvver petty officer came out of an office just inside the gate shouting, 'Fall in here,' and he pointed to a white line painted on the ground. We all fell in line and he shouted, 'Right, pick up your kit.' We all picked up our kit. Then he shouted 'Double march.' He then lead us to anuvver gate that lead to the inside of the main building.

When we got to the gate he said, 'Double march on the spot.' We were still double marching when we got inside the building and the sight that greeted me next I shall never forget. There was a centre ring wiv all little cells branching awf and the place was spotless. Everyfing was gleaming white. Even the banisters leading up to the landings were shining. I found out later that they were polished every morning wiv emery paper.

We were still double-marching when out of a small room came a warrant officer. The petty officer in charge of us shouted, 'Prisoners halt.' I fawt *Fank God for that. I would never have been able to keep it up much longer.* The officer told us to turn out our kit and put it in a nice pile as shown on a board he gave us. Then he gave us a pep talk saying, 'This is the house of correction and I am the master as well as all the other officers here, and before you leave this place we will turn you into men.' Wot I fawt of him at that moment, I could never describe.

He then read out the diet. I could 'ear him say, 'You will receive four ounces of ship's biscuits for breakfast and a mug of tea wiv porridge, and for dinner you will get soup and four ounces of ship's biscuits, and for tea you will get four ounces of ship's biscuits and a mug of tea, and the last fing at night you will get a mug of cocoa, and the lights out will be at nine o'clock. There will be no smoking. For the first fourteen days you will sleep on a bare board wiv no mattress and each night you will put your gear outside your cell and only sleep in your underpants.' He finished awf by saying, 'And there will be no blankets to keep you warm.' I fawt, *They have got to be mad. If this is wot I came to fight for, they can keep it.*

We were then told to pick up our kit. As I bent down to muster my kit togevver, it seemed as though the ground was going round and round. The lad next to me was a bit slow in picking up his kit and one of the petty officers who had been standing by went up to the lad and started shouting at him. The poor kid didn't know wot to do.

The next fing that happened was the petty officer kicked all the lad's kit up in the air and shouted, 'When I say move, lad, move!' I could see tears in the lad's eyes and it was then that I was determined not to let them get at me.

Everyfing in that place was done at the double. At around five o'clock the gate opened and in came the rest of the lads that were doing detention. Some of them looked as if they were ready to drop and not one of them was allowed to talk except when they were shouting out their name and number.

About 5.30 we were all locked in our separate cells and they brought round our tea. The biscuits were the size of cream crackers and as hard as wood. They called them hard tack and that was the proper name for them. I could not eat mine as they were too hard. I found out later that the best way to eat them was to soak them in your piss. The tea was like piss. It had been boiled for hours but it was a drink and that is all I wanted at that time as I fawt my froat was closing up.

At 8.30 the door of my cell opened and a petty officer said, 'Put out your kit, lad.' I took awf my clothes, leaving on only my underpants, and I was told to put my bedboard down and put my kit outside the door. I had no sooner done this when the light went out and I was in complete darkness.

That night I was so cold, I couldn't sleep. I lay awake all night finking of home. At about four in the morning I cried myself to sleep. I must have gawn awf in a dead sleep.

I was awakened by the sound of a big bell ringing and someone banging on my cell door. I could hardly get up awf of the bedboard to have a wash in the cold water that stood in a jug in the corner on a wooden washstand. My cell door was opened and I was told to get dressed. No sooner was the words spoken than someone else shouted, 'Get slopped out, lad.' That meant that they wanted me to slop out the washing water and the chamber pot that I had to use during the night. I didn't know where I had to take it, so I just followed the uvver lads.

Slopping-out time was the only time any of the boys spoke to each uvver. I could hear people shouting, 'Shut that noise up there in the recess.' I emptied my bowl of water and returned to my cell to await my breakfast. When it arrived I couldn't eat it. It wasn't fit for a pig. The porridge I couldn't eat so I just drank the tea and ate the biscuits the best I could.

I spent four days in that hell trap and on the fifth day I just couldn't get awf my bedboard. I felt somefing soft. It was a pillow. I had been taken to the sick bay in the detention barracks.

I lay on the bed and I kept falling into a deep sleep, sometimes waking up wiv a start. Around noon the doctor came to see me and about this time I fawt I was going to die. Arfter he had finished examining me he gave me an injection in the arm and told me he was sending me back to the naval hospital at Gosport. When he left me I could feel the tears rolling down my cheeks and I began to cry like a baby.

That night I was tucked up in a nice warm bed in the hospital and I was told I had suspected pneumonia. Arfter about a week I was able to sit up and eat my food properly. The lad in the next bed said he was going back to Portsmouf barracks. I asked him if he would try and find Jock or Geordie for me and to let them know where I was. He said he would find them if he had to tear the barracks apart looking for them.

Two days later I found out he was a man of his word. As I woke up one arfternoon I could 'ear someone talking. I opened my eyes and saw Jock and Geordie standing by my bed. They both spoke at once asking me how I felt. I was so pleased to see them that I couldn't speak for a moment.

Jock put his hand on my shoulder and said, 'How do ya feel, mate?'

I smiled and said, 'I feel like a bleeding wet kipper.'

'Ya look as though ya have just come back awf ya holidays,' said Geordie.

'It ain't been no holiday where I have been, me old son,' I said.

Jock and Geordie stayed wiv me for about an hour and they wanted to know all about the detention barracks. I told them of 'earing grown men crying in the middle of the night and how we had to double around the parade-ground in full kit wiv 'aversacks filled wiv sand. And how I had to hold a rifle above my head until I fawt I was goind to drop in my tracks, and how it was only sheer determination that kept me going.

I told them of the way a dirty pig of a petty officer would frow a red rusty bucket in ya cell and how ya had to polish and clean it till it shone like a mirror, and if he wasn't satisfied wiv the results he would make ya polish it over and over again until ya fawt ya arms was going to drop awf.

I told them how they made ya lay all ya kit out in ya cell according to regulation orders, and when ya got back to ya cell at lunch time some dirty barsted had kicked the 'ole lot up in the air so by the time ya had laid it all out again it was time to go back on parade so ya missed ya dinner – if ya can call it that.

'I don't fancy none of that,' said Jock. I put my hand on his shoulder and said, 'I wouldn't wish it on my worst enemy, mate.'

Jock used to come and see me every day arfter that and one day he told me he was being transferred to a new naval barracks across the river at Gosport. He told me it was only down the road from the hospital. I spent five weeks in the hospital and while I was in there I was told that I would not be sent back to the detention barracks as I still had some infection on my lung. When I was discharged from hospital they sent me to the same barracks.

Jock was on guard at the gate when I arrived in the lorry, and when he came round the back of the lorry and saw me, he said, 'Ya made it then, ya weak Cockney barsted.' Jock managed to get me in the same mess as him and we were togevver once again. I settled in nicely and I liked the barracks. For one fing old Swain wasn't there and life was a lot easier. And for anuvver I fell in love.

It happened one summer's night. Jock and I had been given free days' jankers (punishment) for coming in late one night so we spent the next free days in barracks. On this particular night it was so warm and the sun was still high in the sky. We decided to polish the mess cutlery on the grass by the fence. That way we could see all the passers-by. I was polishing away like a good'un when Jock said, 'Ay up, Al, here comes a couple of birds.' Little did I know those few words were to change my whole life.

I looked up and coming down the road were two girls. As they walked by I called arfter them, 'Does ya old lady know you're out?' At first I fawt they were going to ignore us but one of them turned round and smiled and that was it. I was hooked for life.

They turned out to be sisters. They eventually came back arfter some persuading and I knew wot one I wanted out of the two. We made some small talk and we found out that their names were Betty and Joan. All the time we were laughing and joking around I couldn't keep my eyes awf Betty. She was five foot two tall, wiv dark brown hair and grey eyes. We arranged to see them in free days' time as we had anuvver two nights of jankers to do.

When they left us, I said to Jock, 'That little Betty is a cracker.' All next day I kept finking about her and I couldn't get down to that fence farst enough when the evening arrived.

We had a wartime courtship like millions of uvvers and we were married the following year. I have had a wonderful married life wiv a wonderful girl and I have had no regrets. She was seventeen when I first met her, and the best-looking bird in Gosport. We done the usual fings in our courtship and went to the usual places like the pictures, and for walks in the park. I just asked her to marry me and she said, 'yes' and that was that.

I shall never forget our wedding day. The night before our wedding day, I got as drunk as a newt and the next morning I had the best of hangovers, so I had to have the 'air of the dog to bring me round. An old friend of mine was my best man and he later married Betty's sister, Joan. Arthur, my best man, had been out wiv me the night before and we certainly put away a few beers. I had to stay in Betty's house overnight as I was still in the Navy and my Mum and Dad were still in Scarborough.

'You can't go back to the barracks in that state,' said Betty's muvver so Arthur and I ended up sleeping in the front room of Betty's house. I could not see Betty when we got back to the house as it was supposed to be unlucky to see the bride the night before the wedding.

The next morning, I said to Arthur, 'My bleeding head, it's killing me.'

'I should fink so wiv wot you drank last night,' he replied. He told me I even tried to sell the wedding ring to a geezer in the boozer.

'Leave awf, I wouldn't do that,' I said. 'Ya bleeding did,' he said. We had a laugh about it and anuvver drink.

Betty's muvver came in and said, 'Come on you two. You'd

208

better get ready to go to the registry office. You don't want to be late.'

I put my best uniform on and I wore a white silk ribbon in front of my naval jumper as all the matelots do when they are getting married. As we had to go from Gosport to Fareham to the registry office, we left the house first. We made arrangements to meet one or two of the lads outside the registry office.

When we got there one of the lads shouted, 'Here comes Cockney,' and before I knew what was happening, I found myself in a boozer just round the corner from the registry officer wiv a double rum in my hand. The landlord of the boozer noticed my white ribbon, and he handed me anuvver drop of rum on the house.

By the time we left that boozer I was well away. As we were coming out of the boozer there was a lorry standing at the side of the kerb loaded wiv sailors, and when they saw my white ribbon they all shouted, 'Who's a silly barsted then?'

'Bollocks,' I shouted back. 'Come down here and I'll fight the fucking lot of ya.'

'Leave awf, Al,' said Arthur, 'they're only kidding.'

There was only one person missing on my wedding day and that was my old pal Jock. I have never seen Jock since we parted at Gosport but I am always finking of him and I pray to God that he came frew that horrible war OK.

I contracted a bad chest frew the pneumonia and in 1943 I was invalided out of tne Navy. I said goodbye to Jock and the rest of the boys and once again I was in Civvy Street. The Navy hadn't learned me a trade. All I learned in the Navy was how to fire a gun and how to kill.

Betty had rented a little house in Gosport. She made it nice and cosy for us and I settled down to being a married man. For the first few weeks I missed Jock and rest of the lads and I was like a fish out of water as I just could not settle down.

A few weeks arfter leaving the Navy they gave me a pension and a small silver badge to wear in my lapel. Written on the badge was, 'G.R. for loyal service.' It must have been worf about tuppence. I slung it in a tin box and it 'as been there till this day. Jerry was still bombing Portsmouf and I had to take Betty down to the shelter at the bottom of the garden at the back of the house every night.

It was a lovely little garden and one day Betty bought some seeds to plant in the garden. While she was out shopping I fawt

I would plant the seeds. Laugh – I got them all mixed up: I had the flowers mixed up wiv the veg. We had collieflowers coming up wiv pansies. When Betty had seen wot I had done we had a good laugh about it and she said, 'You'll never make a gardener.'

'Well, how did I know?' I said. 'We never had a garden where I came from.'

'You mean you never had a garden at the front and back of your house?' she said.

I told her the only fing we had at the front of our house was the boneyard and bleeding rats as big as cats.

While we were living in Gosport I fawt I'd have a go at a nine-to-five job. Of course my first love was busking but only a mug would try busking in Gosport. So I got a job in a timber factory and what a fiasco that turned out to be.

It was all on account of this young bird called Nellie who worked on the nailing machine making boxes. I fancied her from the first time I saw her. The boys nicknamed her Nellie the Nailer. One of the boys who worked on the machine opposite me said she was a right old raver and she was anyone's meat. I fawt, *if you're telling the trufe, mate, this is one geezer who is going to have her.*

Well, I got to know her very well and one day she said to me, 'I bet all the girls chase you, don't they?'

'I've had more birds than you've had hot dinners,' I replied.

'Leave awf, ya wouldn't know wot to do wiv it if ya had it on a plate,' she replied. 'Ya wouldn't like to bet on that, would ya? And if ya fink I am kidding, I'll meet ya in the yard in two minutes.'

'Right, you're on,' she said. I fawt, *she's fucking joking, this bird.*

I told the geezer who worked on the machine next to me, and he said, 'If Nellie said she will meet ya out the back, then she'll be there.' Just then Nellie walked by my machine and winker her eye at me, and at the same time she beckoned me wiv her head to follow her. I fawt, *right ya barsted if that's wot ya want that's wot ya going to get.* As I left my machine I winked to the geezer on the next machine, and he said in my ear, 'Give her one for me, me old son.'

Well, I got out into the yard of the factory, and the gents and ladies' toilets were in the same building, wiv a wall between them. But the wall didn't go right up to the ceiling so anyone could climb over it. I waited for a second or two, and then I whispered, 'Nellie, ya in there?'

'If ya bleeding coming, come and hurry up,' she replied. I was over that wall farster than you could spit.

'Quick,' she said, 'in here,' and she had one of the toilet doors open, and before I knew it she was dragging me in the cubicle. I have never seen a bird strip awf so fast in all my life. Before ya could say 'Moby Dick' she had her skirt and pants awf. There I was wiv the biggest hard-on I have ever had, and she was grabbing hold of me and telling me to hurry up. She then lifted her jumper displaying the biggest pair of tits I had ever seen.

Well, ya might guess wot happened next. I was riding her like a bull rides a cow. We were having a lovely old time when the door of the toilet came flying open and the foreman – who was her husband by the way – got hold of me by the scruff of the neck and pulled me awf of Nellie. The next fing I knew I was kicked up the arse and slung out of the gates wiv my cards and money in my hand, and arfter that I swore I would never mess around wiv married women.

The bombing was going from bad to worse and one night fings got so bad that the next morning I spoke to Betty about going to Scarborough to live wiv the old folk. She was all for it. So we ended up going to live in Scarborough.

Chapter Eleven
Back busking in the smoke

By the end of 1943 my wife presented me wiv a baby daughter that we named Susan and I knew then that I would have to work twice as hard as I was now a family man. I stayed in Scarborough for a while doing odd jobs that my heart wasn't really in as I had never worked for a guvner before. Then one day my wife's sister wrote and told us she was going to marry Arthur, my best man. Betty and I had a laugh about it and I told Betty that all Cockneys make the best husbands.

Arfter Betty's sister had been married for a few monfs she wrote and told us she was taking a house in London and she went on to say that if we liked we could share it wiv her and her husband. I fawt, *Wot a wonderful chance for us to get back to dear old London*. It was like a dream come true as I was always yearning to get back to London.

The old man and the old lady didn't like the idea of us leaving them but we finally made up our minds and left Scarborough for London. At this time Jerry was still bombing London but I wanted to get back so much that I was willing to take a chance.

A few weeks arfter we returned to London the house next door to us became empty so we applied for it and got it. It was in Thomas Street, Stepney. It was a broken-down old dump and all we had was a couple of beds, a few chairs, and an old kitchen table, but Betty soon put fings to rights and we now had a place of our own. We had no fancy barfroom but that didn't matter to me as we never had a barfroom when I was a kid. But we did have two fings – love and laughter. We became very happy in that little place we called home.

Albert was still in the Army and one day he came to see us while he was on leave. I told him that when the war was over he could come and live wiv us and that he and his wife Edie could have the upper part of the house. We talked about wot he was going to do arfter the war and he said, 'There's only one fing I can do and that is to do wot I have been doing all my life – busking.' He spoke about taking a show out on the road and I was all ears as I had always longed to work wiv Albert in the West End.

On the 8 May 1945 the War was over and as the fires of victory were dying down I was hurrying to get the midwife as my wife had started labour wiv our second child. It turned out to be anuvver girl. As she was born on Victory Day there was only one name we could call her and that was Victoria.

Arfter Victoria came Marie. She was born in 1947. Then came Wendy in 1949. By this time I fawt to myself *I am never going to have a son to carry on our name and be a busker like his farver*, and then – bang! – we hit the jackpot and had our first son, Tony. He was born in 1952. Then came Dudley, who was born in 1956.

I now had two sons and I was as proud as a dog wiv two cocks. Mind you, the way I was going on I fink that one was enough. Then the last was Cindy, who was born in 1960. Fank Christ for that – it was bleeding hard work!

None of my sons ever went busking. It was a shame that the line ended wiv me and Albert. Albert's younger son tried it for a few weeks while I was ill once but it didn't work out. The good Lord had uvver ideas: he was killed in a car crash, God bless him. He was a lovely boy, young Derek, and so full of life. He had blond hair, blue eyes and a freckled face and on my day awf we would always go to the pictures togevver and have a right old giggle.

Two days arfter Victory Day my bruvver Albert came to see me as he was only stationed in Kent, and he said, 'It won't be long now before they discharge me.' As he was on a twenty-four hour leave, he asked me if I would like a run out wiv him to the West End to work the slangs (picture queues). I jumped at the chance so awf we went to work.

Albert played the stride (piano accordion) and I bottled. We ended up pulling a big edge (crowd) and everyone was going potty. They were singing and dancing and laughing. It was as though happiness was coming from everywhere you looked – the war was over. The cab ranks (yanks) were going mad and the medzers were all boner (the money was good).

Albert played all the old wartime songs like 'Roll out the barrel', 'When the lights come on in London', 'Run rabbit run', 'Yankee Doodle Dandy', and lots more. We worked till two in the morning and Albert said, 'I've had enough ya jaggs. Let's call it a day.'

Well, when he stopped playing the crowd kept on clapping and asking for more. It was as though they had let go of all the energy they had stored up inside themselves arfter all the years of heartaches and pain. But Albert was all in. Besides, he had to report back to his unit in Kent.

A few weeks later Albert was discharged from the Army and he and Edie came to live wiv us. Poor old London was in a hell of a mess. Some of the old bevvies I had known was no longer there. All our old neighbours we knew were either dead or they had moved away.

One day I decided to go round my old neighbourhood in Bloomfield Street to see if I could find Fred or any of the uvver boys. But it was no use. The old house we once lived in was down to the ground. Jerry had dropped a landmine at the end of the street. He had wiped out free streets of houses and killed nearly all our old neighbours – people we had known since childhood; boys and girls we had played wiv. Everything was just one big mess.

As I stood there, my heart sank to see such destruction. I know the old places were running alive wiv rats and bugs but to those who lived in them it was home. I fawt of all the laughter and tears that those old houses had known. I fawt of all the families that had lived in them.

I saw an old mirror hanging on a wall – all that was left of Tommy's house. It was a miracle how it had not smashed wiv the blast. I stood and wondered how many times lovely Diane had stood there and brushed her hair in that old mirror. It seemed as though that old mirror was left there by God wiv all its past reflections and secrets.

I was about to leave and as I turned to walk away a voice said, 'Hellow, Harryboy.' I turned round and there stood one of my old neighbours. It was old Mister Clark. It was the same old Clarkie wiv his old flat cap and his old stook tied round his neck as it always was.

He was about five foot seven wiv snow white hair, and he used to live a few streets away. He once lived in our street but when his wife died he went to live wiv his son. He was an old man and he loved pigeons. I had known him as far back as I can remember and he never seemed to change. His hair was a little whiter but he was just as I'd remembered him.

214

We exchanged greetings and I said, 'I fawt you had gawn away wiv the family.'

'Who, me? Not me, son. I had me old job to look arfter. Besides, who was going to take care of me old pigeons?' he replied.

I started to ask him about all the old neighbours and went on to tell me who was dead and who had been evacuated. He told me of whole families who had been killed. They were people who I had known as a child and who I would never see again. Inside of myself I was asking God why he had let it all happen. But there was no answer to this madness.

I found out a lot that day and on my way home I was sick wiv greef as I looked at all the destruction. As I was about to say goodbye to old Mister Clark he hit me wiv the final blow.

'Of course,' he said, 'ya know ya old mates have gone, don't ya, son.'

'Wot do ya mean, Mister Clark?' I said.

'Well, them mates of yours you used to knock about wiv. Young Hunter and young Fred what's his name.'

'Wot about them?' I asked.

'Don't ya know, son?' he replied.

'Know wot?' I asked.

'Well, young Georgi got killed in the African desert and young fred went down at sea. He was torpedoed.'

My head began to whirl as I 'eard myself say, 'Oh no.'

Old Mister Clark must have seen the sickness in my face. I could hear him saying, 'Blimey, son, I am sorry. I fawt ya knew about those two boys.'

Wot I said next I shall never know but as I said goodbye to him he walked away shaking his head. I looked up once more at the old mirror hanging on the wall and I fawt about Tommy and I wondered if I would ever see him again. I could feel my eyes burning and as I wiped them I could feel the dampness on my cheeks. All at once I had the feeling of complete loneliness and I felt sick inside. I was in the street where we played as kids but the laughter and the shouting was no longer there.

It was a month later that I saw Tommy. I fawt I was seeing a ghost. I had just got awf of a bus at the top of the market and I saw him rabbiting to one of the stallholders.

215

'Tommy!' I shouted, and the look on his face was one of complete surprise.

'Blimey, Al,' he said as he got hold of me. We both tried to ask questions at the same time in the excitement of seeing each uvver.

'Blimey, you're the last geezer I expected to see. I fawt ya was dead or somefing,' he was saying.

I told him that I was married and that I had two kids of my own and I told him how I went up norf with the old man and the old lady when I came out of the Navy.

He got hold of my arm and said, 'Come on me old son. Let's go and have a bevvy,' and awf we went to the nearst boozer.

'Wot ya fancy?' he said. 'A drop of turps (whisky), Al?'

'I couldn't care a donkey's bollock if I drank prostitute's water the way I feel right now,' I said. We had a laugh and we spoke of old times.

'Did ya hear about Gobber topping (hanging) himself?' he said and went on to tell me how Gobber came home on leave from the Army arfter being overseas for two years and caught Rosie in bed wiv a cab rank. Arfter he had slung the yank down the stairs he smashed a china jug on Rosie's face scarring her for life. Then he stormed out of the house.

'The next morning his old muvver found him hanging from the bannistairs up on the landing.' I was shocked and fawt back to before the War when we'd all said he'd end up doing Rosie in.

'It's funny. Ya know wot, Tom,' I said, 'my old lady said he would end up on the end of a rope and she was right, wasn't she?'

Tommy told me how his muvver had been evacuated to Oxford and how he'd gone to work in the glass factory there, so he was exempt for War Service.

He hadn't changed much. I would know Tommy anywhere wiv his black hair and dark eyes. He was a little fatter. We spoke of Fred and Georgi wiv lumps in our throats, knowing they were gawn forever. We ended up getting well pissed and I took him home to meet my wife. He stayed wiv us all that day as we both fell asleep in the armchairs. He left me about seven o'clock as he had to get his train back to Oxford.

Before he left me he told me that Diane was OK and living down in Oxford wiv him and his mum and dad. I couldn't resist asking him about her, and he told me she had grown to be a

216

proper lady. All the boys were chasing her in Oxford but she only had one boyfriend.

'He's a lucky guy, Tommy,' I said. 'I hope he appreciates her as she deserves the very best.'

'Don't worry about Di, Al,' he said, 'she knows where she's going.'

We said our goodbyes and that was the last I was to see of him. I did see Diane again tho', and I'll tell you about that later.

After the war life went on almost the same in the East End. By this time I had teamed up wiv a guy named Fred Veens. He was a marvellous pianist and we worked well togevver. We used to work all the boozers and sometimes we would spend as much as an hour in one boozer. It wasn't like working in the street but it was still busking.

One night we were asked to work in a boozer every weekend. The medzers was good – that was why we took the job. The name of the boozer was the Barge Inn at Pitsea.

When we first went there we had a moderate crowd but once the word got around we soon built up a good reputation for ourselves. Boy, did we get up to some tricks in that bevvy. Fred would play 'Donkey Serenade' and I would go outside and borrow the old donkey awf the geezer who used to sell winkles and shrimps. Then I'd ride the poor little barsted into the bar and by the end of the night the place was in uproar.

Albert had teamed up wiv a dance team who called themselves the Happy Wanderers. The act consisted of our old pal Ronnie Ross, Micky Glover and Albert. The unusual part of the act was that Mick was a girl – and very nice too. She had a very nice personality and was a very good box player. Ronnie was a great performer and between the free of them they made a very good act. They became well-known round the West End and always drew big crowds.

One day Albert came to me and told me he was going to leave the Happy Wanderers. It was a pity really as they were a good act togevver. They had even been to New York as a publicity stunt for a show called *The Drop of a Hat*. I never did ask Albert why he was leaving Ronnie and Mick. It was none of my business, but as the old saying goes, as one door shuts, anuvver door opens.

A few weeks after that Albert asked me if I would like to team up wiv him. I jumped at the chance.

It took us a week to get the show in trim and to get the strile

217

(piano accordion) player we wanted – and that was my old partner and friend, Charlie.

I shall never forget the day we took that show on the road. Charlie was like one of the family. He had been busking most of his life and he could speak the language, so we was well away wiv him playing for us. Charlie played the bass drum and the accordion at the same time and he was the only joegar who could play for the wallopers and his playing was perfect. He had worked wiv uvver groups, and before the Second World War he was on the stage.

The next fing for us to do was to find a good bottler, so we went and got The Mud Lark. The Mud Lark was only his nickname. His real name was Jim. His act was unique. Long before he became a busker he used to work in a circus. He would lie on the ground and would squeeze himself frew two small steel rings. But the highlight of his act was when he would take a piece of chalk, place it on the ground, walk back about fifty yards, and then run and do a somersault wiv a pick-axe handle and pick up the chalk in his mouf. Old Jim always looked nice and clean wiv his white tee-shirt and white plimsoles and he was a showman frew and frew.

The first day we went out wiv the show it was a huge success. Before we struck up, we had a big edge. Down went the big bass drum and Charlie put on his accordion and we went into action. I was playing the side drum, Charlie was playing the accordion and bass drum, and Albert was messing around in front doing a few tricks wiv his bowler hat.

For our first routine we was dressed as two parsons and this got a lot of laughs. While we was doing the parsons' routine Jim was out bottling. A good bottler would go out as soon as the show started. This way ya didn't miss anyone.

Arfter we had finished the parsons' routine, Charlie would sing a solo, and boy could he sing. Ya could hear him all round the square. This was to give Jim time to get back and get ready for his act.

While Jim was performing, me and Albert was out bottling. This way we had someone collecting all the time. This was in case the scarps arrived to nick ya. In them days if ya got nicked it would cost ya a chinker beonk (five shillings) but as years went by it was increased to a dooey font (two pounds). Little did we know the first day we took our show on the road we was going to become the pride and joy of Bow Street Police Court as they

218

finally arrested us over 575 times for obstruction! This is why ya had to have a bottler out all the time.

Arfter Jim had done his act, me and Albert was back to perform the sand dance and this was the routine that we was known for. We would take awf our frock coats and bowler hats, roll up our trousers past our knees, roll down our long bright-striped shirts, put on the red fez and do an Egyptian sand dance. There must be millions of photos of us doing this routine. While we was dressed as Egyptians we would fit in a lot of gags as there was plenty of opportunity to ad-lib as the traffic went by.

For instance, if we saw a posh car we would go on our hands and knees and bow down to it and this would get a big laugh. One night we done it and sitting in the back of her gold-plated Daimler was Lady Docker, wife of Sir Bernard, the former boss of the BSA motorcycles empire. She was wearing a mink coat and she just smiled and put a pound note out of the window.

I remember one night we was working the Egyptian routine and I spotted a Rolls coming along the road. I said to Albert, 'Down jaggs,' and we went on our hands and knees ready to bow to it. Instead, it slowed down and the chauffeur opened the door. It was a gag sent from heaven. I done no more but I jumped in the Rolls.

'Where to, sir?' said the chauffeur.

'Round the square, me old son,' I said and awf we went leaving Albert still on his knees and the crowd laughing their heads awf.

'I bet they all fink this is yours,' said the chauffeur.

'I bet it got a laugh,' I said.

'If my boss sees me I'll get the bleeding sack,' he said.

'Never mind, me old son,' I said, 'you can come out wiv us.'

By the time we got back round the square, Charlie, Albert and Jim was nowhere to be seen but there was still a big edge there. As I got out of the Rolls they all laughed and clapped.

I was about to close the door of the Rolls when a hand tapped me on the shoulder and said, 'Come on Henry, you're nicked.' It was a scarp we used to call 'Eyes Higher' as he had one bigger than the uvver. Someone told us he got smashed in the ogal wiv a brick.

'Nicked? Wot for?' I said.

'Come off it Henry,' he said, 'you know wot for.'

'OK, John, you win.' I said, and awf we went to Savile Row police station. It was not the first time Eyes Higher had nicked me.

If we had a copper who was a bit flash we would say, 'We ain't walking all the way to Savile Row wiv this lot! Get the fucking van!' By doing this we knew that the crowd would boo him when the van arrived.

They were a good lot of boys those scarps in the West End. We was on first-name terms wiv all of them. The inspectors we called 'guv' as we always showed them respect.

When me and old Eyes Higher met in court the next morning, he said, 'Sorry Henry but I hadn't had a nick all day.'

'That's all right, John me old son,' I said and wiv that old Jeff the jailer came up and said, 'Hello, Henry. How's Albert and Charlie?'

'OK fanks, Jeff.'

'I nicked him getting out of a Rolls last night, didn't I, Henry?' said old Eyes Higher.

'Of course ya did,' I said. 'It was mine, ya berk. I was coming to work wasn't I?'

So arfter that every time Jeff saw me he would say, 'Still running the Rolls, Henry?'

'Yus, Jeff,' I would reply, 'it's parked outside the court,' and we would have a laugh.

He was a nice old boy, old Jeff! He was about six feet tall wiv a bald head, fair complexion, and blue eyes. I always said to Albert, 'He is too nice for that job. He isn't the jailer type.' He must have had some characters frew his hands the time he spent at Bow Street. He always had a good word for us and sometimes on his day awf would come and watch the show and he would always have a chat wiv us like most scarps that nicked us.

They would often come and watch the show on their day awf. We had one policeman who used to bring his wife and children to see the show on his day awf and we ended up doing a show at his daughter's wedding. We done many a show for many of the policemen when they got married.

That's why it came as a big shock to us when one night a sergeant came up to us in plain clothes and said the big chief wanted to see us all the following day at Savile Row nick at two o'clock. He wouldn't say wot he wanted us for when we asked.

'Don't forget to be there,' was all he said.

'I wonder wot he wants us for,' said Charlie.

'Maybe he's going to knight us,' said Albert.

'Ya mean he's going to nick us, more like it,' said Jim.

Well, the next day we all met in Angelo's and Wanda's café.

220

That was the place where we used to change into our props in the back room before we went to work. Angelo and Wanda were two very old dear Italian friends of ours and we would spend hours in their café if it was raining and we couldn't go to work. We had many a laugh wiv Angelo. Well, we had a cup of tea and made our way up Piccadilly to Savile Row. It was 1.55 as we all walked frew the police station door. The sergeant at the desk didn't recognise us as he hadn't seen us in our street clothes before. He had only seen us in our props when one of the boys had nicked us and took us in.

'What can I do for you gentlemen?' he said, looking up from the desk. And then he recognised us. 'Blimey, it's you three. I didn't recognise you all done up,' he said.

It was a funny fing that no one knew us in our street clothes. I can only remember being recognised once and that was in a cafe on the M1. We had just finished a club in Birmingham and we was in a motorway café when a lorry driver came and sat at the table next to us wiv his little boy.

Just as we was about to leave, he came over to our table and said, 'Excuse me, but ain't you the sand dancers out of Leicester Square?' When we told him we were he said to his little boy, 'There, I told ya so. I said it was them, didn't I?' He went on to tell us how his little boy had seen us working in the Square and how he told his muvver about us, and his muvver said, 'Don't be silly, men don't dance in the road.'

Well, arfter that we ended up giving him a big autographed photo of us and that kid was as pleased as punch. As his farver pulled out of the car park he was waving to us out of the cab window.

'There goes anuvver satisfied customer ya jaggs,' I said to Charlie, and that was the only time we was recognised out of our props.

Anyway, back to the police station.

'Right lads, wot can I do for you?' said the sergeant.

Albert told him we had an appointment wiv the 'Big white chief.'

'Hang on, I'll find out,' said the sergeant. And wiv that he picked up a phone and rang the chief's office.

Arfter a moment he said, 'Right lads, take the lift to the first floor and it's the first office on the right as you come out of the lift.' We found the office all right and Albert knocked on the door.

'Come in,' said a voice. As we went in we could see by the look on the inspector's face we wasn't what he had expected as we was all dressed up in our best suits. Arfter the initial shock of seeing us he came back to himself.

'Sit down, gentlemen,' he said and offered us all a seat. Arfter a moment he went on, 'I suppose you are wondering why I have asked you here today. As you know I have been transferred to Savile Row and it has been brought to my notice that you have been to one or two weddings of my constables.'

'That's right, guv,' said Charlie.

'Well I am afraid, lads, it has to stop,' he said.

Well, ya could have knocked me awf of that chair wiv a fart from a sparrow.

'Why, wot's up guv?' asked Albert.

The inspector went on to say it was his policy and that his men was out of order by asking us to perform at their weddings.

Well, I mean how can ya argue with the big white chief himself? So we said we would not go to any more weddings for the lads at Savile Row. Before we left he read us the riot act and told us he wanted no bovver on his patch.

We parted the best of friends.

Chapter Twelve
Our midnight show in Park Lane

The next time we saw the Chief was at the International Police Ball at the Court Rooms in Charing Cross. We ended up having a cup of tea wiv him in our dressing room and it was a big surprise to him to find out that we didn't drink while we was working. We was asked to do a show for them by one of the sergeants who was on the entertainment committee.

As I've said, the scarps in the West End were the best in the country, and if we ever needed them they were there. One Sunday we was doing a pitch in the Square and we had the biggest edge I have ever seen. the show was going like a bomb and out of the blue someone started a fight. Well, these two geezers were having a punch-up right in the middle of the toby (road).

'Swallow it ya jaggs (take no notice),' I said to Charlie. And we went on working.

After a moment or two, Charlie stopped playing and shouted to Albert and me 'Johnalderly ya jaggs scarps (Run mate it's the police).'

We done no more than pick up the props and scarper. We all met round the corner and Jim said, 'I fink they have nicked the two geezers who were fighting.'

Just then the scarps lardy came round the corner and out jumped two plain-clothes scarps. The biggest fellow of the two was Big Mac who we had known for a long time.

'Wot's the trouble, lads?' he asked as he reached us.

'Nuffing, Mac. Why?' asked Charlie.

'Well, we got it over our radio that the Roadsters were in trouble in the Square so we came to see wot was going on,' he said. Just then up came two more scarps.

'Wot's up, Mac?' one of them was asking.

Then up came a young scarp who explained to Mac wot it was all about. By this time we had a nice little edge. We fanked Mac and the uvver coppers for taking our welfare to heart and awf they all went. We gave them enough time to get awf the manor and we went back to work.

Most of the scarps in the West End – though not all of them – treated us right, and we treated them the same. We have had them come up to us and say, 'I haven't had a nick today. Who's going to volunteer to have one stuck on them?' and one of us would volunteer to go to the nick. Sometimes they were sent just to nick us, but we didn't mind as that was one of the hazards of the game.

Not all the scarps were great though. one Saturday arfternoon we had just started a pitch in the Square and was 'arfway frew the bleeding act when in came frustrated Dick, a nasty bit of work if ever there was one, wiv a young rookey copper. Before we had a chance to pack up the props he had us.

'All right, ya're nicked,' he bawled.

'Wot? All free of us?' asked Albert.

'Yes, all three of you,' he replied.

'That's a bleeding liberty,' said Charlie. 'Ya only had me yesterday.'

'That's right and I am having you today,' he replied.

By this time I had the big drum on my shoulder, and Albert was putting the rest of the props in the bag. I fawt, *Bollocks to this barsted. If he wants me up the nick, he will have to get the van.*

So I took the big drum awf of my shoulder and said, 'Right, Dick, if ya want me down the nick ya will have to get the van.' He seemed stumped.

'I can't get a van. They're at Trafalgar Square because there is a meeting down there,' he said.

'That's your hard luck, mate,' I said. 'You and your mate will have to carry the props then, won't ya?'

By this time Albert and Charlie tumbled wot I was up to so Albert firmly said, 'I ain't walking all that bleeding way – never.' All the crowd were on tenterhooks, watching and waiting to see wot was going to happen.

'Well, wot's it going to be?' Chalie chipped in. 'A van or are you going to carry the props?' Frustrated Dick now had to nick us as he had his partner wiv him.

'OK, you win,' he said, and wiv that he said to the young rookey, 'You carry the big drum and I'll take the bag.'

' 'old on me old son,' Charlie said. 'Who do ya finks going to carry this box?' 'Give the accordion to him,' said frustrated Dick pointing to his partner.

Well, we made a pretty sight as we walked along amid the astonished tourists. As we went by, one of the barrow boys standing on the corner wiv his barrow started singing, 'Here we are again, as happy as can be, all good pals and jolly good company.'

'Ya want to watch out, Johnny,' I said. 'He'll have you next.'

By the time we got to the nick the young rookey was well and truly fucked. We saw him about five weeks after that incident and as he came up to us Charlie said, 'You can piss awf for a start. We ain't done a pitch yet.'

'I ain't come to nick ya mate,' said the young copper. 'I've come to say how sorry I was for ya the other week.'

'Oh that's all right, son,' said Albert, 'we know how ya feel.'

Arfter that, the younger copper used to go out of his way when he saw us working and he never nicked us all the time he was at the West End Central.

The West End scarps had a lot to put up wiv, wot wiv the brasses and the Johnsons (ponces) and all the spivvies. There was one team they wouldn't stand for and that was the free-card-trick merchants. They would set up a small folding table in the side doorway of the cinema and they would play a game called Find the Lady wiv free cards. They would find a mug in the crowd and take him for all he had. The scarps were always arfter them and they got knocked awf for more than a two pound fine. It was fifty pounds. But even that didn't stop them. They would come back time and time again.

Apart from the free-card-trick merchants there was the *Old Moore's Almanac* team. They would stop a likely punter and give him some tale about being an ex-serviceman and that they were selling the *Almanacs* for the British Legion. I have seen them take as much as five pounds awf of a punter for one *Almanac*. In my opinion they needed nicking as none of them were ex-servicemen. To us they were all bald 'omes (bad guys).

There 'as always been bad guys in the West End and there will always be. But it's a funny fing, all the bad guys was good guys to us. There was one gangster called Jack. Every time he saw us he would make a big fuss of us and he always bunged a clinker font (five pounds) before he left us. He was about six foot two and the size of a house. But he always had his heavies wiv him. He loved to watch us work and he liked a laugh.

I used to say to him, 'One of these days, Jack, I am going to give you one right in the eye,' and he would laugh his head awf. The newspapers said some bad fings about him but he was always a good'un to us. He asked us to perform at a party one night. Laugh . . .

When we eventually got into his flat in Gerrard Street, Soho, arfter banging merry hell out of the front door as the noise was so loud, we couldn't believe our eyes. There was villains from all around the West End wiv broken noses and collieflower ear'oles all over the gaff. There was a bird dancing on top of a grand piano stark naked except for a pair of old army boots. She had a champagne bottle in her form (hand). Well the fings that bird done wiv that bleeding bottle was enough to rupture a fucking elephant. I couldn't take my minces awf of her.

'If she bungs that bottle up herself any ferver she will knock her bleeding teef out,' said Chrlie.

'Ya must be joking ya jaggs,' said Albert. 'She can take that and four more like it.'

The next fing was I had a big cigar stuck in my norf and souf and a large scotch in my German band. It was just a waste of time telling Jack that we didn't drink a lot. Besides, who wants to argue wiv the number-one gangster in the West End? All Jack kept on saying was, 'Get it down ya, and pick yaself each a bird, boys.' Well, arfter about five scotches we didn't know any more and as regards to putting on a show, well they had had it.

About five in the morning, I woke up under a table in the kitchen and the bird wiv the champagne was in kip wiv two geezers. I found Albert and Charlie asleep in one of the armchairs and Jim was nowhere to be seen. We finally found Jim in the hallway to the flat. I woke them all up and said, 'Come on jaggs, it's gawn five o'clock.' All poor old Charlie could say was 'Oh my bleeding head.' There was bodies all over the gaff. Some of the birds were stark naked wiv nuffing covering them up. We got out of there a bit lively after stepping over all of the bodies.

Jack had a long run in the West End and one night gang warfare broke out and the Law had to step in and soon jack gave up his frone. I don't know how he lost his power in the West End but I know there was trouble and he faded into the background. He must have made a packet before he retired. He had his hands in everyfing and everyone's pockets. You name it and he had a slice of it.

Even the notorious Messina Bruvvers knew how far to go wiv him. They used to run all the brasses in the West End. They were always togevver. Where ya saw one ya would see the uvver and whenever they saw us they would always give us a pound. If we was working as they came by in their big black car we would bow down to them and they would love it. Their driver would slow down and wind the car window and out would come a font (pound). The Messinas would sit in the back of the car and wave like royalty. They were around the West End for a few years but like all good fings it came to an end for them. A certain newspaper reporter, Duncan Webb of *The People*, started writing about their activities and a few of the girls testified against them and they fled the country. But not before they had earned millions from vice.

The West End was really somefing in those days, wot wiv the bright lights and all the fings that went on there: the sound of the traffic; the music of a barrel organ playing in the distance; the ladies and gentlemen in their evening dress. It was a different way of life in those days.'

Of all the brasses I knew in the West End there was one girl I shall never forget if I live to be a hundred. She called herself Fay and she was the cream. She seemed to be above the rest. She was a beautiful looking girl too. She had dark brown hair and brown eyes. She never needed a lot of make-up as she was lovely. Her flat was in Rupert Street. I used to fink to myself when I saw her taking a punter up to her flat, *How can such a lovely girl like her do such a fing as that?* She was a smart girl, too. She looked 'ansom when she was dressed up all in her best for work. It's funny, but she looked like a real lady. There was a few prostitues around Soho who were getting on a bit. They were the free pound touches, but that Fay was tops. It was as if her eyes were always laughing but I knew she was hiding the sorrow that went wiv her profession.

She was French and she told me one night that she came from a little village somewhere in France. She told me how her muvver used to brush and plait her hair when she was a little girl. Her eyes would be laughing but I knew that her heart was crying for that place she called home.

'You know, mon cheri,' she would say to me, 'one of dese days your little Fay will be going back to her momma.'

'Leave awf, Fay,' I would say, 'the West End wouldn't be the same wivout ya. Besides I ain't got no uvver girlfriend, only you.' And she would kiss my hand and say somefing to me in French and laugh.

Poor darling Fay. She ended up wiv twenty-six stitches in that lovely face. The rumour was she wanted out of the game but she had no chance. Arfter they had marked her for life, she just went from bad to worse. She started to drink heavy and take drugs. I found out awf of one of the uvver girls that she finally died in hospital of consumption.

Behind the bright lights and glamour of the West End there is a side the tourist never sees. There's the filth and garbage you would never dream of. They say that if ya stand in Piccadilly long enuff you'll see every nationality under the sun go by. To see the West End with its glamour stripped awf you must go round the back streets in the middle of the night long arfter the spivs and prostitutes have gawn home to bed. You'll see old men sleeping in doorways, wrapped up in newspaper, and drug addicts in a world of their own. Young girls who have left home for the bright lights, just walking around wiv an old battered suitcase. Maybe just around the corner lurking like some dark shadow, there are ponces waiting for a likely girl to put on the game. It is their best time in the middle of the night to catch a young girl straight awf of the train from up norf. They would promise her all sorts and the next fing she knew she was on the game working some ponce who never had the decency to earn an honest living.

There used to be an old lady that used to walk around the West End and, just like the words of the song 'Streets of London', she carried her home in two carrier-bags. She was old and dirty and tired of life. She never spoke to anyone. She just kept on walking. Where she came from and where she went to no one knew but every night she would walk past us wivout a word.

London can be the loneliest place in the world if you are on your own, but to us it meant bread and butter and Leicester Square was our stage. When people asked me wot I did for a living I told them that I worked on the biggest stage in the world. The bright lights meant glamour to the tourist but to us they were our footlights. Some of the biggest stars in the world would come and have a chat wiv us and we have worked wiv some big names too.

I once told Sammy Davis Junior that if he was ever out of work he could team up wiv us to get a few bob. Sammy was appearing at the Hippodrome and he was watching us work in the Square. Arfter we had finished he came up and gave us a fiver and we had a long chat wiv him. He said anytime we wanted to go up to his dressing-room we would be welcome.

'If ya ever need a run-out, Sammy,' I said, 'ya can come out wiv us.'

'I'll consider that,' he said wiv a laugh. We never had the honour to work wiv him. Out of all the big stars we knew and worked wiv Sammy Davis is my favourite. He is a real gentleman.

Apart from the famous, there was the ordinary folk who would come and have a word wiv us every Sunday. Week arfter week they would come and watch us. Like little Tim. We called him Tiny Tim and every Sunday, winter and summer, he would be there with his dad in his wheelchair. It was like a long basket on wheels. Little Tim had some kind of spine disease. Every Sunday he would watch about four shows and on the last show he would put a say saltie (sixpence) in the bottle. We would have a few words wiv him and a few laughs. He seemed to be happy. He loved to touch Charlie's accordion and Charlie would work the bellow while little Tim pressed the keys down and his little eyes would light up wiv happiness.

We never saw him for about free weeks and one Sunday we was just finishing a show and putting the props away when I noticed Tim's farver.

'Wotcher mate, where's the boy?' I said.

His eyes filled wiv tears as he pointed heavenwards and said, 'He is up there watching ya show now, mate.'

I just didn't know wot to say. He went on to tell us how he died. My heart sunk and for the rest of the day my heart wasn't in my work, but like all good showmen the show 'ad to go on, and like all good troupers we carried on wiv the gags and larfter. Tiny Tim was only nine when he died. Where he came from I don't know. He must have been eight when he first came to watch us.

We did so many charity shows that we lost count. We never refused a genuine charity. We were all happy as long as we made people laugh. One charity show we done was for the war-disabled ex-servicemen from the Star and Garter House at Richmond.

Every year the London Taxi Driver's Benevolent Association would take the disabled ex-servicemen on a day's outing. There would be hundreds of taxis all following one anuvver wiv about free ex-servicemen in each cab and they would get a free lunch and a show. It was the first time we were asked to do this particular charity. One of the cab drivers picked us up and took us to Worthing Town Hall where the lunch was laid on for the boys and we spent the whole day wiv them. We had a lovely time and the boys enjoyed themselves.

Arfter we had done the show and returned to the dressing

room I decided to go to the lagingage (toilet). The sight that greeted me when I got there was one I shall never forget and don't want to see again. There in a wheelchair was a young man wiv no arms and no legs and his face was one mass of scars. A male nurse was struggling like mad putting him to piss. I couldn't help looking at him as there was mirrors all round the wall of the toilet. I felt sick wiv the whole world at that moment and I wondered in silence when will men learn to live in peace wiv one anuvver.

As I was about to leave the toilet he must have seen my props and he was trying to say somefing to me. I couldn't make out wot he was trying to say. The nurse explained, 'He is thanking you for the show.' I couldn't shake him by the hand as he never had any. I just put my hand on his shoulder and said, 'That's all right, my son.' As I left the toilet I fanked God for the talent he had given me to make people like him happy for just a few hours. Arfter that show we ended up doing some more shows for the Star and Garter boys.

There was some right old characters in the West End. Two very good friends of ours were Big Ted and Big Jack. Ted was about twenty-two stone and Jack wasn't far from it. Big Ted used to sell papers and he had pitches round the West End. He still works the readers to this very day and I often see him when I'm in town. Poor old Big Jack 'as long since gawn. He used to help Ted wiv his papers. Apart from selling papers they would have a go at anyfing to earn a crust. They were a real couple of boys. Those two were never apart. Where you saw one, the uvver wasn't far behind. They were the two most lovable characters I have ever known and when they were togevver it was one round of laughs.

When poor old Jack died it was left to Ted to have him buried as jack had no relatives of his own. Well they laid poor old Jack out in his best suit and he looked 'ansom and there across his old Derby Kelly was his old watch and chain. Everyone fawt it was gold, but we knew it was brass and worf about ten bob. When the undertaker came to screw him down he said to Ted, 'Are you sure ya want that lot to go wiv him, sir?'

'That is wot he wanted, me old son,' said Ted.

'OK if that's wot you want, sir, but it must be worth a fortune.'

Big Ted stayed in the room while they nailed the big fellow up. Jack, being a well-known character round the West End, was the reason for so many mourners. We all went to his funeral.

Just before we set off for the cemetery, Ted said to the undertaker 'Don't forget to stop at the Crown for a few minutes, guv.' The Crown was the big feller's favourite bevvy. Well, we reached the Crown and all the cars stopped. Before the undertaker knew wot was happening, all the boys piled out of the cars and went into the Crown to have a drink on the big feller. We were all in the Crown knocking back double-whiskeys while the big feller waited outside in his box. The undertaker finally came in to get us all out.

One of the boys said, 'Here guv, cop this, and wiv that he stuck a double whisky in the undertaker's folk (hand) and said, 'Have that on the big feller.'

By the time we left the Crown the old undertaker didn't know if he was coming or going. We finally put old Jack to rest and we all went back to big Ted's place and had a booze up and it went on till two in the morning, and all the boys were saying wot a good feller big Jack was.

A few weeks later the undertaker sent big Ted the bill for the burial. Ted wrote back and told him if he wanted his corn (money) he would have to dig the big feller up and take his watch and chain. I don't know for certain but I fink that old undertaker is still waiting for his medzers up until this day.

We had one guy come up to us one night just as we was about to pack up and go home, and we could tell by the way he spoke he was a proper toff. He asked us if we would like to do a show for him. We asked him where he wanted us to do it and wot time.

'It must be arfter harf past twelve,' he said, and added that he would pick us up in his car and take us to the place where he wanted us to do the show.

We told him that we would do the show for a dateture font (ten pounds). Well, he agreed to the price and said he would come back for us as 12.10.

Well, he was as true as his word. There he was at 12.10 in this dirty big black Bentley. He called us from the window of the car and we all piled in.

'Whereabouts is this job, guv?' asked Albert once we was on our way.

'Oh, up Park Lane, old chap,' replied the geezer. 'Bleeding Park Lane?' I said to Charlie. We should have charged him jagg a does dature fonts (twenty pounds).' I mean to say, Park Lane is where all the nobs live.

Well, he drove up Piccadilly and turned into Park Lane and

231

came to a halt outside a big house. We all got out of the Bentley expecting to go into the big house, but before we could move, this geezer said, 'OK chaps, make as much noise as you can.'

Well, we all looked at each uvver. I mean, it was gawn midnight.

'Ya mean ya want us to work out 'ere, guv, at this time of night?' said Charlie.

'Of course, old chap. That's the whole idea.'

'We can't do that, guv. You'll get us all nicked,' said Albert.

'But you must. I've already paid you,' he said (which was true). 'I'll tell you what I'll do. I'll give you twenty pounds if you do your stuff.'

Well, for twenty quid we would have blown up Park Lane. He went on to say that if we got nicked he would come along to pay our fine.

Charlie done no more, he put on his box and awf we went. Well there was lights coming on in all the houses. By this time this geezer was knocking merry hell out of the side drum. The door of the big house opened and out came a geezer in a long dressing-gown.

He walked up to the geezer who had booked us and said, 'His lordship has sent for the police, sir, and he is very annoyed with all this.' The geezer took no notice and just went on banging the side drum.

By this time we had stopped performing and the whole of Park Lane was lit up like a bleeding christmas tree. A few seconds later the scarps arrived in the hurry-up wagon and out jumped an inspector. His face was red wiv rage.

'What the bloody hell's going on here?' he shouted at the top of his voice.

'It's all right old chap. We are having a little celebration,' said the geezer who had hired us. The Inspector asked him his name and when the geezer told him the inspector was all apologetic and he took him to one side and they had a little chat. Well, we all ended up getting nicked and the next morning at Bow Street the geezer was there true to his word and he paid our fines. All the time we was waiting to be called, the inspector kept calling this geezer, sir.

Arfter it was all over and we came out of court he was waiting for us outside.

'Ah, there you are, gentlemen,' he said as he approached us.

'We showed them, didn't we old man?' he said to Albert, patting him on the shoulder.

'Tell me one fing, guv,' said Charlie. 'Wot's it all about?'

Well, it all boiled down to this. This geezer had had a ruck (argument) wiv his farver-in-law and the only way he could get his own back was to start a rumpus outside his house. He told us that the geezer in the dressing gown was the butler. He shook us by the hand and fanked us all for our co-operation and went on his way.

Chapter Thirteen
Prince Monolula, Mutton Eye, Jock the Paper Tearer
and The Rolling Stones

I'll tell you somefing, I've never seen so many cranks in all my life as there were in that West End. There was an old bird we named Pillow Case Kate. She was about five foot three wiv dirty brown hair, blue eyes and a round chubby face. She used to be a joegar and she would work all the picture queues. We found out that she had a pillow tucked up her coat to make her look feelyfaked (pregnant). It was to make the punters in the queue feel sorry for her. Mind you she had a lovely voice and you could hear her all the way up Piccadilly. Where she came from we didn't know. She would just come and go like the wind.

Then there was old Flowers. Flowers was a right old piss-artist. I don't think I have ever seen him sober. He was always bevvied. he was about six feet tall wiv thin brown hair and brown eyes. He must have been in his fifties. he used to sell flowers round the boozers and every time he sold a buttonhole he would buy himself a drop of scotch wiv the medzers and by the end of the evening he was well and truly pissed. Sometimes while we were working in the Square he would come staggering out into the road right in front of us wiv a carnation stuck behind each ear and his flower basket balanced on his head.

In all the years he was around the West End I never saw saw him drop that basket until one night he got knocked up in the air by a lardy da (car). There was flowers everywhere and old Flowers ended up in the middle of the road on his back. Poor old FLowers was taken to hospital. He was still singing 'Lovely flowers' as they put him on the stretcher. Mind you the driver who knocked him up in the air done us a favour for a few weeks, as he wasn't there to frow flowers at us, as he sometimes did while we were working.

Then there was the Silent Runner. He had long grey hair right down to his shoulders. He always wore a clean white shirt and a pinstripe suit. He used to run everywhere he went and he never spoke a word to anyone. Winter and summer he would run right frew the crowd while we was working. Albert would sometimes run arfter him and it got a big laugh from the crowd. There was a story about him and it went like this.

One night he took his girlfriend to the West End to see a film and she left him in the queue while she went to the toilet. He waited for her to return but she never came back and never saw her again. From that night on he would go to the West End and look at every woman in the queue to see if it was her. He would run from queue to queue. That is why he was called the Silent Runner.

All the old characters in the West End have long since gawn. They were characters that made the West End wot it was. On a Saturday when he was not at the racecourse giving away his tips old Prince Monolulu could be seen around Leicester Sqare dressed in all his finery. He was a very tall man wiv skin as dark as ebony. The head-dress he wore made him look even taller. I fink he came from Nigeria. He was a real giant wiv an infectious hint of mischief in his eyes and a real sense of fun. he was dressed in bright-coloured robes wiv a magnificent head-dress of bright-coloured ostrich fevvers and he looked seven-feet tall.

He would sometimes stop and pass the time of day wiv us and he always left us a tip for that arfternoon. As he left we could hear him shouting at the top of his voice, 'I've got a horse. I've got a horse.' One day we read in the paper that he had passed away.

'Poor old sod,' said Albert, 'the old man used to know him. He had been grafting the races for years.' I fawt, *I bet he is giving his tips to the angels now*.

Sometimes on a winter's night we would walk into the Square and we would hear a portable playing somewhere in the distance and we knew it was old Mutton eye who had been busking from the year dot and who worked wiv my Dad years and years ago when I was a little boy. He could always be seen working the picture queues wiv his little portable organ. On the lid was written, 'A wife and sixteen kids to support, and six all-in wrestlers'. He would sing a few old songs to the queue and then take his old bowler hat round. If he got to a fellow and the fellow didn't put anyfing in his hat, poor old Mutton Eye would say, 'Wot's up, guv, got cramp?'

The reason for calling him Mutton Eye was that one of his eyes was a glass eye, and it kept on running, so the uvver buskers named him Mutton Eye. He wore an old bowler hat and always wore a stiff collar and a bow tie. He was about six foot and he walked very upright for an old man. We would see him going from queue to queue wiv his old portable on his back, and whenever he saw us he would shout out, 'How's the medzers ya jaggs?'

He would stop and spend a few moments wiv us and he would say, 'Ho well, this won't get the old woman a pair of new drawers,' and awf he would go on his way. He just left the West End one night and we were never to see him again. We found out a few weeks later that he had died. He was turned seventy when he passed away. It seemed as though buskers were like elephants – they went away to die. They seemed to leave the West End wivout a goodbye.

For an old man Mutton Eye was very witty. One of his gags was that if we was working a slang and a geezer started to cough, he would stop playing and shout to the geezer, 'That's a bad cough ya got there, guvner. I'll tell ya how to get rid of that. Ya take two dozen Beccham's pills, a tin of Epsom Salts, two dozen senna pods and arfter that bleeding lot, you'll be too frightened to cough.' That gag always seemed to get a laugh from the crowd.

At the end of his act just before he was about to bottle he would shout out, 'I'll soon wipe the bluddy smile awf ya faces, I'll be coming round wiv the bluddy hat in a minute.' Yus, he was a great old character, Gawd bless 'im.

To me all the characters in the West End was like jetsam coming in wiv the tide. Where they came from no one knew and where they went to at night was just as big a mystery. There was characters wiv names like: Jock the Paper Tearer; Yorky the Bosh; Baldy; Stones; Jim the Rings, uvverwise known as the Mudlark; Spoons; Mad George; Mick and Mike; and Nutsy. There was an 'ole string of them.

Mick and Mike used to work wiv a barrow organ and they would be dressed in evening dress wiv top hats and bow ties. One played the barrow organ while the uvver one sang and bottled. The uvver buskers called them the city gents.

Baldy wasn't much to speak of. In fact he was a bit of a nutter. He never had a hair on his head. All he did was to spit on a penny and stick it on his head. He done the same old fing for years.

236

' 'ey Baldy,' Albert said to him once, 'Ain't it about time ya changed ya fucking act?'

'Piss awf,' he replied. 'This is easier than wot you're bleeding doing.' *That's true,* I fawt. *He's not such a nutter arfter all.*

He had been in the West End for years. He was about five foot ten tall wiv brown eyes and bo barnet (Barnet Fair – hair). He wore a ragged old overcoat and baggy trousers. He must have been around fifty-six. Once he had stuck the penny on his head he would dance round, singing, 'Hair, hair, hair, I've got none on me noddle.' Arfter doing this a few times he would then take the hat round.

As for Spoons, he had as much idea of playing the bleeding spoons as I had of cutting diamonds. He used to kip in the dosshouse and he was lousy; he had more crabs on him than they had on Soufend beach. If he came wivin ten yards of us we would tell him to fuck awf.

'Piss awf ya old barsted, and go and have a barf,' Charlie would shout out to him.

He came down from Scotland expecting to make a fortune. The only fing he made was a bleeding noise. He was a small fat little geezer wiv a red face, grey hair and blue eyes and he could 'ardly bend down to play the spoons on his knee. All the time he was playing the spoons he would 'um to himself and he would be going red in the face.

'That fucking Spoons is going to have a bleeding 'ard attack one of these days,' Albert once said.

'The fucking sooner the better,' replied Charlie.

Then there was poor old Stones. The reason for calling him Stones was that he had done fourteen years on Dartmoor for killing a geezer. I don't know wot happened. It was before my time. He was about sixty-two wiv snow-white hair and blue eyes. He wasn't a busker – he used to sell newspapers. He must have seen some sorrow frew his life. His poor old face had more lines on it than a road map. Wot I liked about him was that he was always clean and tidy and very quietly spoken. He was just one of God's children who had fallen by the wayside.

Nutsy the peanut king was a different kettle of fish, and the story goes that he was a very rich man and he had a big house in the country. He was a tall, skinny guy of about six foot tall. He always wore a flat cap and a long white coat. He used to have a wooden tray hanging round his neck wiv bags of peanuts and bars of chocolate on it. He would work all the slangs and ya

237

could hear him shouting, 'Nuts, get ya lovely roasted peanuts a tanner a bag.' We would see him rushing around from queue to queue as fast as he could go. As he passed us he would say, 'Wotcher, lads.' And one of us would reply, 'Ows ya nuts, Nutsy?'

One night Nutsy left his tray outside a café while he went in for a cup of tea. When he came out someone had nicked the bleeding lot and he went mad.

'Wot's up, Nutsy?' I said to him.

'Some dirty barsted 'as nicked all me bleeding stock,' he said.

'Fancy having ya nuts pinched,' Albert said.

'Ya, that's a nutty fing to have done to ya, ain't it me old son?' I said.

'I wouldn't mind,' said Nutsy, 'it cost me firty bob to have that bleeding tray made.'

'Well Nutsy, ya have to see the union, me old son,' said Charlie.

'Wot fucking union?'

'Why, the nutcrackers' union,' said Charlie.

'Oh piss awf,' said Nutsy as he left, raging wiv anger. That little episode put Nutsy out of work for two days while he had anuvver tray made. But arfter two days he was back wiv his lovely peanuts.

Mad George was a latecomer to the West End. When he first arrived he had a woman's hat on and an old fur round his neck. Arfter a few weeks he started coming up dressed as a Chinaman. Then he came up dressed as a Scotsman. Where he got the gear from we didn't know, but he was a right old nutter. He would dress up in all kinds of gear and he was as mad as a hatter. He would sing a song and end up frowing his hat in the air. And if he didn't cop when he went round wiv the bottle he would tell the slang they were all barsteds.

That was the only word he knew as every time we saw him we would say to him, 'Wotcher George, how ya doing?'

'They're a lot of barsteds,' he'd reply.

One morning Charlie and I was at Bow Street as usual and Mad George was there as well. When the magistrate fined him two pounds he shouted out in court, 'You're a lot of barsteds.' That night poor old George was having his supper in the nick. He'd got two monfs for contempt of court. But it made no difference: when he came back to the West End he was still calling people barsteds.

One night we were having a rest by the railings when Mad George came along dressed in a woman's hat and a frock wiv

238

black stockings and hobnail boots and carrying a nice levver briefcase.

'I am going to work your pitch tonight,' he said.

'If ya don't piss awf George my old son you're going to end up in fucking hospital,' said Albert. As always George just laughed. 'Where did ya get the briefcase from, George?' I said.

'I want to sell it,' he said.

'How much do ya want for it?' I asked.

'Ten bob to you,' he replied. 'Piss awf,' said Albert. 'Ya owe us five bob that ya borrowed the uvver night.'

'Well, if that's the case,' I said, 'here's anuvver chinker beonk (five bob) and the briefcase is mine.'

I've still got that bleeding old briefcase and it's still as good as ever.

That George used to drive us up the wall. Every night he would come up to us to ask if he could work wiv us.

'George my boy,' Albert would say, 'how do you expect to work wiv stars like us?'

'Go and join the buskers' union and we will let ya work wiv us,' Charlie once said to him.

'Where do I join that?' he asked.

'Ya got to write to the Chief of Police at Savile Row,' Charlie told him.

'OK, I'll do that,' said Mad George, as he walked away.

'Charlie you'll end up getting that poor barsted nicked,' I said.

'That ain't a bad idea,' said Albert. 'They may put him in the nut farm and that will keep him away from us.'

Geroge never did join the buskers' union and ne never worked wiv us.

One of the oldest-known characters ever to busk the West End was a dear old guy and a very dear friend of ours known as Jack Felton who came from Hayes, Middlesex. He could always be seen walking around the West End dressed in a black evening jacket, black trilby hat, and big boots that he used to make himself. He carried an old battered prop bag which contained all his old props. His boots were a pair of boots wiv the soles and toes extended. They were about eighteen inches long and as he walked he would flop the soles on the ground. In his prop bag he had an old umbrella, wiv a big brass knob for the handle and a tin whistle.

He would stop and pitch anywhere. If he saw a copper coming he would pick up his props and scarper. Jack had been busking for years but he never spoke our language. All he could say was, 'Wotcher jaggs.' He was about seventy-six when he died of cancer. Everybody knew him around the West End. He looked a pathetic little guy, as he was so small and thin. In later years he always worked on his own, but before the Second World War he worked wiv my bruvver Albert and the Luna Boys.

I shall never forget the night he was working outside the Empire Cinema. He had a nice big edge and everyone was happy wiv his performance. Always at the end of his act he would frow his old walking stick in the air and shout, 'That's it folks.' Anyway, on this particular night he frew his old walking stick too high. Well, it came down and hit some old bird right across the nut knocking her out as cold as a mackerel on a fishmonger's slab. The blood began to run like a river all down the old bird's boat race. Her hat was knocked to the back of her head and her glasses were being held on by one ear'ole.

Well, poor old Jack didn't know wot to do. He just turned round wiv his norf and souf open. Someone went and phoned an ambulance and while they were waiting for the meat wagon to arrive all that poor old Jack could say was, 'It's an accident jaggs.' The husband of the old bird was going to do all sorts to poor old Jack. He was going to sue him for every penny he had.

The next to arrive was the scarps to find out wot was going on. The last we saw of poor old Jack was when he was being lifted up into the hurry-up wagon by two big burly coppers. That time poor old Jack's feet didn't touch the ground. All he could say to the two burly coppers was, 'It was an accident, ya jaggs.' We heard afterwards that the old bird felt so sorry for poor old Jack that she didn't even press charges and on top of that she bunged Jack a chinker font (five pounds) for his trouble. When he told us about the fiver, Albert said, 'Ya don't want to make a 'abit of it, ya jaggs. Not everyone can afford a fiver to have their nut split open.'

'That's true,' said Charlie.

Poor old Jack lasted for a few more years in the West End and then he faded out of the picture. Albert always knew where Jack lived and we used to go and visit him. He lived in a neat little council house wiv his wife and they always made us welcome. Once when we were at a theatre near Jack's home we went round to see him, and we took him back wiv us to see the show. Arfter we all met in our dressing-room his old eyes were full of happiness and he was so excited. I know now just how he felt.

240

He lasted a couple more years and then he died of cancer. My bruvver Albert went to see him in the hospital, and he told me he had lost so much weight that he looked just like a little baby lying in the bed.

'I wouldn't like to have seen him like that,' I said to Albert. 'I'd sooner remember him as he was, wiv his big boots, bobtail coat, and battered old prop bag.'

They put him to rest while Charlie and I was in Canada. When Albert told me the news I was shocked. Jack was a busker of the past that you will never see the like of again. He was a real character.

The most lovable character in the West End was an old lady by the name of Lil. She was one of the old flower sellers. She was a Cockney and must have been seventy if she was a day. She was the most lovable girl I knew apart from my old mum. Her hair was as white as snow and she had bright red rosy cheeks. Every night we would see her wiv her barsket of red and white carnations, and as she came towards us she would say, 'Wotcher, my old darlings. How's it going?' She would stand and watch us do our show and never missed the bottle. At the end of a show she would come over to us and give us all a sprig of heather and say, 'There you are my lovelies, that's for luck.' Then she would bid us goodnight and go on her way.

One night Albert said to me, 'Ya know wot, jaggs, we haven't seen old Lil for some time have we?' Then I realised I hadn't seen her. There are no more flower girls in the West End. It is a fing of the past. The flower girls of Piccadilly are long since gawn.

There was one old character in the West End called Charlie the Boot Black who lost his leg in the 1914–18 war and had an old-type wooden leg that strapped over his shoulder. The joints of it were very stiff so sometimes it got locked.

Well, one Saturday he had been polishing shoes all day in the Square and he wanted to go for a piss. Well laugh . . . he couldn't get up as his wooden leg was stuck.

'Hey, give us a hand to get up, boys,' he shouted. 'Me bleeding leg's gawn on the blink and I am breaking me fucking leg for a slash.'

Well, no matter how we tried we couldn't lift him up.

'Stop messing about, Charlie,' said Albert. 'You're bleeding heavy.'

'I ain't messing about,' said Charlie. 'Me bleeding leg's got stuck.'

'There's only one fing for it, Charlie,' I said. 'I'll have to go and get a bucket awf of the geezer in the piss 'ole and ya'll have to do it in that.'

'Why can't ya unstrap ya wooden leg and take the bloody fing awf?' said Albert.

Arfter about fifteen minutes we finally got him to his feet and he went to walk away to the laggingage when he fell flat on his boat race. His bleeding wooden leg had got stuck again!

We managed to get him in the toilet, and got some butter awf of the toilet attendant to grease his wooden leg. Every time we saw him arfter that we would say, 'How's ya wooden leg, Charlie?'

Poor old Charlie didn't show up on his pitch one day and we found out he had been knocked down by a bus and died in hospital.

'I wonder wot they will do wiv his wooden leg,' I said.

'If his old bird had any sense she would burn the barsted as it was always getting stuck,' said Charlie.

'Besides, who wants a second-hand wooden leg?' said Albert.

We have seen all the old characters leave the West End. Some of them died and some just faded away.

There was some very good acts around the West End at that time. You would see busker arfter busker waiting to work the same queue. We had a code amongst the old-time buskers that each would take their turn to perform to the queue. It was different wiv our act. We had our regular pitch in Leicester Square. Sometimes we would move up outside the London Palladium to work to the queue before they went in. The London Palladium seemed to be part of us. Apart from working outside we have also worked inside wiv stars like Jo Stafford and dear old Robert Morley and Red Skelton, and many uvvers.

One time when we had to go to the Palladium we met the Rolling Stones, and we ended up sitting on the stage having coffee wiv them and I found them a great bunch of lads. At the time we met the Rolling Stones we were appearing at a festival in Gloucester. We had to do two shows a night to big crowds. Out agent sent us there for a week. While we was there he phoned Albert to tell us that he had a film job for us at the Palladium with the American comic Red Skelton who was the star of the movie.

We arrived at the Palladium around ten o'clock the next morning, just as the Rolling Stones had finished working so we

242

all settled down to a nice cup of coffee. We sure needed it arfter dashing all the way from Gloucester. That was the part of the business that I liked most, all the travelling from one place to anuvver. Arfter being introduced to Red Skelton we were fitted out in pearly kings' costumes as the film was for American TV.

Red Skelton was a very nice guy and he treated us like big stars. He wanted to know all about the busking side of our life and he became very interested in all we had to tell him. We tried to learn him some of our lingo but he just couldn't get the hang of it. That arfternoon we finished filming around four o'clock.

As we came out of the Palladium stage door to put the props into the car Albert said, 'Oh no!' and I could see he was looking towards our old motor and there on the windscreen was two parking tickets.

'I'll kill that fucking warden if I get hold of him,' said Albert.

'You've got some hopes. I bet the old barsted is hiding round the corner laughing at us,' said Charlie.

'Oh well,' I said, 'it makes a change from getting nicked for obstruction, don't it.'

As we were piling all the props in the boot of the Lardy Da Charlie said, 'We will never make Gloucester in time for the first show.

'Yus we will if ya put ya toe down Charlie,' I said, and put his toe down he did. I don't fink that old twelve-year-old green Vauxhall of ours had ever been driven so fast before. I always said to Albert, 'That fucking colour's unlucky,' as it was always breaking down and that day was no exception.

We was making good progress, and we were just going frew a little town when all of a sudden smoke started coming from under the bonnet of the car.

'Blimey, wot the fucking hell's that?' shouted Albert.

Charlie pulled into the kerb and we all got out to see wot was wrong. By this time the smoke was bellowing out as black as soot.

'Lift the bonnet up ya silly barsted,' Charlie shouted at me. I lifted the bonnet and there was smoke everywhere. Being a small town we soon attracted a small crowd and they were all laughing at us.

'Aye, aye, Charlie, we've got an edge,' said Albert. 'Bottle ya jaggs.'

'The fucking car's on fire and you talk about bottling,' shouted Charlie. Everyone was laughing and then I tumbled wot they were laughing at. In our hurry to make good time, we had left the Palladium still wearing our props. Charlie was saying somefing about it not being the radiator as he had only stuck it togevver wiv sticky tape the day before.

We finally guessed wot the trouble was. One of the rubber leads had started to burn. While we had all our heads under the bonnet up came a young scarp to see wot all the fuss was about. He took one look at us and said, 'Wot's going on here then?' I felt like saying 'We are waiting for a bus, guv.'

We told him who we were and wot had happened to the old motor. He started to laugh and said, 'Blimey I fawt you were the Keystone Cops.'

We fixed the wire by taping it up the best way we could and after wishing the copper good luck we went on our way.

As we started up the old motor the crowd began to cheer and wave. We were more than late for the first houses but Charlie kept on driving. We got in the carnival grounds wiv seconds to spare and by this time we were all sweating bottles of ink. We started to unload the props from the boot of the car when the stage manager appeared and said 'There's no need to panic, boys. I've got a stand in for you just in case you never made it back in time.' Well, I could have hit him wiv a pair of prostitute's knickers arfter all the worry we had in getting there.

Show business is like that, there is a lot of worry attached to it and no matter wot kind of trouble we ran into we would always turn up to fulfil the contract. I can honestly say that there are some very nice people in show business and I am proud to have been associated wiv them.

People like the lovely Susannah York. We took part in a short film wiv Susannah called *Scene One Take One*. At that time she had just come to the screen. In it we had to do our act outside a cinema. Susannah played the part of a nun and she was on the run from a convent. She came to ask us if she could do our act wiv us to get some medzers for food. We showed her wot to do and she done very nicely. She got up to all sorts of fings in that film, including taking part in a bank robbery.

She is now a big star and 'as made some great films including *The Killing of Sister George* and many uvvers. Arfter we had finished the film and had been invited to the first showing we were all invited to her house for a cheese-and-wine party and we all had a good time. When I see her on the silver screen now I feel proud to have been associated wiv such a smashing lady as Susannah.

On Saturday we would start work around midday and work until about four, have a break, and start work again around 6.30 and work on to nine o'clock at night. One complete show would last twelve minutes. That's if the law left us alone and that was very seldom. It was very hard work on a Saturday walloping ya cobblers out, there on the hard cobbles. By the time the night was out we were all in and ready to call it a day, but I loved every minute of it. Sometimes on a Satuday we did twelve shows. We never did a firteenf one as that is an unlucky number.

On Sunday we would start work around 2 pm and when we got to the Square our regular punters would be waiting for us. Sometimes on a Saturday we would get nicked two or free times and that would hold the job up as we would have to walk all the way to Savile Row, spend about twenty minutes in the nick and walk all the way back to Leicester Square.

Sometimes when it rained we would meet all our old friends, the cab drivers in Angelo's café and have a bit of a giggle. There wasn't many cab drivers who didn't know us in the West End. They were a good bunch of boys and they never missed a chance of helping us out wiv a gag. We knew a lot of them by first name like Morrie, Ginger, Solly, Ben, Frank, and so on. Charlie would put his box on and Albert would play the side drum and we would have a bit of a singsong. It was more like an old-time music-hall than a café. Wanda and Angelo used to love us going in there as Angelo loved to hear Charlie play. We would have the cab drivers singing at the top of their voices.

By 1962 our summonses were mounting up, but to us it was just one of the hazards of the game. We were in and out of Bow Street police court like bleeding yoyos. No matter how many times they nicked us we never made a fuss. They were a grand bunch of coppers and if we could do them a favour we would do so.

One night we were waiting to start work when a copper in plain clothes came up to us. He flashed his warrant card and as he did so, thinking he was going to nick us, Albert said, 'Leave awf, guv, we ain't even started work yet.'

'Don't worry, Albert, I ain't going to stick one on ya,' he said.

'I just want to know if you will do a show for us at the International Police Ball tonight.'

'We will do a show for ya on one condition, guv,' said Albert. 'What is that?' asked the copper.

'Well we will do it providing none of them foreign coppers don't nick us.'

The copper laughed and said, 'You're a lot of barsteds. Are you going to do the job, yes or no?'

'OK, guv, you win. Wot time do ya want us there?' asked Albert.

'Around nine o'clock,' he said.

'OK, guv, we will be there,' replied Albert and awf went the copper to the ball, saying he would see us later.

Well, we went to work that night and on our second show, two young coppers came steaming in and nicked us.

As we was on our way to the nick, I said to one of the coppers, 'I bet we are out of the nick before you can say "Bollocks".'

'How do you make that out, Henry?' one of them asked.

'Never ya mind, my old son,' I said and he gave me an old-fashioned look.

When we got to the nick we all piled in and as we got inside I saw one of the inspectors that we knew very well.

'Hello boys, how's things?' he asked.

'Not bad guv,' I said, 'but I'll tell ya one fing. If we ain't out of here in ten minutes there's going to be a lot of sorry coppers tonight.'

'How come, Henry?' he asked.

And then we told him about the job we had at the police ball.

'Well we can't let the lads down, can we?' he said. 'All right constable, give them a warning this time.'

'Yes sir,' said one of the coppers who had nicked us.

When the inspector went out of the room the copper said, 'You are a crafty barsted, Henry. No wonder you were so certain you wouldn't be in the nick so long.' And we all laughed about it.

'It's not wot ya know in this world, me old son, it's who ya know,' I said.

'OK, you win,' he said.

'How do ya fink we are going to get all the way up to Charing Cross Road wiv all this bleeding lot?' said Albert, meaning the props.

'All right,' said the copper, 'a nod is as good as a wink to a blind horse,' and he went outside and got the van to take us to the ball.

'I feel like bleeding Cinderella going to the ball,' said Charlie.

'Ya may feel like her ya Jaggs, but you sure don't bleeding look like her,' I said.

When we got to the ball there was thousands of coppers, fat ones, skinny ones, even black ones.

'Fuck me,' said Charlie, 'if only the Devil was to cast his net now, wot a bleeding catch he would have.'

The show went down well and as soon as we walked onto the floor everyone knew us. And oh boy, did we take the piss out of those coppers and they loved every minute of it. Arfter the show everyone wanted to buy us a drink and a lot of them were surprised to find out that we didn't drink. It's a funny fing but a lot of people fink that all buskers are bevvy merchants, but not us. We may have just one to be polite but that was all.

One of our favourite gags when we got nicked was to demand to be taken to the nick by van. In those days the old police vans had no partition between prisoner and driver, so when the hurry-up wagon arrived we would all march in frew the back and out again frew the uvver door by the driver's seat. The crowd would roar wiv laughter and the poor old coppers would go as red as beetroots but they took it all in good part.

The best day for us to work was Sunday and I remember on one lovely Sunday arfternoon in the summer we had a big crowd of about twelve hundred people watching us. That arfternoon there were a lot of big stars rehearsing for a royal charity show at the Odeon Leicester square, stars like dear old Tony Hancock, Liz Frazer, Kenneth More, Warren Beatty, Joan Collins and many more.

On our second show all the stars came out to work wiv us. Tony Hancock said to Albert, 'What can I do, chum?' 'Ya can have the best job of the lot, me old son,' said Albert, 'ya can bottle.'

Well Tony ended up bottling and Kenneth More played the side drum. We all had one big giggle and by the end of the show the road was completely blocked and we had stopped all traffic. We were all working away like good'uns when I saw out of the corner of my eye a young scarp coming towards ut.

'Varder the scarp ya jaggs,' I said to Albert.

'Nanty ya jaggs (take no notice mate),' he replied and we went on working. The copper came right in at us and said, 'Right lads, you're nicked.'

'If ya nick us, mate, ya will have to nick the geezer on the side drum and the geezer who's doing the bottling,' said Albert.

When the copper saw who was playing the side drum and who was doing the bottling he went as red as a baboon's ars'ole and he just walked away. All the crowd clapped and started to sing 'For he's a jolly good fellow'. That poor little copper didn't know what to do. We saw him a few days later and he said, 'I shall never forget that as long as I live,' and he never nicked us again.

Mind you, there was one or two coppers who weren't so good to us. There was one sergeant (I don't fink he had a farver) that used to nick us every time he saw us. And it was frew him we got all our publicity in the national papers. The press began to take notice of our legion court appearances. As a matter of fact he did us a favour because it was frew him that we got an agent and this agent gave us some lovely work all over the world and that's how we was able to work wiv all the big stars and to meet royalty.

When our dear old Dad passed away it was as though someone had taken a big slice of our lives and frown it to the wind. As farvers go, my farver was an angel. He died of a heart attack at the age of sixty-free. We got the telegram around four o'clock in the afternoon, and like all good troupers we put on a brave face. But that night there were two broken-hearted clowns trying to laugh but all the time we were finking of our dear old Dad.

We got to Scarborough as soon as we could. Our poor old Mum looked like a little-girl-lost. She had had so many happy years wiv our old farver and her poor old blue eyes were red wiv crying. I don't fink she could have cried any more as there was no more crying left in those poor old tired eyes. She had done all her crying through the years when she nursed our farver frew all the eye operations he had had. As Albert and I stood and looked down at that old work-worn face in the coffin, I wanted to say, 'Sorry Dad.' I wanted to say how sorry I was that none of us boys could take him by the hand and lead him round his dear old London busking as he did long ago. But it was too late. God was his guide now . . .

My life I owe to my farver and the way he taught me to live it. There is only one regret I have in my life, and that is that I wasn't

248

wiv him when he passed away. But regrets don't come cheaply. He was the best farver anyone could wish for and we all loved him to the end. To me there was never a gentler man than my Dad.

Chapter Fourteen
Threatened with clink

When Albert and I came back from Scarborough after the funeral, life went on for us as usual – and the summonses kept coming. But it was always a laugh when we went to court, certainly not the solemn place most people imagine it to be. Like the morning when they had 'Rosie', the queer, who had been knocked awf the night before for soliciting in Hyde Park. The sergeant behind the desk at Bow Street was sorting out Rosie's personal belongings and a young constable was writing down his effects.

'One handkerchief, one bunch of keys, one lipstick, one jar of Vaseline,' the sergeant shouted out.

The young constable looked up and said, 'What's the vaseline for, sergeant?' And there was one roar of laughter from all the boys who was waiting to be put up in the dock.

'If you don't know wot it's for, lad, then I am certainly not going to tell you, am I?' said the sergeant.

Rosie was grinning all over his face and was obviously delighted he had found a virgin. Rosie went up before the beak and got a ten-pound fine and a warning that the next time he would be sent to prison. He paid his ten-pound fine and as he went frew the door he said to the sergeant, 'I'll be seeing ya me darling.'

'Piss awf before I bang ya up again,' said the sergeant and Rosie went out smiling.

The number of characters that went frew that Bow Street Court was quite unbelievable. You could always get a laugh while you was waiting to be called in front of the magistrate. Old Jeff the jailer used to take it all in his stride. On our way out we would say, 'See ya tomorrow Jeff,' as we knew we would get nicked again that night. Getting nicked to us was just like paying rent for the pitch.

The only time we couldn't work Leicester Square was if there was a premiere at one of the cinemas round the Square. That meant that the Queen or some uvver member of the Royal

250

Family would be visiting the cinema for the big first night. When this was the case, the police would cordon awf the Square for the Royal visitors. And that would be the only time we would give up our pitch to anyone. If this was the case we would move up to work outside the London Palladium.

One night the Palladium doorman said, 'What's up, boys? Ain't ya working the Square tonight?'

'No mate,' said Albert. The bloody Royal Family's working it tonight.'

'Ya, and I bet they don't get nicked for obstruction,' added Charlie.

I got to think that it would be a giggle to old Prince Philip and the Queen appearing in front of old Mr Barraclough the magistrate at Bow Street in the morning. Old Jeff the jailer would have certainly stuck his chest out then. I wondered also if he would have lent them the money to pay for their fine like he did for me on one occasion.

It happened like this. I was late in getting up and I had to be at Bow Street Court by 10.30 am. I got to the underground all right wiv the silver I had in my pocket, but it was about 10.40 am when I got to the court. I surrendered my bail to Jeff as usual and he unlocked the main door and said, 'Good morning, Henry.'

'Good morning, Jeff. Ya alright mate?' I said.

'Yea not bad,' he replied.

I went in to wait my turn to appear in the dock. The same old routine followed and I was fined two nicker. I bid Mr Barraclouch good morning and then I went downstairs to pay my two pounds. I put my hand in my pocket and to my surprise I realised I had no money. I fawt, *That's fucked it. I've left my medzers behind.* And then I remembered I took the money out of my pocket the night before and dropped it in the dressing table drawer.

The sergeant behind the desk said, 'How much, Henry?'

'Two pounds,' I said. 'But ya'll be lucky if ya get it. I've left me bleeding money at home.'

'Well, if ya haven't got it ya'll have to send out for it,' he said. Just then Jeff came into the office wiv some papers, and he saw me going frew my pockets.

'What's wrong, Henry?' he asked.

I told him wot I had done and put his hand in his pocket and slipped two pounds in my hand and said, 'Here, I'll see ya tomorrow.' I couldn't believe it.

'Fanks Jeff,' I said. 'You're a toff. I'll pay ya back tomorrow.'

251

I knew I was bound to be nicked that same night and I did pay Jeff back his two nicker the following morning. But it was a lovely gesture by old Jeff. He was the nicest copper I've ever met.

The taxi drivers in the West End were a great bunch of lads. If we was working and one of them saw a copper making his way towards us he would pull up alongside, wevver he had a fare in his cab or not, and give us the lowdown that the Law was on its way. We saved ourselves many a fine wiv the help of the old London cabby. And we could always bank on getting a laugh from a cabby. We had one who would drive up to us while we was working and he would stop his cab for Albert and me to get in. We would get in one side and out the uvver. Those cabbies would do anyfing for a laugh.

November the Fifth, Guy Fawkes Night, was always a dodgy night for us to work. There was bound to be one joker in the crowd. One Fireworks Night Albert and I was doing our act as usual in the Square – we had come to the sand-dance routine and we were about twenty yards away from Charlie dancing up the road and Charlie was looking our way in case we should break awf to do some kind of gag – when I saw this geezer walk by the snake-tin and drop somefing in it. I fawt he had cropped some medzers so we went on working the routine.

All of a sudden there was a terrific bang and the tin went about fifty feet in the air spilling its contents – which, incidentally, was a woman's bra tied to the end of a banna whistle wiv a bit of fishing line. Well, poor old Charlie shit 'iself as he didn't know wot 'ad 'appened.

'Fuck me, it's sabotage,' I said to Albert.

The next fing was that the tin came down and coshed Charlie right across the nut. It was a good job he had been wearing his bowler or he would have been knocked out cold. The crowd saw it as one big joke and they were laughing their heads awf. Charlie tumbled wot had happened so, wivout batting an eyelid, he went on wiv the show. The poor old tin was all buckled and bent. The whistle and the bra we found on top of one of the phone-boxes in Leicester Square. We straightened out the tin and the show went on as usual. A little fing like that didn't stop The Roadsters from working.

It's a funny fing but we never got nicked by the traffic wardens for parking in the West End. I will tell ya the reason for this. We did a show at one of London's most famous hospitals and we worked a gag into the act where Albert did a somersault and

252

landed on his back. He just lay there on the floor pretending to be dead and I would shout out, 'Is there a doctor in the house?' Being a hospital this got a laugh.

Well, arfter the show was over one of the young medical students came up to us to congratulate us on our performance.

'Wot you want to complete that gag where Albert goes on his back on the floor,' he added, 'is a doctor's stethoscope. You could pretend that you are giving him an examination.'

'That's a good idea, son, but where the bleeding hell are we going to get one of those fings from?' said Charlie.

'You leave that to me, old chap,' said the student. And with that he left the room.

About five minutes later he returned wiv a brown paper bag. He called me to one side.

'Here you are, old chap,' he said. 'This is just the thing for that gag.' I looked into the bag and there inside was a brand new stethoscope. The fings we did later wiv that stethoscope was nobody's business. We had some right old laughs with it.

One of our favourite gags was to leave it on the dashboard of the car whenever we parked it. We usually would park around the back of the dental hospital in Orange Street and leave it where it could be seen. In all the five years we had that stethoscope we never got nicked once by the traffic wardens. They fawt we were bloody doctors.

Sir Mortimer Wheeler, the archaeologist and television personality, used to pass us every night and would say, 'Good evening, gentlemen,' and we would reply, 'Good evening, guv.' He was a real gentleman. he always raised his hat to us as he approached us. The Yanks used to love us and we made several American friends and every time they came to London they would come and see us. Apart from the Yanks there were people from all over the world.

I shall never forget the night we walked back onto the Square arfter being told by one of the magistrates at Bow Street we would get sent to prison if we appeared in front of him again. We got nicked on the Saturday arfternoon and we had to appear at Bow Street on the Monday morning. Albert and I surrendered our bail to old Jeff as usual and to us it was just a normal day.

'Good morning Albert. Good morning Henry,' said Jeff as he unlocked the door leading to the cells.

'Morning Jeff, how's fings wiv you?' I said as we passed the time of day wiv him for a while. The drunks and the layabouts were being called and before we knew it one of the court coppers shouted 'Albert Hollis and Henry Hollis.' Albert and I went up the stairs leading to the court and we said good morning to one or two of the coppers that we knew.

When we got in court instead of our old magistrate Mr Barraclough there was a new magistrate on the bench, Mr Geraint Rees, a distinguished-looking man with grey hair and gold-rimmed glasses. The copper who read out the charge claimed we were singing and dancing in the street and playing an instrument. I don't know if the magistrate fawt we was drunk or not but he asked the copper if we had had any previous convictions and when the copper told him we had been in court over four hundred times before, he nearly fell awf the bench.

He looked at bofe of us and said, 'I am going to fine you each two pounds but if you come up in front of me again I will order you to find sureties to be of good behaviour and if you fail to find sureties you will go to prison.'

Well, ya could have knocked us down wiv a fevver. I didn't want to go to prison for making people laugh. All the people in court looked at us and I don't fink they could believe their ears.

As we came out of the court to go and pay the fine, one of the coppers who we had known for years said, 'Blimey, that's a shock. Wot are you going to do lads?'

'He can go and piss in the fountain in Trafalgar Square,' I said. 'I am still going to work tonight.'

Wot ya fink, jaggs? poor old Albert said.

'Let's pay the fine and then we can thing about it,' I said.

As we was paying the fine old Jeff came up and said how sorry he was to hear about it all. When we got outside the court we got pounced upon by newspaper reporters and they all wanted to know what we was going to do.

'Well we just can't give up wivout a fight, can we?' I said to one of them.

A reporter from one of the London papers was very good to us. He asked us if we could go back to his office wiv him and he would consult his legal department for us to see where we stood. But it was no use. The law was the law and there was nothing we could do about it so we decided to have a meeting at home wiv Charlie to see wot we was going to do.

When the evening papers came out that night we were big

news. There was healines like 'THE BUSKERS SAY FARE-WELL' and 'WEST END SEES THE LAST OF THE FAMOUS BROTHERS'. And next day we were everywhere in the papers. The *Daily Mail* reporter, under the headline 'THE ROADS-TERS ARE TOLD IT'S CURTAINS' wrote:

For two middle-aged men in moth-eaten frock coats, pyjama jackets, Tommy Cooper fezes and hobnail boots, all the world is definitely not a stage. Particularly as they and their one-man-band want to do their busking act in London's traffic-bound Leicester Square. A magistrate, Mr Geraint Rees, made this clear to the three – the Roadsters – yesterday at Bow Street Court when he presented them with their second £2 fine this week for causing obstruction. And he warned them, 'If you come before me again I shall order you to find sureties to be of good behaviour. If you fail to find the sureties you will go to prison'. The Roadsters, Bert Hollis 49, his 38-year-old brother, Harry, and their (one-man) band Charlie Hilleard 59 – walked dejectedly from the court. Huge crowds used to gather in the Square to watch their act. Policemen on the beat summed up the situation and generally left them alone. Then their 'stage' became a one-way street. The Roadsters – Bert and Harry, live in Cherston Road, Loughton, Essex and Charlie in Northborough Road, Streatham, S.W.16 – regard themselves as a tourist attraction.

And the *Daily Mirror* carried the headline, THE BUSKER BROTHERS FIGHT FOR THEIR STAGE. The *Mirror* story went like this:

A famous part of London's West End evening scene – two toothbrush-moustached buskers who have tap-danced to delighted crowds for 30 years may soon disappear. Twice in four days Albert and Henry Hollis have paid fines at Bow Street for causing obstruction in Leicester Square where thousands have watched their slapstick dance routine. Outside the court where they each paid £2 yesterday Albert said, 'Fines have cost me £30 in the last few weeks. They are trying to drive us off the streets and it looks as if they will succeed.' Last night the brothers and Albert's wife Edith took a rest from their nightly street act to stay at home in Cherston Road, Loughton, Essex. Albert said, 'The police started picking on us about Easter. We are being taken to court so often we are thinking of changing our name from the Roadstars to the Bow Street buskers. We will try Leicester Square again but if we get another summons as soon as we start we will have to leave the West End and play at Petticoat Lane or the Portobello Road Market.

The controversy was kept going by the *People* who that Sunday carried a long piece about us which had the headline 'PART OF LONDON DIES'. In it the reporter said:

Apparently London night life can find room for motorists – those strained grey creatures shuffling their cars through the hopeless streets of the West End. But authority will not tolerate colourful characters who bring rud joy, a certain merry disturbance and a zest for pure night-out happiness to millions of people. The cries of London fade away . . . I will miss the buskers should they fade away and die in the established order of things.

When we were having all the publicity in the national papers one showbiz personality, Marion Ryan, wrote to one newspaper and said, 'The old buskers in Leicester Square should be given the freedom of the city or the O.B.E. instead of being threatened with jail. But we didn't want the OBE. All we wanted was to be left alone to get an honest living.

With all this publicity we knew the police would be specially on the lookout for us so arfter a long discussion we decided to take the show to the East End where we had started busking many years before.

The following day we walked the streets of the East End and we were sick inside. We worked where the old market in Chris Street used to be, but it was not the same. It had all been changed. The market had all been closed in. Then we went to the same gates at West India Docks where I used to hang around as a kid. It showed me how fings had changed over the years. I wasn't happy to be back. There were too many sad memories.

I looked at the tired grimy houses and narrow streets. I watched the smiles in the timeless cockney faces. I should have been happy in a nostalgic way. I was back in the old East End where it all began for me as a small boy, but my heart was heavy. My laughs were forced. I could see the end of our living and a piece of old London dying as we daren't work the West End any more.

Arfter a few pitches I said to Charlie, 'How's the medzers ya jaggs?' 'The way fings are going, ya jagg we won't even have our fare home,' he replied.

Arfter we had finished our act and packed up the props, I said to Albert, 'There is only one fing for it jagg. We will have to go back into the West End and take a chance on getting nicked again.'

'Wot, and go inside for it?' he replied.

'It's that or fucking starve,' said Charlie.

We ended up phoning a good friend of ours who was a reporter on one of the newspapers and we told him wot we was going to do. He fanked us for the story and he said he was going to see us all right for the evening papers. And there it was in big headlines: 'THE SHOW GOES ON: LONDON'S FAMOUS BUSKERS RETURN TO WEST END'.

Around 7.30 that night we walked back to our old pitch in Leicester Square and to our surprise we found there were people on bofe sides of the road. they were waiting for their beloved buskers to perform. As we walked out into the road there was applause and cheers from the crowd. I was near to tears.

I looked at Albert and said, 'We are home my old son. Let's go. Let's show them,' and we went into our act.

That night all went well and we got a full night's work in. All the time we had people coming up to us and saying how sorry they were to read about our trouble and they were telling us to put up a fight as we were a part of dear old London.

The following morning we had a phone call from an agent called Norman Crumby. He phoned Albert and asked us if we would like to go on the inside for a while. We jumped at the chance as we would be able to have some respite from the Law. We went down to his office in Orpington to meet him. He asked us if we would like to go on tour wiv a show promoting a certain brand of cigarettes. He also promised us plenty of work arfter that.

We decided to take his offer. Albert said it would give the West End a rest from us, as none of us wanted to go to prison for making people laugh. Wherever we went wiv the stage show we were a great success. The first show we did was wiv the then slimline Bill Maynard, before he had such a hit as Selwyn Froggitt.

It was while we were working wiv him at Poplar Town Hall that

257

I met once more my first love. It was the first time we had been back to Poplar since the war but this time it was not at the old Town Hall that I knew as a child, it was a new modern building wiv a stage as big as the London Palladium's.

On the last night of the show, Charlie, Albert and I were sitting in our dressing-room having a rest before the last house. Suddenly there was a knock on the door. It was the stage-door keeper.

'Come on in whoever ya are,' shouted Albert. The door opened and the stage-door keeper put his head round the door and said, 'Which one of ya is 'enry?'

'That's him pop,' said Charlie. 'That ponce over there.' I looked up from a paper I was reading.

'Wot can I do for ya, pop?' I asked.

'There's a man and a woman to see ya out back. The woman says she knows ya.'

'Hurry up jaggs, it could be a fan,' said Albert. Or it could be some bird you've stuck in the family way,' said Charlie.

'Piss awf, Charlie,' I said, 'ya know I don't do fings like that.'

I followed the stage-door keeper round the back of the stage to the stage door. As I approached the stage door I could see a smartly dressed woman dressed in a smart blue costume. She had her back to me and I noticed her jet-black hair fell softly on the back of her neck. Wot I saw from the back I liked very much.

Just as I got to where she was standing, I heard the man say, 'Here he comes.' This guy I didn't know from Adam.

Just then the woman turned round and, as she did so, she put out her two hands to me and said 'Hello, Al.'

I recognised her at once. My heart was racing so fast I fawt it was going to bust, and my legs went like jelly. The next fing I knew, we were locked in each uvver's arms, and all I could say to her was, 'Di, Di, it's you.'

She smelt so sweet, and she felt so warm. Arfter a moment we let each uvver go, and I could see tears coming from her lovely dark eyes.

'Don't cry, there's nuffing to cry about,' I said.

Wiping her eyes wiv a white lace handkerchief she turned round to the man who was wiv her and said, 'I'm sorry, Jim, this is Al. Al, this is my husband, Jim.'

I shook him by the hand and I knew at once he was the man for her by his handshake. My old Dad used to say to me, 'Son, you can always tell a man by his handshake.'

'I am pleased to meet ya, mate,' I said.

Arfter the introduction was over we talked about old times. Diane told me that Tommy had emigrated to New Zealand and was married wiv a family of his own. As she talked I was finking of how lovely she still was. She was a real mature woman now.

But she was still the same Diane I had known as a child and I will remember her till the day I die. The guy who she had married was obviously in love wiv her, but he would never have the love for her that I once had. Ya see, we had first love, and first love is the best. Nuffing can change that. And that was the last time I saw Diane.

It was on this tour that we had the privilege of appearing in the presence of H.R.H. the Duke of Edinburgh. It was at Grosvenor House for the Lords Taverners. The show went like a bomb and there was a lot of lords and ladies there apart from some of the biggest stars in show business. It took us all day getting ready, wot wiv washing all the props and running frew the act to make sure everyfing was OK.

We left home about 7.30 as it was November the Fifth. There was the usual crowd in Trafalgar Square letting awf fireworks and singing.

I kept saying to Albert, 'Are you sure we have everfing?'

'Everyfing is there ya jaggs,' he replied.

'I hope so,' I said. 'We don't want no slip-up in front of the old Duke, do we?'

Ya see I was the worrier of the act and I liked to know where everyfing was.

When we got to Grosvenor House the Duke's car was outside.

'Blimey, Charlie,' I said, 'he is already here.

'That's to make sure he gets a seat,' said Charlie and we all laughed as we went frew the doors.

Once inside a geezer came up to us and said, 'Can I help you, gentlemen?'

'Yes mate,' replied Albert, 'we're here to work in front of the Duke.'

The geezer gave a smile and arfter looking at the letter we had he said, 'Come this way lads,' and he showed us into a big room.

When we got inside there was Tommy Trinder, Lionel Blair, the late Sid James, Richard Hearn (Mr Pastry) and lots more stars. None of them recognised us until we got into our props and then they all started to talk to us.

259

'I thought it was you, boys,' said Lionel Blair.

Well, we all had a nice time swopping gags and having a laugh.

'Have ya seen the old Duke yet, Sid?' I asked Sid James.

'Yus,' he said, 'he is sitting right in front of the door as you go out onto the floor. If ya look through that door you will be able to see him.'

We all had a look frew the door and there was the man himself, sitting right at number one table.

'Blimey, Charlie,' I said, 'you will have to be careful or ya might 'it 'im wiv the stewed plum (drum).'

'When I get out there I am going to ask him to move his chair for a gag, so I can get by wiv the drum,' he replied.

'Ya can't do that.'

'Who can't?' said Charlie. 'You watch me.' And he was as good as his word.

It was our turn to perform and Charlie went out first as usual. As he got to the Duke's chair he shouted, 'Do ya mind moving ya chair, me old son.'

Well, I fawt the place was going to fall apart wiv laughter. Everyone started to clap and cheer. I don't know if it was for wot Charlie said to the Duke or if it was because they recognised the old drum as Charlie put it down. Charlie gagged around for a while as he was putting on his accordion. Then he struck up and out went Albert and yours truly. As we went into the act so they clapped and cheered. The show went as good as any uvver show we had ever put on and the applause was fantastic.

We had to pass the Duke's table on our way back to the dressing room and he was still laughing as we reached his table. One of the party on his table said, 'That was wonderful, gentlemen.'

'Fanks, guv,' said Charlie, and we made our way to the dressing room.

Arfter the show was over the Duke came and shook hands wiv us and he said how much he had enjoyed the show. He asked us if the police were still chasing us.

'We don't mind, guv,' said Charlie. 'It's part of the game.'

The Duke laughed and said, 'I hope you last for many years to come.'

That wasn't the only time we were to meet the Duke. Charlie said we should put 'By appointment of H.R.H. the Duke of Edinburgh' on the old stewed plum.

'Leave awf,' said Albert. 'We can't do that. You'll get us nicked.'

'That will make a bleeding change, won't it,' I said. 'This is wot they call a busker's command performance,' I said of our show for the Duke.

The next night, when we went into the West End, the uvver joegars wanted to know all about it. We were the envy of all of them and we were really proud.

Before the Second World War Charlie had done a lot of stage work. He'd worked wiv a number of accordion bands and he used to tell me about some of the capers he got up to at some of the digs he stayed at. Like the time Charlie and one of the boys from the band got back to the digs late and the landlady had locked them out.

'Well, I don't know about you, mate,' Charlie said to his mate, 'but I ain't staying out here all bleeding night,' and he went round the back of the house to climb into the upstairs bedroom window.

To get into the window Charlie had to climb onto a pigeon shed and he ended up covered in pigeon's shit from head to foot. He told me he couldn't move for laughing and his old suit was in such a state that he had to frow it away. For the rest of the week he walked around in a pair of flannels that he borrowed from one of the boys in the band. Charlie was at home wevver he was performing on the stage or busking in the open road. Ya see, he was a trouper and a showman and I learned a lot from him. Charlie was the eldest of our group and he never finished busking until he was seventy-two.

He once said to me, 'Ya know wot, Al. If I had my time over again I would still do the same. I've had a lovely life wiv God's help.'

It was a pity as Charlie never had any children to carry on the old act in Leicester Square. It's a funny fing but as ye get older ya seem to look back over the years and ya don't fink of tomorrow or wot it might bring. I always fawt I would go on busking forever but the good Lord planned it otherwise.

Anuvver six monfs and a hundred summonses later we were still busking in Leicester Square but at the same time our agent was providing us wiv some very good work. Although I liked working

261

on the stage and doing cabaret I was more at home busking. You can't seem to understand the feeling I used to get when I used to walk out into the Square and start them laughing at the antics of the act.

It was different to being on a stage. We had the whole road to work in and at night we had the cinema to provide us wiv lighting. The Yanks used to love us and take photos of us working and the crowd loved to see us get nicked as they knew it was one big laugh wiv the scarp who nicked us.

Sometimes the crowd would boo the unfortunate boy in blue and he would go blood red and I would say to him, 'There y'are old son, they're singing your song.'

'I've got to nick ya, Henry me old son, as I don't know who is watching me,' the copper would reply. Ya see, they could never trust one anuvver in case one of their mates was in the crowd and he would report him to the guvner at the nick the next morning.

We never worked during the day in the West End as they were all working pecks from the offices. It was the tourists we were arfter. Our time for starting work was around seven in the evening and we would work up until 9.30. In that time we would entertain around five fousand people. Mind you, not all of them dropped in the bottle. If they did we would have been stone rich.

The next lot of gangsters to arrive in the West End were the Kray twins, Ronnie and Reggie. They used to drive by us every night while we was working and there was always a bit of silver from them but they never interfered wiv us. We knew them by first names as they was born in the same district as Albert and I. It's a funny fing how all the gangsters come and go. As one lot got nicked so anuvver lot would take over. The times I've heard a new police chief say he was going to clean up the West End. They have no chance. there will always be villains in that astonishing area.

It is the same wiv prostitutes. My old mum used to say, 'The bigger the whore, the better the luck,' and she was right. I have never seen a prostitute skint. I remember one of the girls coming up to us one night in the Square and she said she was going to retire from the game. She told us she had already bought a cottage in the country and she was now finking of buying a car. She then produced a pile of catalogues and when we looked at them they were all from Rolls Royce.

'Blimey ya jaggs we are in the wrong game,' I said to Charlie.

Mind you, she was a wide bird. Most of the prostitutes used to work for the mob and if they didn't do their quota of business Gawd help them. They had to pay for their flat. One girl told me she paid sixty pounds a week for one room. And then there was the maid to be paid for an all the french letters to buy. No prostitute would let a punter go wiv her wivout a french letter. Mind you there were the old slags who would knock around Hyde Park and you could have one of them for around ten bob. That's if you wanted to take a chance and risk getting a dose of the Albert Docks.

Around 1964 we were the talk of the West End wiv all the summonses we were getting. There was never a day passed that we didn't get nicked. Sometimes we got nicked twice a day but we took it all in our stride. One Satuday I can remember getting nicked free times right awf. We was no sooner in the nick that we was out again and back in the square about an hour arfterwards. We must have paid out a fousand nicker in fines. By getting nicked like that on a Saturday we had to work late to make up for the time we spent going to the nick.

Once I had a letter wiv ten pounds in it and all it said was, 'This is to help you pay for the fine when you get arrested on Thursday night.' I don't know who sent it but by the look of the handwriting it was from an educated person.

When we were having all the publicity we had hundreds of letter wishing us well. They were all addressed to Albert's house in Loughton, Essex.

'There ya are jaggs, someone loves us,' said Albert. 'Look at all this fan mail.' There was even a letter from Tiny Tim's farver. We had letters from showbiz personalities saying how sorry they were to hear how the law was chasing us. We had a lot of good people on our side, but it made no difference. The fines were still piling up. They finally nicked us so many times that we ended up in *The Guinness Book of Records*.

Chapter Fifteen
100 summons later

We had pet names for all the coppers who used to knock us awf. Names like Eyes Higher, Baby Face, Ten to Two Feet, Frustrated Dick, Pluto, Smiley, Bubbles, Flash Gordon, and Snozzle.

Flash Gordon was the farstest copper on two legs. His name was Gordon so we called him Flash Gordon. Ya had no chance wiv him. He was in the crowd like a shot from a gun and before he nicked ya he would say, 'Right, you're nicked,' and awf ya would go to the nick.

Old Snozzle was a right old mug. One night he came steaming into the crowd and before he could capture any of us we all ran. I dived into a phone box, took awf my bowler hat and glasses and moustache and pretended I was making a phone call. He walked right past me. That night I saved myself two pounds.

I remember one night Eyes Higher, the copper I mentioned earlier, chased us round the Square. Albert and I ran into a boozer and Eyes Higher was outside wiv his mate waiting for us to go but I said to Albert, 'I ain't going out there. He nicked me last time.'

By this time all the people in the pub was laughing their heads awf as we were in our Turks' gowns and red fezes. The guvner behind the bar fawt it was a big joke.

'You're a pair of cowards,' he said. 'Why don't ya go out and let him nick ya?'

'Leave awf guv,' said Albert. 'He nicks us ever time he sees us.'

Well, old Eyes Higher kept looking over the top of the window at us. The guvner gave us bofe a bevvy and every time Eyes Higher looked over the top of the window I held up my glass to wish him good health. Well, this went on for about twenty minutes and Eyes Higher wouldn't move away from the pub.

'There is only one fing for it jaggs,' I said to Albert. 'We will have to surrender.' And wiv that I tied my hanky to the end of my walking stick and poked it frew the door. Old Eyes Higher went mad.

'Come out Henry, you barsted and get nicked,' he said, and out we went.

All the way to the nick he kept saying, 'I suppose you fink that was funny.'

'Wot's the matter wiv ya?' I said. 'You getting miserable in ya old age?'

The next morning in court we found out that he had been going mad all day wiv the toofache and he wasn't in a very good mood when he nicked us.

'Why didn't ya tell us ya had the toofache?' I said. 'I would have brought ya a drop of Scotch to take the pain away.' Poor old Eyes Higher. He took it all in good part.

The reason why we called one copper Baby Face was that he was so young-looking. We never had much trouble from him. I fink he only nicked us about twice all the time he was in the West End. Ten to Two Feet (whose feet pointed out like the hands on a clock) nicked us about six times.

Frustrated Dick was a right old barsted. Every time we saw him he wanted to nick us. One night he came up to us while we was standing having a rest.

'I don't want no trouble from you lot tonight,' he said.

'Leave awf guv,' said Charlie. 'We haven't even started work yet.'

'I'm just warning you,' he replied.

'Why don't ya piss awf and go round Soho where all the ponces is and nick a few of them?' said Albert.

'I can't go round Soho,' he said. 'I am on this beat tonight.'

We ended up going for a cup of tea. By the time we got back he was gawn. We went to work and just as we finished he came round the corner and nicked all free of us. We gave him a right old bollocking on the way to the nick but it made no difference. We were nicked and that was that.

Old Pluto wasn't a bad copper. He did sometimes give us a break. We called him Pluto because he had big ears and baggy eyes. I fink he nicked us about four times. One night he nicked me and on our way to the nick I said to him, 'Do you sleep at night when you nick geezers like me?'

'Look Henry,' he said, 'it is only my job I am doing. If I am sent out to nick you I have to nick you and that is all there is to it.'

I suppose he was right but it seemed funny to us wiv all the

265

scum there was in that West End they picked on us and we were only making people laugh.

Smiley was always smiling so that was how he got his name. If he nicked ya there was no messing about. He just sent for the van and that was that. I suppose it was better than walking.

Bubbles was OK too. He must have nicked us about eight times. Every time arfter he nicked ya he would say, 'Sorry, lads.' But his 'Sorry' didn't pay the fines . . .

A guy once said to us, 'Why don't you pack it in and get a proper job?' I asked him wot type of job could we do as we knew nuffing else but busking.

'If you fink this is easy, matey, you come out there and have a go,' said Charlie.

'I haven't got the guts,' said the geezer and that's wot you have to have; plenty of guts to put up wiv the hardship.

Winter can be very hard. Sometimes we would stand about for hours before we could have a pitch and maybe at the end of the night we took about firty bob between the four of us.

The only time we left our pitch in Leicester Square was on Derby Day. We would travel down to Epsom to the races. I used to like working the race course as it made a nice change. There we would meet up wiv all the Joegars and Pikeys (gypsies). We knew a lot of them and their families and we would swap stories. Old Prince Monolulu would be there shouting, 'I've got a horse, I've got a horse.' There would be spivs, pickpockets, and all kinds of villains.

Arfter the races were over we would all meet in a café and the stories you would 'ear was out of this world. There was the Wind Bag boys. They could sell ya shit wrapped in brown paper and get away wiv it.

Epsom was one big fairground. My favourite was the jellied-eel stalls. I'd always have two basins of jellied eels. They were 'ansom. At Epsom we put on the same act as we did in the Square. The only difference was we had to take a dancing mate wiv us as we had to work on the grass.

The wind-bag boys used to offer all sorts of fings, not just shit, but when the punters bought the packet there was hardly anyfing in it. I've seen women pay five pounds for a sixpenny brooch out of Woolworths. It's a funny fing, the punters stood for it year arfter year.

The uvver buskers included Mutton Eye wiv his portable; Jim the Rings wiv his somersault act; and Baldy was there once wiv his penny stuck on his noddle.

There was one guy there who would tell us the most fantastic stories. Like the time he told us he earned sixty pounds in coppers and he tied it behind the back of his bike on the carrier. 'That's a load of cobblers,' I said to Albert. 'Do you know how much sixty pounds of copper weighs?'

'Don't take any notice of that berk,' said Albert. 'He hasn't earned sixty pounds in all his bleeding life.' You could bet ya life. We was the cream of the buskers and we never earned sixty pounds a day.

People ran away wiv the wrong idea. They fink you earn a fortune busking. I can say we earned enough to keep our families on but we never earned a fortune. It was the same in my farver's time. He earned just enough for us to live on. I could never imagine me working in a factory. It would be like being in prison.

I shall never forget the time we all got nicked for not paying self-employment stamps. Albert and I was at home getting ready to go to work when there was a knock on the door. It turned out to be a geezer from the National Insurance Office.

'Wot bleeding insurance cards?' I said.

'You must have an insurance card,' he said.

'I've never had an insurance card in all my bleeding life,' I said.

'You should have one. Didn't you get one when you left school?'

'Wot bleeding school? I never went harf of the time,' I said.

He then asked Albert about his insurance card and Albert laughed in his face and said, 'We don't need cards on our job, guv. We work for our bleeding selves.'

'But you do,' he said. 'You have to pay self-employed stamps.'

'Who said so?' asked Albert.

'Why, the government,' he said.

'Well, ya better go and tell the bloody government to pay them for us,' said Albert.

Well that upset this geezer a bit and he went as red as a beetroot and the next fing he said was, 'Well if that's the case I will have to prosecute.'

'You can do wot ya bleeding like, mate,' said Albert.

'You'll be 'earing from our office,' said the geezer and awf he went.

267

About free weeks later we all had a letter telling us we were to be prosecuted by the National Insurance people for not buying these stamps.

'Wot can they do to us?' I said to Albert and Charlie. 'I never knew we had to buy any bleeding stamps.'

Well, the time came for us all to go to court. It was different from Bow Street where we knew all the scarps. We was all called into the dock one at a time and I was first. There was two old geezers and an old bird on the bench. The geezer from the insurance office started to tell the court about me not paying stamps. Then the old geezer asked me wot I had to say.

I told him I had never bought a stamp in all me life. He asked me wot I had done for a living, and I told him I was a busker and he couldn't understand wot it was all about.

I said that buskers didn't pay stamps.

'They do now,' he said, looking over the top of his glasses.

'How come?' I said.

'Because it is the law,' he said, still looking over his glasses.

My dad didn't pay self-employed stamps and he was a busker,' I countered.

'That's because in the old days self-employed stamps were never heard of,' he replied.

'Well, I hadn't heard of them now,' I replied.

Arfter he had asked how much I earned in a week they all got up and went into a room at the side of the court.

Arfter about ten minutes they came back and the old geezer said, 'We have considered your case and we have no alternative but to fine you the sum of one hundred pounds.' Well, I fawt I was going mad or somefing.

'How much?' I asked.

'One hundred pounds,' he replied.

'I can't pay that. They only fine two nicker at Bow Street.'

'This is not Bow Street and this is a different offence,' he said and then asked me how much I could afford to pay a week.

When I got outside I told Albert and Charlie wot happened.

'They've all gawn bleeding mad,' said Charlie. 'We didn't know anyfing about self-employed stamps.'

'It ain't no good telling them that, ya jaggs,' I said, 'they won't listen to ya.'

Well Albert and Charlie bofe got fined the same, as the geezer from the insurance office told the magistrate that we all worked togevver.

268

When we all got outside the court Charlie said, 'That's a turn up for the bleeding book. We'll all end up skint by the bleeding time we have paid them barsteds, ya jaggs.'

Well, there was nuffing else we could do so we all 'ad to pay up like good'uns. When we told all the uvver joegars none of them would believe us.

'Ya want to go down the bleeding insurance office and tell them ya don't pay any self-employed stamps,' I told one of them. 'Ya'll soon find out if we are kidding or not.'

'Not bleeding likely,' he said. 'Let sleeping dogs lie, that's my motto,' and awf he went to do anuvver slang.

The next time I saw him he was at Bow Street Court one morning arfter he had been nicked the night before.

'Wot are you doing here me old son?' I said.

'It's a bleeding liberty,' he said. 'I got nicked for obstruction last night by a little snotty-nosed copper.

'Wot ya beefing for?' I said. 'Ya want to be like us. We get nicked twice a week.'

'Yea, I know,' he said, 'but I don't draw crowds like you and your bruvver do I?'

'No, that's true, but it's all part of the game. Are you going to plead guilty?' I asked him.

'Wot ya fink I should do, Harryboy?' he asked me.

'Well, if I was you, me old son, I would plead guilty and get it over wiv,' I told him.

Well, he took my advice and he got fined a nicker.

When he told me I said, 'That will teach ya to stand on ya bleeding head in the middle of the road and sing "Any Old Iron".'

'Oh, cobblers,' he shouted to me over his shoulder as he left the court.

One week the scarps had a purge on and they nicked anyone they could lay their hands on. They nicked barrow boys, brasses, and all sorts. It used to happen like that whenever a new inspector took over. They all started awf by trying to clean up the West End but not one of them succeeded and they never will.

That week we got nicked seven times. I said to one of the young coppers, 'What's the matter? Have you got a new guvner up Savile Row, son?'

'Yes,' he replied, 'And he's going to clean up the West End.'

'I wish I had a nicker for every time I've heard that when a new guvner takes over,' I said. 'I'd be a very rich man,' and we bofe laughed on our way to the nick. The young copper knew I was right. He would have to be a genius to do that wiv all the villains about.

As I said, the purges only lasted a week and soon everyfing went back to normal. The brasses were back at work and the barrow boys were back on their pitches.

One week Charlie caught the 'flu but he insisted on going to do a show in Guildford. The show was for Johnson's Wax Company and we was on the bill wiv Bob Monkhouse. As we walked onto the stage we got a wonderful reception from the audience. We went into the act and we were working like good'uns when out of the blue there was a crash and Charlie stopped playing. All the audience roared wiv laughter. I looked round and there on the floor was poor old Charlie all tangled up in the drum and accordion.

The leader of the band was laughing his head awf and he said, 'Wonderful, you want to keep that in the act.'

'Wonderful, be fucked. He's fainted,' said Albert.

I stepped forward and said, 'We are sorry about this ladies and gentlemen, but my partner got out of bed to come and do this show for you.'

We carried poor old Charlie back to the dressing-room and the manager sent for an ambulance. The ambulance arrived and when they took Charlie out to the ambulance you would have fawt he was the greatest star in the whole world. Well, they took him to hospital and Albert and I went wiv him.

You can imagine the strange looks we got when they saw two geezers walking in in bobtail coats and hobnail boots. They wanted to keep Charlie in but he wasn't having any, so he discharged himself. When we got back to the hall where we had been doing the show we got treated like royalty.

'Wot the bloody hell happened?' I said to Charlie.

'It was constipation,' he said.

'Constipation be fucked. Ya sure ya old ticker is OK?' said Albert.

That night I drove Charlie home and for the next few days he was in bed. Wivout Charlie we couldn't work so Albert and I had a rest too, but as soon as Charlie was all right we was back in the Square entertaining the crowds. I missed the old West End wiv its lights and all the people we knew. Most of all I missed the characters and the laughs we had wiv them. I don't go to the West End now when I'm in London as it brings too many memories for me.

Memories like the time we were filming wiv a French film company. We ended up not getting paid for the job and Charlie pushed the director on his arse in the middle of the road. We soon got our money the following day. I can't remember the name of the film. I fink it was a documentary. We was always getting film crews coming up to us in the Square asking us to do little jobs. All they wanted us to do was to perform while they took shots of us.

Jack Bentley of the *Sunday Mirror* took us down one day to the studios to meet Cliff Richard. It was a publicity stunt. We had a right old day out and I enjoyed it. We had coffee wiv Cliff and Melvyn Hayes, star of *It Ain't Half Hot, Mum*. At the time Cliff was filming *Summer Holiday*. He treated us like gentlemen and we even borrowed his dressing-room to change in. We spent the whole day wiv him and his friends.

We became the cream of the buskers in our day. We would put on a fifteen minute show right in the middle of the road in Leicester Square and we became know to millions by our black frock-coats, bowler hats, and hobnail boots, and when we done our sand dance routine we would change into candy-striped shirts and Tommy Cooper fezes. But we was wearing the red fez a lom ime before Tommy Cooper.

People knew us by the name painted on the big brass drum. I've carried that old bass drum for miles and it's no joke trying to scarper from the scarps wiv that strapped to ya back. On Sunday we would draw a big edge as all the tourists would come to Leicester Square to see us. I fink we done more for the tour trade than any uvver group in the country. We was going when the Beatles was just a twinkle in heaven, and we done charity show arfter charity show.

It's a funny fing – nearly all the big stars that we met wanted to know about the busking side of our life but I don't fink any one of them would like to have tried it. I am proud to have been associated wiv names that read like somefing out of *Who's Who*: Sammy Davis Jr; John Gregson; Bruce Forsyth; Sid James; Tony Hancock; Liz Frazer; Warren Beatty; Kenneth More; Susannah York; Bill Maynard; Michael Holliday; Red Skelton; Cliff Richard; Joan Collins; The Rolling Stones; Sir William Connor (Cassandra of the *Daily Mirror*); Donald Zec of the *Daily*

271

Mirror; Lionel Blair; James Robertson Justice; Tommy Trinder; Terry Scott; Melvyn Hayes; and many more. Then there were the most famous people of all like H.M. the Queen and the Duke of Edinburgh; Lord Louis Mountbatten; Sir William Oliver; the Ex-Prime Minister of Canada, Mr John Diefenbacker, and many uvvers. I shall always be grateful to our agent, Norman, for the chance he gave us to see such wonderful people.

Famous people would stop and pass the time of day wiv us. Poor old Freddie Mills would pass us every night on his way to his club in Charing Cross Road. He would always give us a bit of silver in the bottle. Poor old Fred. The law found him dead in his car one night. He had been shot. He would come up to us and in his own quiet way say, 'How's it going, lads?'

'Not bad, Fred. How's yaself?' one of us would reply.

He would chat a while and as he left he would put his hand in his bin and put a bit of silver in the bottle and say, 'See ya, me lads,' and awf he would go wiv his black curly hair and a big smile. He was a great sportsman.

We started to do a lot of cabaret and one night we had a cabaret to do at Orpington for the Orpington Chamber of Commerce. In the arfternoon Albert and I decided to go to the cinema. Little did we know that while we was watching the film someone was nicking our car outside in the cinema car park. It was the same car that we had at Gloucester. We couldn't afford anyfing else.

When we came out Albert said, 'Some barsted's nicked the bleeding motor.'

Well, the manager of the cinema phoned the law and arfter a while the scarps arrived in a police car. We told them who we were and arfter taking a statement and the number of the car the copper said, 'Don't worry, boys. We will soon find it for you.'

'It's all right for him to talk,' I said. 'Wot about the show tonight?'

'Blimey, I forgot all about that!' said Albert.

Well, when we got home we searched out all the old props we could find and, like all good troupers, we went on and done the show. The next day the car was found at Bishops Stortford and all the props were intact.

That wasn't the only time we had no props to work wiv. We had a week at Burnley and we was on the bill wiv Joan Turner. I was the first to arrive at the club and I was waiting for Albert and Charlie to arrive. Finally they showed up and I said to

272

Albert, 'Let's get the props out of the car first, then we can have a cup of tea.' Well, we went to the car and Albert's boat race went white.

'Wot's up, jaggs?' I said.

'I've left all the bleeding props behind,' he said.

'Oh no,' said Charlie.

Well, we phoned the house and Albert's wife told us that her bruvver had found the props in the hall doorway and he was on his way wiv them. The manager of the club was very nice about it.

'Don't worry, boys,' he said. 'If they are here by the second harf it will be OK.'

Albert's brother-in-law arrived just before we was due to go on in the second harf of the show and we had one frantic rush to get into our props. The show went like a bomb and the manager came up to us in our dressing-room when we had finished our act and said, 'That was worth waiting for, boys.' I made sure arfter that that we never left the props behind again.

On anuvver occasion we had to fly to Paris to entertain the US troops at the airforce bases. We had to go all over France. When we arrived at our hotel we got the shock of our lives when Charlie opened up his accordion and all the base fell out.

'Blimey, wot the bleeding hell's happened to me bleeding box?' shouted Charlie.

We set to work putting all the base back and we were sweating bottles of ink as we had to be ready to be picked up by car to go to one of the bases.

'I'll kill that bluddy porter at that airport if I ever see him again, that French bastard,' Charlie was saying. Then all of a sudden the phone in our room rang.

When I answered it a voice said, 'Is that the Roadstars?'

'Yus mate,' I replied. 'Wot can I do for ya?'

'I am just ringing to tell you that you won't be needed for tonight's show.'

'Fanks very much, mate, you've saved our bacon,' I said.

When I told Charlie he said, 'Fank God for that. I would have 'ad to go on playing 'arf a bleeding box.' We all had a good laugh and settle down to putting fings right.

Before we went to Paris our agent said to us, 'If I were you, boys, I would take some tea and sugar with you as it will cost you all a fortune over there the way you all drink tea.' So we decided to take a small camping stove, some tea, sugar, some milk

273

powder, and an enamel jug to make our morning tea in. Each morning one of us would get up and make a jug of tea.

Everyfing was OK until Charlie said, 'Why don't we get some powdered soups and have some for lunch?'

'Charlie boy,' I said. 'They should pickle your brains and put them in a museum. That's wot I call a good idea.' So awf I went to the supermarket to buy some powdered soups.

That lunchtime I filled the jug wiv water and lit the camping stove. The water was boiling lovely.

'Bung the powder in now. It's boiling,' I said to Albert.

Well, ya never seen such a mess in all ya life. As Albert put the soup powder in the boiling water it came all over the side of the jug and ran all over the carpet – laugh! There we were, all free of us, on our hands and knees like a lot of old charladies cleaning up the carpet. Arfter that we stuck to tea.

One night we had to go about ninety miles out of Paris to an air base. On our way back, the car we was travelling in, which belonged to the American Army, broke down and we spent the night in a farmhouse wiv some old Frenchman and his wife because the bloke that was driving it could not fix it. The wife couldn't speak English but the old boy had been in the First World War and he knew a bit. They made us very welcome. Our driver could speak French so it made everyfing OK. In the morning the old lady gave us a lovely breakfast. We fanked them the best we could and went on our way in a car that our driver had to hire.

We never used to include Jim in the act when we did cabaret so he never came wiv us to Paris. But whenever we went to work the Square we would get in touch wiv him and would all meet in Angelo's café.

One week we had no cabaret work on our books so we decided to return to our old pitch in Leicester Square. We arranged to meet at Angelo's as usual. Arfter waiting for about an hour Jim still didn't show up. Poor old Mudlark had no family. He lived in a bedsitter in Shoreditch. All we knew about him was that he came from circus stock but he never mentioned anyfing about a family.

Arfter a while Charlie said, 'I fink we'd better go and see wot's wrong wiv the silly old bugger.' So awf we went to Jim's lodgings.

When we got there his landlady told us he had been taken to hospital and had been operated on during the night for a rupture.

'He never told us he had a rupture,' I said to Albert and Charlie.

'The poor barsted 'as being doing 'is act all this time wivout saying a bleeding word.'

Arfter Jim came out of the hospital we gave him the job as bottler as he could no longer do his act. Poor old Jim lasted for a few more years wiv us and then he passed away and once more there was a bit of old London laid to rest.

When we lost Jim we had to have anuvver bottler. We decided to keep it in the family and Albert's wife Edie became our official bottler. And a good job she did of it too. It wasn't the first time Edie had been bottling. She had also taken the old man out round the East End. She was our bottler right up until we went to Canada.

We finally got rid of our old car, arfter doing hundreds of miles and having a million laughs wiv it. Albert swopped it for a Dormobile and it turned out to be a good buy. Everywhere we went we slept in it and that way we saved money on digs. We finally used it to change in arfter Angelo closed his café and moved to Wells Street.

It had nice little curtains up at the windows and a nice little gas-stove in one corner. Sometimes on a Saturday we would have a break and Edie would make tea for us on the stove. Arfter tea we would go back to work for the rest of the night.

One Saturday we got nicked twice before five o'clock. Albert said to me on the way back from the nick to Leicester Square, 'There's bound to be a fird nick ya jaggs before the night is out.'

'Next time we will have to make a run for it,' I said.

'I will keep my eyes open,' said Charlie, 'and if I see a scarp coming, I'll give ya the wire and ya might have a bit of a chance to scarper.'

Well, we arrived back in the Square and stood back on the pavement to have a smoke before starting anuvver show. We were lucky we had done free more shows wivout getting nicked.

On the fourf show we were working the sand-dance when Charlie shouted 'Johnalderly ya jaggs.'

I looked up and saw our favourite sergeant coming towards us at top speed. As I was picking up the big drum I said to Albert, 'Scarper Jaggs,' and we bofe ran round the back of the Square towards Orange Street.

'Johnalderly to the lardy ja jaggs,' shouted Albert to Charlie.

By this time the sergeant was well on our heels. We got to the Dormobile and Albert opened the back door for us all to get in. Laugh – ya should have seen us all diving frew the back door. I stuck the big drum up Charlie's arse and knocked him arse over head inside the Dormobile. We got in by the skin of our teef, Albert pulled the curtains over the windows and we all sat down to get our wind back.

'Varder ya jaggs for the bold ome,' I said to Albert.

Albert looked out of a crack in the curtains and started to laugh his head awf.

'Wot's up, jaggs?' said Charlie.

'Come and look at this silly barsted,' said Albert. 'He can't make out where we have gawn to.'

We all looked out of the window, and there was our favourite sergeant standing scratching his head wondering where we had gawn to. One minute we were there and the next we were gawn.

'Blimey,' said Charlie, 'that was close.'

'Ya can say that again, Jaggs,' I said.

'There is no point in getting nicked again today,' said Albert. 'We might as well turn it in.'

Chapter Sixteen
A right royal surprise

Over the years there has been some big changes in the West End. When we worked Leicester Square we had the traffic to contend wiv, but now no traffic is allowed to go frew the Square. If it had been like that when we worked there we would not have had all that trouble wiv Old Bill, but then we would not have been known world-wide. The traffic didn't worry us in Leicester Square, we were so used to it. If I stepped out into the road to stop a car and to pretend to clean its bonnet I knew it would stop. If anyfing did go wrong I fink the crowd would have lynched the driver as the crowd loved it.

I shall never forget the night a German film crew came to us and asked if we would appear in a film. It was a short documentary about London and they wanted to film our act. We said we would if the medzers was right so we made arrangements to see the producer the following morning at the Rembrandt Hotel.

'It ain't no good of all free of us going to see the geezer,' said Charlie, so I was elected to go.

I found the hotel all right and I was shown up to the producer's room. When I got inside there was about five uvver geezers there and a palone and they was having some kind of a party. The producer gave me a large scotch and said how pleased he was to see me. Two large scotches later I fawt, *It's about time I asked the geezer how much he is goind to bung us for the job*, but he was well away wiv all the bevvy he had had. I said to myself, *Harryboy, when in Rome do as the local punters do*. So I got stuck into the bevvy and started to enjoy myself.

It turned out that the bird was a German film star and I got on wiv her liked a pig in shit. By this time the bevvy was flowing like water and yours truly was well away. As I am not normally a bevvy merchant I didn't know wevver I was coming or going. Around four o'clock the bird passed out and she was in a right old state. Her hair looked as though it had been combed wiv an egg-whisk and one of her false eyelashes had come adrift and it was hanging down her cheek.

'Fritz,' I said to the producer, 'you'd better take that bleeding eyelash awf of her face before she slashes herself to death wiv it.'

He burst out laughing and he took the eyelash awf and stuck it under her nose.

'She looks like bleeding Hitler,' I said.

All of a sudden it went quiet. One minute they were all laughing and the next they were all looking at me. I fawt, *If they want a punch up they can have it.*

Then the producer burst out laughing and said, 'Ha, you make bloody good joke, Harry.' I fawt, *I can't see anyfing funny in it, but if they finks it's a joke it's all right by me.*

A few minutes later there was a knock on the door and in came the hall porter.

'Vot is it?' asked one of the film crew.

'Is there a Mr Hollis here, sir?' asked the hall porter.

'No there is no one here of that name,' answered the crewman.

'Hold on, that's me ya berk,' I said.

The hall porter looked at me and said, 'You are wanted on the phone, sir.'

I went to get up to follow him to the phone.

'You can take it from here, sir,' and he pointed to a phone on a small table by the bed.

As I picked up the phone a voice at the uvver end said, 'Is that you ya jaggs.' It was Albert.

'Are ya still there?' he was asking.

'Yus,' I replied.

'Wot about the job? Have you made a deal yet?'

'Well, to tell ya the trufe jaggs, they're all bevvied up here and I've had a few meself and I can't get no sense out of the geezer,' I replied.

'Well ya better blow it out before ya get too bevvied as we have got to go to work tonight,' said Albert.

'OK, I'll meet ya in the Square around seven,' I said putting the phone down.

I fawt, *I've got to do somefing about getting this geezer to see sense,* so I walked over to where the producer was sitting and said, 'Now Fritz, wot about this bleeding film? Do you want us to do it or not?'

'Ya the film is OK,' said the producer.

'Right then, how much is the job worf?'

'How much do ya vont?' he asked.

278

'Well if ya put it like that me old son shall we say free hundred nicker?'

And to my surprise he put out his hand and said, 'Done.' I fawt, *He's a nutcase. No one would ever pay us that.*

Then I remembered wot Charlie had said the night before about getting a retainer.

'Wot about a bit now to show good fair then?' I said.

'Ya,' he said wiv a smile. 'Now how much do you vont?' he added as he pulled a cheque book out of his jacket pocket.

'Well, Fritz, if ya put it like that shall we say 'arf now and the rest when the job is done, me old son?'

'Ya that is good,' and before I knew it he began to write out the kite. I watched him write the figures 'One hundred and fifty pounds' and I made sure he got the name right. I shook hands wiv the the rest of the team except the bird who was still flat out on the settee and I left as happy as a pig in shit.

As I had not eaten that day I made my way to the nearest café for a meal. I felt very pleased wiv myself and while I was waiting for the grub I took anuvver look at the kite to make sure it was OK. I was wondering wot the boys would say when I told them how much I got for the job. I left the café to make my way up west for the Square. I got there around 6.30 and I went straight to Angelo's café to await the appearance of Charlie and Albert.

Charlie was the first to arrive and as he came up to me he said, 'Well, ya jaggs. How did ya get on wiv them Jerries?'

'Not bad. I charged them free hundred nicker,' I replied putting my hand in my pocket for the kite I had been given.

'Leave awf jaggs,' said Charlie. 'They won't pay that kind of medzers.'

'Who won't? There's bleeding harf of it,' I said as I put the cheque on the table. Charlie's eyes nearly came out of his head when he saw the cheque.

'Fuck me,' he said. 'One of you must be mad. It's either you or that geezer.'

'It ain't bleeding me,' I said.

'He must have been well pissed to stand for that, or you must have the cheek of the devil,' said Charlie.

'I don't give two monkeys,' I said. 'I got one hundred and fifty nicker awf of him, and we have the rest to come tomorrow when we finish the job.' Just then Albert and Edie walked in.

'Oi, jaggs wot ya fink this little ponce 'as done?' Charlie was saying to Albert.

279

'Nuffing would surprise me, he sounded well pissed over the blower,' replied Albert. But he was as surprised as Charlie when he saw the cheque.

We spent the following day filming and Charlie kept saying, 'Wait until the geezer tumbles about the medzers ya jaggs.'

At about five o'clock the director called it a day and we had finished. I went up to the producer and said, 'Well Fritz, everyfing OK me old son?'

'Ya, very good,' and he put his hand in his pocket and pulled out a cheque and said, 'There you are. This is for you. This is what we agreed upon.'

I took the cheque wivout looking at it and put it in me pocket. I shook hands wiv him and said, 'See ya round, Fritz me old son.'

'I've got the medzers jaggs,' I said to Albert and Charlie, and we made out way towards Angelo's café.

On our way I pulled out the cheque to give it to Albert as he used to look arfter the finances of the act. I looked at the cheque and I fawt I was seeing fings. There before my eyes was written, 'Pay three hundred pounds'.

'Blimey jaggs look at this bleeding lot!' I said and handed the cheque to Albert.

When he saw it he said, 'Blimey! That geezer 'as slipped up. He must have forgotten about the medzers he gave you yesterday.' Old Charlie was all for cashing it.

'Leave awf ya jaggs,' said Albert. 'We can't do that.'

'I know, let's go to their hotel tomorrow and see wot he 'as got to say about it,' I said. And the following day we done just that.

We arrived in the Rembrandt Hotel about eleven in the morning and the film crew was busy packing their gear. The producer was sitting on the bed reading some papers. He looked up as we entered the room.

'Ha, gentlemen,' he said as he got awf the bed, making his way towards us wiv his hand outstretched. We shook hands wiv him and he said it was nice to see us again before they left for Germany.

Arfter we'd all had a drink I explained wot we was doing there. He looked at the kite and said, 'No, that is right. You have don a good job.' I fawt, *You can come again me old son*. We had anuvver bevvy and chatted for a while. Then we said our goodbyes and all free of us went out smiling.

'That was boner, ya jaggs,' Charlie said. 'We'd better let you

280

do all the bookings from now on, jaggs,' and we all had a good laugh.

That night, arfter we had finished working the Square, I said, 'I fink we should all have a few days awf so we can give Old Bill a rest from nicking us.' Well Albert and Charlie was all for having a good rest.

So the next day we cashed the two cheques and had a share-out. I went awf to have a few days wiv my old Mum in Scarborough. Albert went down to Somerset and Charlie went down to Brighton to do some fishing (he never used to catch any though).

When I got to Scarborough I told my old Mum about the film we had just finished and she told all her neighbours that her two sons were film stars. I had a lovely few days wiv her and I took her out and about all the time I was there. When I left her waving the train out of the station I saw for the first time how old and tired she looked. I stood looking out of the train window until she was out of sight. Not long arfter that she left us for good. I still hold her dear to my heart.

One morning, arfter being nicked the night before, I was making my way on the underground to Bow Street magistrates court to surrender my bail. I had to rush around a bit as I was late in getting up. As I was about to get out of the train at Covent Garden I felt a sharp pain down the left-hand side of my body and a pain across my chest. I tried to shake the pain awf by moving my arm about but it was no use. I began to feel hot and sweat broke out on my forehead. I decided to sit down on a seat for a while. I didn't know then that this was God's way of telling me to slow down.

Arfter a while I began to feel a lot better so I made my way to the court to get fined the usual two pounds. I didn't say anyfing to anyone about that little episode and by the time I got home I was my old self again but the fawt of it never left my mind as I knew there was somefing wrong. I was afraid to go and see a doctor in case there was somefing wrong wiv my ticker so I went on working.

You see us buskers (real buskers that is) are a superstitious lot. If we found a medzer medzer (farthing) in the bottle we would frow it over our shoulder and spit and we would never whistle while walking under an archway if the day was a Friday.

I remember going frew Blackwall Tunnel one night wiv my old Dad. We were going to work at Lewisham. 'arfway frew the tunnel I started to whistle.

'For Gawd's sake, son,' said my old Dad, 'don't ever whistle going frew a tunnel or an archway on a Friday. It's bad luck to a busker.'

'Who said so Dad?' I asked.

'It's a known fact among buskers,' he replied. 'I'll tell ya wot son. If ya grandfarver heard ya he would go mad.' Since then I have never whistled while going frew an archway or a tunnel on Friday. It is the same if ya spill the sugar. It is supposed to bring ya bad luck for the rest of the day. Or we would never turn a loaf upside down once a slice 'as been cut from it. It meant that you would have a bad illness.

Where these superstitions came from I don't know, but that's the way it is. It's the same if you whistle in a dressing-room. It is supposed to bring bad luck to the show. Some big stars carry some little trinket about wiv them to bring them good luck. My old grandfarver was a very superstitious man and he seemed to have handed it down to my old Dad.

The highlight of my life was when I actually met Her Majesty the Queen. I couldn't believe that little Al from Poplar was actually talking to Queen Elizabeth II. None of me friends, Fred, Bomber, Gobber and Georgi, could have been wiv me but I wished they were.

The right royal surprise took place at Expo 67, the celebration of Canada's first hundred years in Montreal. The Road Stars had been invited to appear at the British Pavilion as typical London buskers. It was a wonderful break for us, except for poor Albert.

Albert had had to return home to England three weeks before this great occasion. You see, a few monfs before we got the contract to go to Canada, Albert's youngest son got killed in a car crash and Albert took it pretty hard. His son was only twenty-one when it happened. He tried to work on the best he could but I knew he wasn't himself and all at once he was beginning to look old. Charlie and I did all we could to help him get frew, but by the time we went to Canada he was really ill. Still, like all good troupers he tried to carry on.

On the 1 June 1967 he had a nervous breakdown and he had to return home to England wiv his wife Edie. The doctor said it

282

was because of the loss of his son. Albert went home by boat as the doctor said the trip would help him to get better. We saw them awf and I knew it was going to be the last time we were going to work togevver. When he left it was as though someone had cut awf my right arm. When you have been partners as long as we were it comes hard when you have to break up.

So on the day we met the Queen it was our old pal Ronnie Ross who took the place of Albert. Ronnie is a good performer and a good showman. Ronnie had taken my place once before when I was ill. he was one of the buskers we had worked wiv in London. I had to get in touch wiv our agent to let him know about Albert's illness and Ronnie was the next best one to take his place so about free days arfter Albert went home Ronnie came out to Canada. And boy was I glad to see him when he arrived, as Charlie and I had to work for free days on our own and that made extra work for us. It was so hot the sun belted down all day so you can imagine wot it was like to dance in the fick bobtail coat and bowler hat. Ronnie soon got the hang of fings and he settled down nicely.

The meeting wiv the Queen took place on Monday 3 July 1967. It was a very wet morning and we were told to be at the Expo site by 9.30 that morning. We were all given special passes to get into the site.

When we arrived, one of the mounted coppers on the gate stopped us and told us to wait.

'Wot's it all about?' I asked Charlie. 'Wot have they stopped us for? She's our Queen and no fucker is going to stop me seeing her.' Arfter a few seconds the copper came out and said, 'OK, you guys. You can go through.'

'You try and stop me, old son,' I said, and frew we went.

When we got to the British Pavilion we was met by Sir William Oliver who was in charge of it.

'Good morning lads,' he said. 'Not a very nice one, is it?' I fawt, *Ya can say that again, mate.*

We went into a big office and as I was asking one of the girls for a cup of tea there came a voice from behind me.

'You must be joking, Henry.' I turned round to find it was Sir William Oliver.

'Blimey, guv,' I said, 'I am dying for a cup of tea.'

'You will have to wait until this is all over,' he said. 'What do you think the Queen would say if she found us drinking on the job?'

'I'd offer her a cup, Gawd bless her,' I said.

'No tea and that's that,' said Sir William.

My throat by now was parched but fortunately there was coffee laid on for all those who had been invited.

We waited there for the great lady to arrive and about 10.30 the phone rang and someone said they were on their way. Anuvver fifteen minutes and we were all lined up to meet her.

'I am going to ask her how the kids are, ya jaggs,' said Charlie.

'Leave awf,' I said, 'ya can't do that.'

She looked so nice. She was dressed in a pink floral coat wiv hat to match. As she got close to us my knees went like jelly. I was the first one she met out of the free of us. She put out her hand and said, 'Good morning.' I was afraid I would break her hand, as I have a very strong handshake.

'Good morning, ma'am,' I replied and Sir William Oliver told her who I was.

She asked me how I liked Canada and I said, 'It's not bad. It's not as good as Leicester Square.'

Wiv that she gave a real hearty laugh then she moved on to Charlie. I stood there in a daze and thought of my old teacher Gibbo and the day he said to me, 'Hollis, you're scum, you'll never make anyfing of yourself,' and managed a wry smile.

'Good morning, miss, if ya can call it that,' said Charlie.

She said how right he was, then she moved on to Ronnie Ross.

At twelve o'clock the sun came out and it turned out to be a lovely day, a day I shall never forget.

We also met John Diefenbacker, the Ex-Prime Minister of Canada at Expo. We had a long chat wiv him. He asked us about how we liked Expo and how long we was there for. Then we had our picture taken wiv him. He shook our hands and said it was a pleasure meeting us. he was a very nice guy.

It was also in Montreal that we met Lord and Lady Mountbatten. We were performing to the crowd at Expo and we had just finished and was having a rest when Sir William Oliver came down the steps wiv Lord Louis.

'Look, jaggs,' I said to Charlie, 'it's the old man himself.'

'Well I'll be fucked,' said Charlie. 'So it is.'

They made straight for us and as they got up to us we said, 'Good morning, sir.'

'Which one of you was in the Navy?' said Lord Louis.

'It was me, sir,' I said.

He then introduced us to his daughter and he went on to ask

me about my service. I told him all he wanted to know and then we had our picture taken wiv him. We all shook hands and he said as he went, 'Keep up the good work, lads.'

I don't know wot the police at Savile Row would have said seeing us making friends wiv such great people.

Anuvver thrill for me was being invited aboard the Royal Yacht *Britannia* two days before we actually met Her Majesty. One day we were performing at Expo 67 and arfter we had done our show two naval officers came up to us.

'A nice show,' said one. 'I enjoyed it very much.'

'Fanks, mate,' said Charlie.

Then the uvver guy said, 'Would you consider coming aboard the Royal Yacht?' I fawt, *This guy has got to be joking.*

'Ya want us to come on the Royal boat?' said Ronnie.

'Yes,' replied the officer wiv a smile.

'How much are you going to pay us?' asked Charlie.

'Leave awf, Charlie,' I said, 'you can't ask the lady herself to pay us.'

'Her Majesty will not be there I'm afraid but there will be a lot of titled people there,' said the officer.

Well, we agreed to do the job for nothing so at eight o'clock a car arrived for us at our digs and we was on our way to the Royal Yacht.

I shall never forget that night as long as I live. I fawt as I was going up the gangplank, *Not bad for a snotty-nosed kid from the slums.* As we went up the gangway, I said to Charlie, 'Keep ya bleeding hands awf the crown rocks.'

'They have hocked them to pay the crew, jaggs,' said Charlie.

When we got to the top of the gangway the officer who we met that arfternoon was there to meet us.

'Good evening, gentlemen,' he said and wiv a gesture of his hand he said, 'come this way.'

We followed him down a gangway to the wardroom. When we got inside there was enough gold braid to sink a battleship. He asked us wot we wanted to drink. We gave him our order and he told a steward to fetch the drinks for us.

Well, that night we put on a good show and got well pissed in the bargain. The crew of the Royal Yacht enjoyed every minute of the show. We were then shown round the yacht. We were showed every cabin except the great lady's.

'Ya know why they didn't show us her cabin, ya jaggs?' said Charlie.

'Why?' I asked.

'Well, they didn't trust Ronnie wiv his beady eyes, did they?'

By the time we left the *Britannia* we were well bevvied. It took me all my time to get Charlie down the gangway to the taxi that came to take us back to the flat that we had rented while we were in Canada.

We certainly paid for our visit to the Royal Yacht the following morning. Charlie had a right old hangover. When I woke him wiv a cup of rosie lee he said, 'Blimey, jaggs, wot a bleeding party.'

'I told ya not to drink wiv us naval boys, Charlie,' I said. 'Ya know wot Charlie, I fawt that geezer was kidding when he came up and asked us if we would do a show on the Royal Yacht.' 'So did I,' Charlie replied. 'But all I know is this bleeding hangover ain't kidding.

We worked in Canada wiv that grand old Frenchman, Maurice Chevalier. He was a grand old man and he treated us as though he had known us for years. It was wonderful to have big stars like him treat us the way they did. The bigger the star the better they treated us. Once while we was talking to him one night in Canada, someone started talking about dying and I can remember him saying that he was not afraid to die.

'Leave awf, Maurice,' I said, 'you're only a saveloy yet.'

'Wot is dis saveloy?' he said. When I told him it meant boy he laughed his head awf. Yes, he was a grand old gentleman and his death is a great loss to showbusiness.

We made several TV appearances while in Canada and the Canadian people took us to their hearts. Everywhere we went at Expo we was recognised and the amount of autographs we gave away was out of this world and we loved every minute of it. We were invited to party arfter party and everywhere we went we were made welcome by our hosts.

There was one place that we worked at every day at Expo, and it was called the Garden of the Stars. There we would draw big crowds like we used to draw in the Square. We performed twice a day at the Garden of the Stars and we drew about two thousand people each time we performed.

Chapter Seventeen
Farewell Leicester Square

Arfter Ronnie came out to Canada to take the place of Albert, we continued working to big crowds. By the end of June it became very hot and it was no joke having to work in our very heavy black clothes. By the end of the day we were tired out and ready for old Uncle Nod. By July we were doing eight shows a day.

I woke up one morning and everyfing in the world seemed lovely. I had no idea wot the end of that day was to bring. At 9.30 our car arrived at our flat as usual to take us to the Expo site. By 10.30 we were in our dressing-room getting ready for the day's work. Even at 10.30 in the morning it was quite warm. We chatted away to each uvver about the day's work and by eleven o'clock our jeep arrived to take us to our usual pitches. We packed the props in the jeep and went on our way waving and laughing to the crowds as we went.

By two o'clock that day the sun was blazing down on us wiv all its might. We broke awf around 2.30 for a break and refreshments.

'I could drink the water out of a dirty flannel,' I said to Charlie. 'I am so bleeding firsty, ya jaggs.'

'Ya ain't kidding, jaggs,' said Charlie wiv a laugh. I downed two ice-cold cokes and a large hamburger and I was ready for work once again.

All that arfternoon I fink I ate that bleeding hamburger a fousand times – it kept repeating on me.

By four o'clock that arfternoon I fawt I was having a bad touch of indigestion, but I carried on working. By the end of the last show I was fucked. And while I was sitting in the dressing-room waiting to go on I fawt, *I wish to God it was over*. I was really in pain.

I told Charlie and he said, 'Why don't ya try a cup of hot water, jaggs? It might get rid of it.' I did as Charlie suggested but it was no use.

'Come on jaggs, it's the last show,' said Ronnie. Let's get it over wiv and then we can all have a bluddy good night's kip.'

Well, I went on to do the last show but how I carried on I don't know. All frew the show I was in severe pain.

That night the sweetest words I have ever heard was when Ronnie said, 'Goodnight, God bless.' And then there was the applause and the audience shouting for more. As I left the stage I fawt, *Fank God that is over.*

I made my way to the dressing-room and as I went to sit down I had a terrific pain in my chest and then I blacked out – and that was that.

I woke up next morning in hospital and I was told by one of the doctors that I would never be able to perform again. The strain had become too much. I had had a serious heart attack. As he was telling me, I fawt to myself, *This guy is nuts, I'll be back in the old Square before he's got time to change his bleeding white coat.* But I was never more wrong in all my life.

All the time I was in hospital Charlie and Ronnie came to see me every chance they had. My only worry while I lay in hospital was that Betty and the kids were so far away. But I knew I had my dear friend and partner Charlie there if anyfing went wrong.

Arfter four weeks the doctor told me they were going to fly me home and that I would have to report to my own doctor when I got back to England. All the time I was finking of the contract I had wiv the Canadian Government and that on the uvver hand I wanted to be home wiv my Betty and family. So on 18 August 1967 I said goodbye to Charlie and Ronnie and left for home.

As I left, Charlie said, 'Don't worry, jaggs, ya can have a nice rest and when me and Ronnie comes home we will have plenty of work to do. But I was never to work wiv them again.

Ronnie and Charlie carried on at Expo 67 till the end of the contract. As the plane got higher and higher I looked out of the window and I could see the Expo site hundreds of feet below, and I knew that somewhere down there the Road Stars were still entertaining the crowds at Expo 67.

Betty and my children were waiting for me when I stepped down awf of the train at Scarborough and when I saw them I knew I was home.

When I first got home I felt safe. But arfter a few weeks I was like a lion in a cage. I just couldn't come to terms wiv my lot. I was told by the specialist at the hospital that I would have to take fings easy and I would not be able to work at my job again. Arfter a monf or so I settled down to wot God had allotted me and I had to be content to be home in Scarborough wiv my family and friends instead of rushing all over the place doing shows here there and everywhere so I just took fings in my stride. But my heart cried out for the bright lights of dear old London. But it was of no use. I was finished as a street busker for good. As the years have gawn by I have learnt to live wiv my lot and I have now joined the ranks of official layabouts.

Charlie carried on working until he was seventy-four and then he gave up and retired. As for Ronnie he is still busking to the crowds in Leicester Square.

I don't fink of London any more as it is of no use to sit and mope over the past, so I am content to live here in Scarborough wiv all my friends – like Peter Jaconelli, who was once Mayor of Scarborough, and his bruvver Alfie who I have known for a long time. Alfie and I have had some right old giggles over the years whenever we met. The Jaconelli family have been trading in Scarborough for years, and are well-known frewout the norf. The amount of people that Peter Jaconelli has helped out is uncountable. Peter's in the *Guinness Book of Records* for eating the most oysters. He should also be in it for his help to mankind.

Anuvver dear friend of mine is Fred Feast, alias Fred Gee of Coronation Street. Fred and I sometimes meet on a Saturday in our favourite boozer, The Equestrian, where the landlady Jessie Brown and her son Michael treat us like one of the family. Michael must be one of the youngest landlords in the norf – and a bluddy good job he does of it too.

I have always found the northern people to be very friendly and outspoken. And though it takes them years to accept you, once they do you have a friend for life.

A news reporter once called me a converted Cockney. I told him no matter how much I love Scarborough I will always be a Cockney till the day I turn me toes up. I once did a chat show wiv Jack De Manio. And in the course of the interview, he mentioned that I now live in Scarborough, and he went on to say what a lovely place Scarborough is. I felt like saying to him, 'Ya don't 'ave to tell me that, Jack me old son.' To me Scarborough is the most beautiful place in the world, but it will always be my second home. My first home is dear old London where it all began for me so long ago. But I have no yearning to return to London. I have too many nice people around me in Scarborough and the air is so fresh and clean. I sometimes sit on top of the cliffs and look out to sea, finking back on my life.

Betty and I have had some happy times togevver in Scarborough and we have had some unhappy times too. Our children have been our life and we love every one of them dearly, and i consider myself to be a very lucky man for having such a lovely brood. Mind you, there have been times when I could wish them awf the face of this earf, but we wouldn't part wiv one of them for all the world. To Betty and me, they are worf their weight in gold.

I am glad that I was a busker. I learned fings while walking the streets of London as a boy wiv my farver that I would never have learned if I had been working in a factory from eight in the morning till six at night. I learned how to stand on my own two feet and not to expect fings to come to me free. I now know that nuffing is free in this life. Ya have to pay one way or anuvver. I've also learned that life is precious.

If God said to me, 'Harryboy, you can have one wish before ya die,' ya know wot that wish would be? I wish I could give every new-born baby the kiss of life to help it on its way.

Arfter suffering my first heart attack while working in Canada I can honestly say that I am not afraid of dying. So when I had my second one in 1972 it didn't worry me at all. I knew that if I didn't recover I would leave the reins of life in the capable hands of my dear wife. I knew she would take care of my family. I haven't been a lucky guy frew my life but it was the luckiest day of my life when I met my wife. She 'as stood by me frew all kinds of trouble and nursed me frew my illness and no man could ask for more from a woman and I love her dearly.

As I have told you before, I haven't been a good boy all frew my life as far as women is concerned. I've had my share of birds. I could name one bird who is a big star now who I could 'ave gone to bed wiv any time I wanted to. But once was enuff.

I even had a little midget. She was free foot four inches tall. I didn't enjoy her much. All the time I was wiv her she reminded me of a little girl. Everyfing she wore was tiny. She had to climb on a chair to open the door. It was embarrassing. I got on a bus wiv her one night when the conductor came along wiv the fare.

'Two to Charing Cross Road, mate,' I said. He clipped the

tickets and said, 'Here, guv, one and a harf to Charing Cross Road.' After that I gave her the brush awf.

I've had a few chorus girls too while working in some of the shows. It's easy if you're a top of the bill act like we were in some of the shows we did. Ya see, we were stars in our own right. I have worked wiv acts that were small names on the bill, while we was top of the bill. Now some of those names are big stars. I always said to my bruvver, Albert, that success came to us late in life. If we had had the same chances when we were young, we would have taken advantage of them. Instead they came too late.

In the course of writing this book, I have had cause to return to London so you can guess I paid a visit to my old Leicester Square. I stood there for a while, living the past of years ago. I looked at the old Square where we once danced a million dance steps. No more was the old characters who made it such an amazing place – like old Charlie, the boot black who had a wooden leg. Or Jock, the paper tearer, working the queues of the cinemas round the Square.

However I was delighted, on my last visit to London, to see that there was still one of the old buskers working in the West End. He is the only original busker left now, and he is my old friend and one-time partner Ronnie Ross. At sixty-six, Ronnie can still be seen working in the West End with his wife Peggy as his bottler. Ronnie and his bruvver Joe came to London in the forties. Ronnie comes from a long line of theatrical people. His farver was of old-time-music-hall stock, in the days when music hall *was* music hall.

The last time I saw Ronnie, I said to him, 'Blimey, I fawt you packed it in ya jaggs!'

He told me he had slowed down a bit, but as for packing it in, he wasn't ready yet. He is keeping up one of the oldest traditions. Once Ronnie 'as gawn he will be the larst, but until that day comes, you can still see him bashing it out on the cobbles of dear old London. It is nice to know there is still someone there of the old school.

I have ridden out the storms of life and I have survived all the turbulences that life 'as dished out to me frew the years. The waves of life have sometimes been choppy, but wiv God's help I have survived all the blows. I have been knocked down a few times, but I've always come back fighting.

As I stood in Leicester Square talking to Ronnie about days long since gawn I felt like crying.

'It is so said to see wot they have done to our old Leicester Square,' I said to Ronnie, 'They have turned it into a cess pit for winos and oily lamps (tramps).'

I said goodbye to Ronnie and looked around the Square for the last time. Where we once danced they have now put down flag-stones and flower pots, but instead of being full of flowers they are full of rubbish. I fawt to myself, *The architect who planned this lot wants nicking for obstruction of the highway.*

Our old Leicester Square 'as gawn forever. As I stood there I fawt of that old song, 'It's a long way to Tipperary' and the line that goes 'Goodbye Piccadilly, farewell Leicester Square.' Wiv a lump in my frote I turned my back on the old Square forever. They may have taken our stage away from us, but they can't take away the memories of it. They will live wiv me until the day the angels close my eyes.

Glossary 1
Buskers' language – Palaree

Bald	Bad
Batarlies	Shoes
Beonk	Shilling
Bona	Good
Bottle	Collect the money (during busking)
Buffer	Dog
Capella	Hat
Dateture font	Ten pounds
Dooey	Two
Edge	Crowd; audience
Feely	Child; kid
Feelyfake	Pregnant
Feely ome	Boy
Feely palone	Girl
Flat	Working man; conventional
Font	One pound
Jaggs	Mate; friend
Joegar	Busker
Johnalderley	Scram; run away; scarper
Lagingage	Toilet; lavatory
Medzer	Halfpenny
Medzer font	Ten shillings
Medzer medzer	Farthing (quarter of a penny)
Medzers	Money
Miltog	Shirt
Mungy	Food
Nant	Nothing
Ogyalglazers	Spectacles; glasses
Ome	Man
Palaree	Language; talk
Palone	Woman
Pecks	People
Saltie	Penny
Saysaltie	Sixpence

Scarping ome (scarp)	Copper; policeman
Scotches	Legs
Slang	Picture queue
Strill	Musical instrument; piano accordian
Toby	Road
Tray	Three
Traysaltie	Threepence
Traysalties	Breasts; (threepenny bits – tits)
Varda	Look
Wallop	Dance (tap-dance)

Glossary 2
Lingo – Cockney and rhyming slang

Albert Docks	Pox; VD
Barnet	Hair (Barnet Fair)
Beano	Seaside outing; feast
Bevvy	Pub; beer; booze; drink
Bin	Pocket
Bird	Prison
Boat-race	Face
Bottle	Buttocks; bottom (bottle and glass - arse)
Boney	Boneyard
Box	Accordion; concertina
Brasic lint	Poor; broke (boracic lint – skint)
Brass	Prostitute
Bubble and squeak	Greek
Buppy	Bread
Burnt cinder	Window (winder)
Bushel and peck	Neck
Butchers	Look (Butcher's hook)
Cab rank	Yank; American
Cain and Abel	Table
Carsey	Toilet; lavatory
Charabang	Coach
Coster	Fruit-stall holder
Cufflink	Chink; Chinaman
Derby Kelly	Belly
Dolly mixtures	Pictures
Duke of Kent	Rent
Earwig	Listen
Firm	Gang
Fork	Hand
Front wheel skid	Yid; Jew
Grass	Police informer
Greengage	Stage
Heavy	Bodyguard
Hurry-up wagon	Police car

Johnson	Ponce
Kip	Bed
Kite	Cheque
lardy Da	Car
Licker	Parsley gravy
Lord Mayor	Swear
Meat wagon	Ambulance
Mince Pies	Eyes
Moldies	Loose change
Nick	Police station
North and south	Mouth
Oily lamp	Tramp
Old Bill	Copper; police(man)
Oliver Twist	Wrist
Peter	Cell
Pikey	Gipsy
Poke	Money
Pop	Pawn (hock)
Punter	Customer
Readers	Papers
Rocks	Jewels
Rozzer	Police
Ruck	Argument
Saucepan lid	Kid
Saveloy	Boy
Scarper	Run away
Speckty	Rotten apple(s)
Stock	Scarf
Strides	Trousers; knickers
Ticker	Heart
Turps	Whisky
Winnypeg	Leg